CRITICAL ACCLAIM
FOR *TRAVELERS' TALES*

"The *Travelers' Tales* series is altogether remarkable."
— Jan Morris, author of *Journeys*, *Locations*, and *Hong Kong*

"For the thoughtful traveler, these books are an invaluable resource. There's nothing like them on the market."
— Pico Iyer, author of *Video Night in Kathmandu*

"This is the stuff memories can be duplicated from."
— Karen Krebsbach, *Foreign Service Journal*

"I can't think of a better way to get comfortable with a destination than by delving into *Travelers' Tales*...before reading a guidebook, before seeing a travel agent. The series helps visitors refine their interests and readies them to communicate with the peoples they come in contact with...."
— Paul Glassman, Society of American Travel Writers

"*Travelers' Tales* is a valuable addition to any predeparture reading list."
— Tony Wheeler, publisher, Lonely Planet Publications

"*Travelers' Tales* delivers something most guidebooks only promise: a real sense of what a country is all about...."
— Steve Silk, *Hartford Courant*

"*Travelers' Tales* is a useful and enlightening addition to the travel bookshelves...providing a real service for those who enjoy reading first-person accounts of a destination before seeing it for themselves."
— Bill Newlin, publisher, Moon Publications

"The *Travelers' Tales* series should become required reading for anyone visiting a foreign country who wants to truly step off the tourist track and experience another culture, another place, firsthand."
— Nancy Paradis, *St. Petersburg Times*

THE GIFT of BIRDS

True Encounters with

Avian Spirits

THE
GIFT *of*
BIRDS

True Encounters with
Avian Spirits

Edited by

LARRY HABEGGER AND
AMY GREIMANN CARLSON

TRAVELERS' TALES · SAN FRANCISCO

Credits and copyright notices for the individual articles in this
collection are given starting on page 319.

We have made every effort to trace the ownership of all copyrighted
material and to secure permission from copyright holders. In the event
of any question arising as to the ownership of any material, we will be
pleased to make the necessary correction in future printings. Contact
Travelers' Tales Inc., 330 Townsend Street, Suite 208, San Francisco,
California 94107. www.travelerstales.com

Cover and interior design by Diana Howard
Illustrations by Randy Johnson
Page layout by Patty Holden using the fonts Cochin, Stuyvesant,
    and Castellar
Distributed by Publisher's Group West, 1700 Fourth Street, Berkeley,
CA 94710.

Library of Congress Cataloging-in-Publication Data
The gift of birds: true encounters with avian spirits/collected and
    edited by Larry Habegger and Amy Greimann Carlson.—1st ed.
        p.   cm. — (Travelers' Tales Guides)
    ISBN 1-885211-41-4
    1. Bird watching Anecdotes. 2. Birds Anecdotes. I. Habegger, Larry.
II. Carlson, Amy Greimann. III. Series.
QL677.5.G54 1999
598—dc21   99-36686
                                                        CIP

First Edition
Printed in the United States of America
10 9 8 7 6 5 4 3 2

A March morning is only as drab as he
who walks in it without a glance
skyward, ear cocked for geese.

— ALDO LEOPOLD,
A SAND COUNTY ALMANAC

Table of Contents

PART II — *Kindred Spirits*

PART III — *Odd Ducks*

PART IV — *Brushes with Divinity*

PART V — *Ascending Song*

Introduction: Mockingbird Summer

LARRY HABEGGER

I CAME HOME ONE EVENING THIS SPRING TO the rollicking song of a mockingbird in the trees outside my house. The song filled an empty space in me I'd forgotten existed, because it was the voice of a long lost friend I thought I'd never hear again. But he was finally back, or one of his progeny was here in his place, singing the same song that had filled my nights with inexpressible joy just a few years before.

It was a time I've come to call my mockingbird summer, a unique period in my hillside neighborhood in San Francisco. We'd always had mockingbirds here, but this one was something else. His song began late one spring afternoon and continued into the evening, just outside my window, through the dinner hour and on into the night. I opened my window wide before bed and stuck my head out into the darkness. That mockingbird just sang and sang, up and down the scale, sounding like a cat, then a squirrel, a chattering chipmunk, a warbler, a jay, an oriole. His repertoire was boundless and he continued singing as I drifted off to sleep. His music lightened my dreams and he was still at it, or at it again, when I awoke at dawn.

It was a virtuoso performance, one not to be repeated there or anywhere else, I thought, but that evening he started up again and continued his song well into the night just as before. After several consecutive nights of this irrepressible song I began to expect it, and indeed all summer it went on, every night, all night. He was singing as if this was all he was ever meant to do, as if his entire reason for being was wrapped up in his singing through the night, spreading joy into the dark, silent world.

That "nightingale" outside my window reminded me how much pleasure birds had given me throughout my life. When I was a boy of nine or ten I spent many thrilling mornings rising at dawn, grabbing my father's binoculars, and racing off to the woods surrounding a marshy lake about a half mile from home. Etched in my memory are images of those pink mornings when the world was a-chatter, the shrubs busy with wrens and juncos, the trees alive with woodpeckers and thrushes and robins, the lake swarming with mallards and coots, and terns swooping above.

I can still see the sunny morning in a nearby park when I lay on my belly, propped on elbows, binoculars trained on a flicker hammering an oak tree so close the bird filled the entire frame, his colors radiant in the sunshine. I can see the black and white flash of a red-headed woodpecker flying

from tree to tree. I can hear the morning call of a mead-
owlark on a wooden fence, see the black V on the yellow
breast as brilliant as it appeared in my Peterson field guide.
I remember dusty ballfields where I saw small, unremark-
able birds that on closer inspection had two tiny rabbit ears,
a feature that seemed so exotic I couldn't believe what I was
seeing. Peterson showed that they were horned larks, a
species I didn't know existed and wouldn't have believed if
I had.

In those childhood years birds took me into the woods,
out to the meadows, onto the margins of lakes and swamps.
By drawing me into the outdoors they gave me a precious
gift—an appreciation of nature—and drew from me a certain kind of love. Love for them, for their surroundings, for
the wide world they and I inhabited.

Later in life, when I'd moved to San Francisco and
found a house on the side of a hill surrounded by gardens
with a broad window looking out upon the bay, I one day
heard a familiar clicking that seemed louder than normal.
There to my surprise was a hummingbird who had flown in
a side window and was futilely trying to escape out the picture window. By the time I arrived to usher him out he had
expired on the sill. I couldn't believe he had died so suddenly and I leaned close to look for signs of life. His ruby
throat gleamed, his iridescent green back shimmered, but
his eye seemed a tiny black orb with no light whatsoever.
He was still as the sill on which he lay. Gingerly I picked
him up and laid him in the palm of my hand. He was so light
he seemed weightless. It was like holding a ray of sunshine,
a piece of heaven so pristine it seemed a link to all of the

natural world. I suddenly saw myself as a bundle of atoms just like this still hummingbird in my hand, part of this grand and incomprehensible world, but a being still energized by life force, which seemed to have abandoned this poor bird.

Not knowing what to do, I moved toward the open window and carefully laid him on the outside sill, hoping that by some miracle he would revive. My fingers had barely released their touch when he leaped into the air, hovered for a second looking at me, and darted off into the trees, leaving me awed, the recipient of a divine vision.

Ever since, I've thought of that incident as a miracle, a visitation from a supernatural spirit to tell me to pay attention, to look beyond my daily human concerns and to appreciate my connection to the world. In this way that hummingbird and his cousins have kept me grounded, helping me reach a fuller understanding of my place on the planet. I am part of the web, as we all are, whether we like it or not, and nothing we do in our ambitious human lives can change that. When a chickadee flits within a few feet and turns her head, when a robin gives us a sideways glance, they're telling us we're just like them, neither more nor less, and in important ways their welfare is our welfare.

Over the years, when I've been talking with my mother on the phone from Minnesota we've always been interrupted by news of the birds outside her window. I can feel the sheer joy in her voice as she exclaims that a cardinal has appeared at the feeder, brilliant red against the snow. The cardinals are a sign of resilience in the harsh winter, a reminder that the frozen mantle over the earth can be endured. In the spring, when the icy patches are stubbornly fending off their inevitable melting, the sight of a robin is enough to raise her voice an octave. The robin means springtime, the receding of winter's hold on the land and the breaking open of a world of possibility and redemption.

Like the mockingbird who sang all night, every night as if his life depended on it, birds have given me the gift of life, nothing less. They have carried a torch to light the path, imploring me to recognize my place in the natural order, and not to miss a thing because it will all be gone so fast. The white-crowned sparrow singing in the morning and at dusk is calling not just to his mate but to me, telling me to take note of the blooming roses, the rich light of sunset washing across the hills.

The writers in this collection have received similar gifts. Their stories explore countless ways that birds have illuminated their lives, whether discovering the restorative power of bird feeders, carrying on a conversation with a raven, losing oneself among thousands of penguins, or tending a flock of wild urban parrots. Their stories range around the globe, from tracking rare cranes in Siberia to following a honey guide in South Africa. Many are deeply personal, many take on a much wider meaning.

But one thing is universal, as I learned during my mockingbird summer: in their ability to lift us above our worldly concerns, birds themselves are a precious gift, if only we are receptive enough to listen to their song.

A note on spellings: Throughout this book we've chosen to spell the names of birds with lower-case letters rather than with capitals, following the advice of standard dictionaries rather than the traditional practice of ornithologists. Both approaches have their merits, but we chose to side with the dictionary to avoid inconsistencies.

I

Vivid
Encounters

Gift of Seed

PETE DUNNE

*A simple bird feeder restores
a lost spirit.*

THE HOUSE SMELLED OF TURKEY AND echoed with the sound of grandchildren. We opened arms and hugged.

"Hello, Dad," I said.

"Solstice cheer!" he exclaimed. "Hurry up. There's something I want to show you."

My father turned, and a grimace twisted the smile from his face. He started toward the glass doors that open onto the deck, and though his legs are long, his steps were pained and short—a result of the Lyme disease that had taken much of his agility and very nearly his life.

We gained the doors and, like a child peeking around the corner on Christmas morning, he leaned forward, studied the bird feeders with binoculars, then relaxed.

"He's not there now," he whispered. "Wait."

3

We did wait. Father and son. Watching chickadees and sparrows, waiting for the new bird that had joined the ranks of my father's feeder regulars.

I saw my mother in the kitchen, working her usual culinary magic. Our eyes met, and we exchanged greetings along visual pathways. In response to my cocked eyebrow, she nodded in the direction of the feeders and smiled.

It was good to see the smile. It had not been there the last time we'd been together.

"We have to find something to catch his interest," she had implored more than urged back in October. "He can't get around like he used to. He can't use his hands very well. If he just sits in a chair all day, we're going to lose him."

"What about putting up some bird feeders out back," I suggested. "A couple of tube feeders filled with sunflower seeds for chickadees and finches. A platform feeder with millet for sparrows. A thistle tube to keep the goldfinches fat and sassy and—maybe some suet. Mom, a feeding station offers more color that a fish tank and more action than a meat counter when ground beef goes on sale.

"It's perfect," I continued. "Hours of entertainment. You get to know all the regulars and itch for each new arrival. You cheer on the chickadees, laugh at the nuthatches, and chastise the evening grosbeaks for hogging all the sunflower seeds.

"Besides, if keeping Dad sharp is the key, wait till he tries matching wits with squirrels. It's easier to keep the kids out of your pies than to keep squirrels out of your feeders."

"All right," she agreed. "Let's try it." That was two months ago.

"It was here just a minute ago," my father promised. "It likes the thistle feeder," he added to hold my attention.

"*There!*" he shouted as a bird flew in, claiming a perch. "That's it! Is that a redpoll?"

"That's a common redpoll," I affirmed, studying the puffy ball of feathers with the crimson cap. "Great bird!"

When he turned in triumph, I saw that the smile was back on his face, and the gleam in his eyes would have rivaled that of any child in the room. To look at those eyes, you'd never guess they'd ever known pain.

Having lived his whole life in New Jersey, Pete Dunne is director of the New Jersey Audubon Society's Cape May Bird Observatory in Cape May Point, New Jersey. He is a consultant to the Peterson field guide series on birding and the author of many books including *Hawks in Flight*, *The Feather Quest*, *The Wind Masters*, and *Small-Headed Flycatcher: Seen Yesterday, He Didn't Leave His Name and Other Stories*, from which this story was excerpted.

Stripped Naked

DAVID ABRAM

*Sometimes a raptor can
rattle your feathers.*

ALTHOUGH THE INDONESIAN ISLANDS ARE home to an astonishing diversity of birds, it was only when I went to study among the Sherpa people of the high Himalayas that I was truly initiated into the avian world. The Himalayas are young mountains, their peaks not yet rounded by the endless action of wind and ice, and so the primary dimension of the visible landscape is over-whelmingly vertical. Even in the high ridges one seldom attains a view of a distant horizon; instead one's vision is deflected upward by the steep face of the next mountain. The whole land has surged skyward in a manner still evident in the lines and furrows of the mountain walls, and this ancient dynamism readily communicates itself to the sensing body.

In such a world those who dwell and soar in the sky are the primary powers. They alone move easily in such a zone, swooping downward to become a speck near the valley floor, or spiraling into the heights on invisible currents. The wingeds, alone, carry the immediate knowledge of what is unfolding on the far side of the next ridge, and hence it is only by watching them that one can be kept apprised of climatic changes in the offing, as well as of subtle shifts in the flow and density of air currents in one's own valley. Several of the shamans that I met in Nepal had birds as their close familiars. Ravens are constant commentators on village affairs. The smaller, flocking birds perform aerobatics in unison over the village rooftops, twisting and swerving in a perfect sympathy of motion, the whole flock appearing like a magic banner that floats and flaps on air currents over the village, then descends in a heap, only to be carried aloft by the wind a moment later, rippling and swelling.

For some time I visited a Sherpa *dzankri* whose rock home was built into one of the steep mountainsides of the Khumbu region in Nepal. On one of our walks along the narrow cliff trails that wind around the mountain, the *dzankri* pointed out to me a certain boulder, jutting out from the cliff, on which he had "danced" before attempting some especially difficult cures. I recognized the boulder several days later when hiking back down toward the *dzankri's* home from the upper yak pastures, and I climbed onto the rock, not to dance but to ponder the pale white and red lichens that gave life to its surface, and to rest. Across the dry valley, two lammergeier condors floated between gleaming, snow-covered peaks. It was a ringing blue Himalayan day, clear as a bell. After a few moments I took a silver coin out of my pocket and aimlessly began a simple

sleight-of-hand exercise, rolling the coin over the knuckles
of my right hand. I had taken to practicing this somewhat
monotonous exercise in response to the endless flicking of
prayer beads by the older Sherpas, a practice usually
accompanied by a repetitively chanted prayer: "*Om Mani
Padme Hum*" (O the Jewel in the Lotus). But there was no
prayer accompanying my revolving coin, aside from my
quiet breathing and the dazzling sunlight. I noticed that one
of the two condors in the distance had swerved away from
its partner and was now floating over the valley, wings outstretched. As I watched it grow larger, I realized, with some
delight, that it was heading in my general direction; I
stopped rolling the coin and stared. Yet just then the lammergeier halted in its flight, motionless for a moment against
the peaks, then swerved around and headed back toward
its partner in the distance. Disappointed, I took up the coin
and began rolling it along my knuckles once again, its silver
surface catching the sunlight as it turned, reflecting the rays
back into the sky. Instantly, the condor swung out from its
path and began soaring back in a wide arc. Once again, I
watched its shape grow larger. As the great size of the bird
became apparent, I felt my skin begin to crawl and come
alive, like a swarm of bees all in motion, and a humming
grew loud in my ears. The coin continued rolling along my
fingers. The creature loomed larger, and larger still, until,
suddenly, it was there—an immense silhouette hovering just
above my head, huge wing feathers rustling ever so slightly
as they mastered the breeze. My fingers were frozen, unable
to move; the coin dropped out of my hand. And then I felt
myself stripped naked by an alien gaze infinitely more lucid

and precise than my own. I do not know for how long I was transfixed, only that I felt the air streaming past naked knees and heard the wind whispering in my feathers long after the Visitor had departed.

David Abram is a philosopher, ecologist, and sleight-of-hand magician who has lived and traded magic with indigenous cultures on several continents. He is the author *The Spell of the Sensuous: Perception and Language in a More-Than-Human World*, from which this story was excerpted.

A Pelican Frenzy

PAMELA CONLEY

*A dip in the sea becomes a close
encounter with the food chain.*

VERY JANUARY, MY HUSBAND DENNIS AND I like to head south. We migrate late because we like to be home for the holidays. In years past, we have visited Mexico, Belize, Honduras, and Guatemala. This year we are looking forward to birding in Trinidad and Tobago; land of the hummingbirds, it is called by the native inhabitants.

In preparing for our January vacation, I was remembering many of our past adventures of climbing Mayan pyramids, birding rainforests, and snorkeling the world's second largest barrier reef. In looking back, I thought about one of my most intense birding experiences.

We had driven a Volkswagon over the high mountains from Oaxaca to the coast. It took us six long hours and we were hot and out of steam when we arrived at the lazy

Mexican beach resort of Puerto Escondido. I jumped into my swimsuit the minute we got into our room and headed for the beach. The cool water was gloriously refreshing and I began to swim. An older gentleman was swimming too, and we began to tread water and converse in an easy, relaxed way.

Suddenly, I felt my foot hit a fish and then the ocean began to explode around us. I froze with fear.

I looked up and saw a hundred pelicans swarming down on us. Some were landing as close as two feet away. Splashes were erupting everywhere, and in the center of this hysteria I realized that they were swooping in on a school of fish and we were in the middle of a feeding frenzy. Pelicans are among the largest of living birds and to see these primitive-looking creatures with a wingspan of six to seven feet descend next to me was to make me think of old horror movies where the prehistoric flying reptiles swooped down and snatched poor human victims, usually a screaming woman, to fly away and never be seen again.

Then understanding replaced panic and I watched in awe as pelicans scooped up fish with what appeared to be gallons of water. They would hold the fish momentarily in their pouches, long enough to squeeze the water out of the corners of their mouths, and then they would tilt their heads upwards and I'd see the fish through the thin skin of their pouch disappear down their throats.

I dove down to see what this chaos would look like from beneath the surface and the exploding noise was muffled immediately. I looked up to see bobbing bodies with long legs and webbed feet with long toenails. The water erupted

with turbulence as a pelican dove down next to me, snatch-
ing up one of many silver flashes and then propelling himself upwards with strong webbed feet. I have no idea how
long this frenzy lasted, but when it finally ended it stopped
as suddenly as it had begun. The quiet was almost deafen-
ing. I looked at the older gentleman who peered back at me
in shock and then I yelled a huge emotional war-whoop and
waved my arms in excitement. I felt alive and vital, but
mostly I felt privileged to have shared such a moment with
these magnificent birds.

Pamela Conley was an international flight attendant for eighteen years and
an international travel consultant for a major insurance company for eight
years. She is now a freelance writer and still traveling and bird watching
when not in her redwood garden in Northern California. She writes a weekly
nature and birding column for *The Bodega Bay Navigator*.

Hardwired

RON NAVEEN

Beware the Penguin-Cognition Delusion.

BAILY HEAD VISITS ALWAYS SEEM MEMORABLE, especially when the chinstrap breeding season is in full swing. The unfolding spectacle is fairly described as *sensory overload* or *biological overload*—there simply is too much to see. Baily Head is so hard to reach, and it's rare to be able to visit at length, without time pressure. Today, I want to see my *chinnies* going through all the motions—to see them in full breeding regalia, in all their glory. But just as important as studying chinstrap breeding biology up close and personally, I want to address one lingering difficulty head-on: My never-ending *penguin-cognition delusion.* PCD is a natural phenomenon—a cognitive fallacy that afflicts everyone who comes to the Antarctic Peninsula. It begins when you initially encounter penguins in relatively *small* numbers—say twenty here, thirty there, perhaps a few hundred over the course of a particular visit. You're having such a great experience with these ten, twenty, or a hundred penguins, enjoying their antics so much, you can't possibly imagine seeing more intriguing behaviors and happenings. *But there always will be something new. And there always will be many, many more of them.*

I've countered some of this delusion by returning again and again to the Peninsula between early November and late February. This frame encompasses all of the action—the entire brushtailed life cycle. I've seen much: chinstraps and adélies returning in the austral springtime, joining the gentoos who have stuck around at favorite fishing spots during the winter. Courtship and copulation. Chick-rearing and -fledging. Chicks heading to sea. Adults molting. And then I've observed all of these penguin venues lapse back to their stark, naked autumn calm. Therefore, I feel bonded with the relatively small cohort of penguin researchers like Gain, Bagshawe, and Lester who were able to witness the entire show.

But there always is something new, always *more* to see. Experience can't assuage one significant aspect of this pleasant malady—a completely natural misapprehension of *size*. Even now, after all of my field time, I continue straining at times to comprehend and absorb the *whole* show. Eyes dilate and swell, as my field of vision attempts to capture the full grandeur of a jam-packed rookery like Baily Head. Nostrils inflate with the most horrid, nitrogenous perfume imaginable. Ears ache and shake from the noise. At Baily Head the sensory overload translates palpably to thousands—actually, tens of thousands—of screaming, volatile krill-balls, spread over a vast landscape, in multitudes of colonies and groups that are virtually impossible to count one by one.

I keep pinching myself, remembering I'm a small-town kid who once thought that going to the big city was a big deal. Baily Head is a really big deal—my synapses overwhelmed not by traffic or people, but by penguins. During my first significant penguin encounter—the few hundred chinstraps at Entrance Point—I had no idea what was unlocking in the inner and not-so-deep recesses of my consciousness.

They're unusually curious and willingly interested in examining us; face-to-face, without inhibition. But wild penguins aren't used to hand-feeding, so their close approach has nothing to do with looking for food handouts. Penguins are a bit nearsighted, so if you get down to their level and avoid any sharp or quick movements you create a safety zone, and it's not uncommon to have one prancing all over you, checking you closely with its beak. I thought my initial hundred animals were a terrific experience, but truth be told, this wasn't definitive. Sure, it was my initial, face-to-face, toenail-to-boot meeting—and there's no question I loved those chinnies at first sight. But something was missing. I was tasting some of the icing, without any bloody idea regarding the size of the cake. I remember Frank Todd telling me that first day about the hordes at Baily Head, bemoaning that we wouldn't be visiting it on our intended rotation of sites. It was something to tuck in the memory bank for the future, though Frank added, inimitably, that it was *a bitch to visit*.

The next season, working on another ship, the *Lindblad Explorer*, I got closer. Mike McDowell, the expedition leader, had considered landing at Baily Head, but conditions were substantially less than ideal. As a sidelight, after the passengers were safely ashore at Whaler's Bay, inside Deception's flooded caldera, Mike copped a Zodiac and took me over to the small bay near the Sewing Machine and Needles, directly beneath Baily Head's towering rim. In the rain and fog, we climbed to the top, for Ron's Little Preview. My jaw dropped, the Big PCD in full bloom. It was wall-to-wall penguins, with activity everywhere. Spread below were what I conjured to be a *gazillion* chinstraps. Who can count that high? Under the rim—in the direction we'd just climbed, two hundred feet below—streams of chinstraps raced to a ledge above the rolling sea, nervously waiting a chance to jump in. Their demeanor suggested prowling leopard seals roaming the shoreline. A dream was fueled, a magic and magnetic attraction—a promise to return again and again.

So this early December day is a rekindling. I feel a chaotic, life-affirming thrill watching the scrappy chinstraps rushing back to mates, high in the hills. Ineluctably, powerfully, I'm drawn to large penguin colonies in the breeding season. Penguins' lives are normally fast-paced and riotous, but the calamity seems heightened during this particular stretch of time. Drama, pathos, and high comedy weave inextricably over the penguin landscape—all to be enjoyed, assuming I can trudge uphill successfully and savor the action from the front-row seat.

They rumble on the entrance beach and assault the crushed stones with explosive energy, surfing beachward on muscle-tight chests, resembling millions of energized lemmings. Perched on a slight rise of beach, just short of the surf, I have a stage-center seat in an IMAX theater of chinstraps, who spew and smash, 3-D fashion, right into my lap and just past my eyes. More whams, bangs, and pops. All are sparkling clean from their feeding runs offshore, their narrow black chin stripes glistening against the pearly white and wet neck feathers. Their immaculate appearance is negated in only one respect: after these healthy krill runs, their feathery cummerbund barely contains a newly acquired yet temporary plumpness. They are rather stuffy-looking, and all that seems to be missing is a top hat and chauffeur. Beady yellow eyes slit my countenance, trying to shrink my towering height. Shaking and trimming quickly finished, they anxiously prance inland and upward toward the colony's center. Hungry, incubating spouses await them. Call it herding behavior or troops on a mission, these hardwired chinstraps lust ahead with little delay. I note few deviations from the preordained plan. They can't be denied, and nothing stops the onslaught.

There is a constant flow of chinstraps up and down along the stream—hordes leaving or returning en masse. The chinstraps' orientation today is British: the uphill throng moves left of the stream, with the downhill throng to the right. Many of the chinstraps don't have the patience to walk the edges and ford straight through the stream, irrespective of the water's pace and depth. All of them make it, though some are better than others at finding stepping-stones in the middle. Some sink in the gushing water to their bellies, some to their throats, a few even swim across. None of this effort seems a bother. They're troops on a mission—with an important job to do, and nothing, certainly not some swift-flowing meltwater, is going to interrupt them. They emerge quickly and continue waddling forward, wherever they're going. The shape of the meltstream changes each season. The ash surface is easily gouged. Much depends on the amount of winter snow and how quickly it melts. But the stream never stops flowing. Even when the year's snowfall has gone, the stream will be fed by Deception's glaciers and ice cap.

Baily Head's mold represents aeons of volcano-altered rock. Ultimately, on its higher reaches, as it transforms into a holy synagogue of chinstraps, the colony becomes a striking amalgam of green mosses, orange lichens, and pink penguin guano set against the volcanic motif of gray, black, and white. It is a perfect place to study or, as some would say, endure penguins. The landscape is characteristic of Deception's violent past, substantially littered with explosive remnants and huge, pockmarked bombs. The guano smell takes some time to ignore. The guano also has a way of invading one's gear and pores, where it remains and defies both strong detergent and extended aeration.

The protein explosion is another indication of the chinstraps short window of opportunity—a tight, two- to three-month frame to quickly find their mates, court, copulate, lay, incubate, and fledge this season's young. If a chinstrap winds up with the same mate from last year, the result is more circumstantial, as opposed to true love. The pair bond depends on the female's return to last year's nest site and how soon it follows that of the male, the pair not being together during the off-season. The male chinstrap will return as early as possible to set up shop, the more experienced breeders accessing the taller, more rugged nesting sites that have been blown free of snow by the howling spring Antarctic winds. The male claims his turf, unfurls his rousing ecstatic display, and expects that she'll be there, shortly....

Penguin sex is critically important. And because Antarctic penguins do so well at reproducing themselves, they have survived extraordinarily well as species. Darwin would be proud. They are prime examples of successful evolution in action. We humans seem to ponder our value in starkly individual terms, often critiquing our individual prowess intellectually, physically, sexually, or according to some other narcissistic measure. And while some of us contemplate whether we're headed for heaven, hell, or something in between, some of us too easily ignore that the true test of successful evolution actually ties to our collective success as a *species*. Our one-on-one successes are rather irrelevant.

Examining penguin reproduction, therefore, casts a slightly different light on our slight niche in Earth's scheme of things. They take a pounding and keep on ticking, so to speak, and I'm rather confident they have no appreciation of individual worth. They're too programmed, too hardwired. Nothing seems to divert them from their mission. There's no time for kissing and foreplay—they proceed virtually straightaway to copulations, assuming mates successfully find each other when the breeding season commences. There is no rest and they undoubtedly get weary from meeting the chicks' endless demands. Their window of opportunity is so, so short. That's why I've come. To witness them, firsthand, tackling the obstacles—spreading the genes to another generation. To see the chaos—a potpourri of courtship in full flower—it's best to get to Baily Head in early December, and to get to as high a vantage point as possible. I'm right on time.

Two nests away, I see another variation of this mutual greeting. It's a low bow-and-hiss affair, with the two chinstraps dropping their heads forward with extended necks, then slowly twining their heads and snaking them skyward, showing the sides of their heads to one another. With beaks closed, they each emit a low, guttural *awwhhhhhhh*. In the middle of the oval, one chinnie starts a vigorous ecstatic display, its beak to the sky, and is loudly and swiftly joined by eight to ten others. It's hard to quell the anthropomorphism, but the higher reaches of Baily Head present a wild scene— a veritable soap opera of growls, snubs, charges, stark jealousies, and fights.

These are the concerns: Have the males made it back to the little pebble nests that served as home last season? Has the female in the pair survived the winter? I want to see more males loudly croaking for their mates and sweating out the wait. Will they divorce? Do chinstraps have affairs? Well, it all depends.

The clock ticks.

Next to me, another stand-up fight has reached the knockout and knockdown stage. Both combatants are bloodied. The stronger of the two forces its chest at the other, whacking it with a stream of flipper blows. One of the punches mashes the other penguin's face and knocks it to the ground. Going for the kill, the victor stomps on the loser's belly, then boldly stabs and grabs the other's neck with it's beak and pushes it downhill. The blow's momentum and the steep incline cause the losing bird to tumble unimpeded until it disappears over the edge of the hummock. The victor raises its beak to the sky, erupts into another ecstatic, with wings outstretched, screaming wild and repetitive *∂uh-ARGH'-ARGH'-ARGH', ∂uh-ARGH' ARGH'-ARGH'* calls as it jaunts over to its nest, which I hadn't initially noticed. The two mates exchange some *quiet mutuals*, again this low bowing followed by raising their twisting necks slowly, growling their low, orgiastic moans. Blood still flows from the combatant's face, but these are superficial wounds that will disappear, washed by the sea, during the next feeding run.

What's happened is this: Mr. Chinstrap returned a few days ago to his previous year's nest site, awaiting his mate's return from her off-season jolly. Where is she? Will she make it back with reasonable dispatch? He waits. A few days overdue — no problem. But now, almost a week has passed. His hormones are escalated to fever pitch. The coming season is all too short and there's no time to diddle. He's also starving. Patience has evaporated. In utter frustration, he's courted and mated with an unattached female who happens by.

The denouement arrives with the original Mrs. Chinstrap, who finally returns and finds a young intruder in her nest. And Ms. Wrong, after a veritable heavyweight championship bout, is the one who, presumably, just got pummeled mercilessly and tossed downhill. Mr. Chinstrap, no doubt, has lots of *'splaining* to do. But Mrs. Chinstrap doesn't hold much of a grudge. She can't. Time's too short. The now reunited mates again twist their heads to the ground, then in unison raise their necks and beaks skyward, accompanied by more low, groaning *awwhhhhhhh*. Shortly they will copulate, repeating the act two or three times, and within two weeks their two eggs will be laid, two to three days apart.

Above me, saucer-shaped lenticular clouds birthed by strong katabatic winds over the Bransfield indicate foul weather arriving imminently. But this scene must be savored, at least briefly. I've reached Baily Head's highest ridge. At this level, the peak of mating has passed. A number of clutches are complete, one mate incubating, the other away, feeding. The panorama is extraordinary. Toward the island's interior, for mile after mile, specks of chinstraps gleam like jewels against the volcanic landscape.

The ridge line undulates up and down like a vast curtain. The nitrogenous perfume and increasing wind rustle various thoughts. Among these chinstraps, I sense a powerful freedom and an immense privilege. I've come to witness a particular spectacle and I haven't been cheated. Darwin marches on.

On the high rim, I stretch prone, lying quietly, simply taking in as much as I can—still dealing with my PCD. One returning chinnie is pounded and pecked along the route back to its nest. Another holds in its beak a rock that's twice the size of its head. Three pairs erupt into mutual ecstatics, their hot breaths spiraling upward. Below, an endless stream of chinnies rises through the fog now enveloping the meltstream. A few are fast asleep with beaks tucked under wings. Do they have REM sleep?

Seeing chinstraps firsthand—having this eyeball-to-eyeball experience—is special. Six chinstraps scurry forward, skipping closer and closer. A few bend over in their characteristic, snake-necked posture, slowly raising their head to engage my stare. Their deep and darting yellow eyes articulate a new path—a contemporary yellow brick road, inviting me to appreciate their lives and to connect with them.

Which brings Albert Einstein to mind. Despite his own revolution of quantum mechanics, he never wavered from believing that the universe is governed by discoverable laws in which a God-like mystery inheres. In his words: "God does not play dice." But, having tackled such mysteries and having integrated their concomitant complexities into his everyday life, he reportedly viewed preachers and their preaching as blasphemous. It was in this sense: Einstein had seen more majesty than they had ever imagined, and he felt that their sermons weren't the result of firsthand sweat and experience, that they simply weren't talking about the real thing.

I hunker closer to the ground, my head poised at chinstrap eye level. My reduced size surely entices their penguinesque curiosity. My legs stretch across the outside edge of this high pink and green breeding oval, left elbow propped on the ash, head lowered to *Pygoscelid* height. There are ecstatic displays and raucous *∂uh-ARGH'-ARGH'-ARGH'*, *∂uh-ARGH'-ARGH'-ARGH'* calls from two birds barely beyond my boots' reach. Other chinnies stride over, dipping beaks into my parka's folds and crevices, inspecting my nooks and crannies. One gives my face a close going-over, and jumps back when I exhale. Within five minutes, a few have crawled around my back, and one prances on my hip and on the side of my chest. It stops, raises beak to sky, and begins an ecstatic roar from my highest point. I feel like I'm part of the scene, a bona fide part of them. Or, in Walt Whitman's words:

> I think I could turn and live with animals,
>   they are so placid and self-contain'd,
> I stand and look at them long and long.
>
> They do not sweat and whine about their
>   condition,
> They do not lie awake in the dark and
>   weep for their sins,
> They do not make me sick discussing
>   their duty to God,
>
> Not one is dissatisfied, not one is dement-
>   ed with the mania of owning things,
> Not one kneels to another, nor to his kind
>   that lived thousands of years ago,
> Not one is respectable or unhappy over
>   the whole earth.
>
> So they show me their relations to me,
>   and I accept them,
> They bring me tokens of myself, they
>   evince them plainly in their possession.

> I wonder where they get those tokens,
> Did I pass that way huge times ago and
>   negligently drop them?

They have no fear. As Robert Cushman Murphy suggests, a chinstrap has a special "kind of *bon camaraderie* if he meets you where he has no reason to resent your presence." Murphy recounts Arthur G. Bennett's story of croaking to chinstraps and having one respond by popping into his boat and soon falling into a doze—apparently planning to stay and sleep unless evicted. Yes, knowing them is life-affirming, the profuse reward for those lucky few of us who've gazed into the eyes of chinstraps.

They are hard to fathom: they have a relatively short longevity, survive an environment I can't tolerate, and continually humble me with routines that effortlessly get them through their frenzied lives. Can't fly—but they are remarkable swimmers, migrating as much as two thousand miles if necessary. How do I relate to a creature that's succeeded so well, whose numbers have blossomed into the millions? No doubt, with awe and respect—and some curiosity about still-unexplored ties between them and us.

I pick up a few unclaimed stones and offer them to the chinstrap who now ambles inquisitively at eye level. It grabs one token with gusto, as if it's stolen a great prize, and scampers quickly toward its mate and chicks on the far side of this pink guano lek. But abruptly, as if it's hit a solid wall, it stops, turns completely to catch my eye, then bows deeply. I return the homage with a nod of the head and a wave of my right hand. It croaks, raises the stone to the sky, shakes its bill, then runs away frantically, no glances back.

I want to be free, like them. They simply are. Never planned, hardly contemplated, and not asked. I don't want to be an actor locked in a role that others dictate. My short time needs to be its own legacy. I dream a new paradigm, conjuring hazy views of unexplored territory, an unending quest for a better understanding of penguins, and recognizing, humbly, our biological ordinariness.

So give stones to chinstraps. And dream of humans risking greater connections. Imagine our résumé evolving from uncontrolled consumer to enlightened participant in the scheme.

Ron Naveen is the founder and CEO of Oceanites, an organization dedicated to raising public awareness of the world's living marine resources. He is the author of *Wild Ice, The Oceanites Site Guide to the Antarctic Peninsula*, and *Waiting to Fly: My Escapades with the Penguins of Antarctica*, from which this story was excerpted. He lives in Washington, D.C.

What the Raven Said

JIM NOLLMAN

*An interspecies odd couple tries to
build bridges for the future.*

A RAVEN GLIDES IN LOW OFF THE ARCTIC
plain, lands ten feet in front, then walks right up
to me. I am lying on my side, using a backpack for
a pillow, reading a book. Now I sit up tall and stare. The
bird responds by pulling its head back although it moves
not an inch. I decide, for no good reason, that it's a male. He's
not large by raven standards, about the size of a football.

The raven is standing so close I could reach out and
touch him, although I decide against it. His long scimitar
beak could render real damage to my hand if he found
offense. He cocks his long beaked face this way and that as
if trying to figure out the best way a bird, whose eyes are
arranged on each side of his head, might stare directly into
the eyes of a human being whose eyes are set on a flat plane.
I wonder if the bird may actually solve what is to my mind

27

an insoluble problem of eye contact, because it soon starts croaking and squawking and cooing in a whispery, soothing tone meant only for my ears.

He searches my eyes. I get an idea, rush to my tent, search a pocket of the backpack to find a small bamboo Jew's harp carved by an Ainu craftsman in Northern Japan. I rejoin the raven, hold the instrument against my lips and start plucking it back and forth with the thumb of my left hand. *"Boing, bo…boing, boing, boing, boing, boing"* goes the harp in syncopated four-four time. The raven moves a step closer, stares at the instrument as if a careful examination might help him pick up a new riff or two to add to his own wide repertoire of sounds. He starts croaking, a sound generated deep inside the gullet. It reminds me of a housecat from a parallel universe who purrs his contentment two octaves below, and at half the speed of, a normal housecat. Twenty minutes pass, a veritable eternity in the annals of interspecies communication. We're still at it. The blend of baritone purring and boing-boings has evolved to sound like a didgeridoo accompanying an overtone singer from Tuva. Our bond is sealed.

I'm played out. Need a break. Stand to take a long walk out on the vast uninhabited plain of the MacKenzie River Delta in northern Canada. The raven follows twenty feet behind and ten feet above me. Our recent music-making has made me acutely aware of every sound emanating from the flat, scrubby plain. The beat of the bird's wings adds a catchy counterpoint to the pad of my sneakers pressing earth. He flies ahead and lands, apparently trying to serve as my guide. When I arrive at the spot, he takes to the air again and lands another few hundred yards in front. I follow him for about a mile, quite willing to surrender whatever subliminal itinerary I might have to the bird's own. To what treasure will he lead me? A thousand-year-old cache of walrus ivory incised with spirals, swans, and stick figures beating on flat skin drums? Or perhaps to a raven's treasure: the rotting corpse of a lemming.

When I suddenly head off on my own, mostly to test the winds of my own contrariness, I justify the new course in my mind as "an experiment in interspecies communication." The bird makes not a sound, but takes to the air to trace my tracks. Within fifteen minutes, without knowing precisely when or how it happened, I notice that the bird is leading again.

When I return to camp several hours later the raven stands on the peat, never more than a yard's length away as I cozy up to a smoldering campfire and stick my cheek against the ashes to breathe the coals to life. I am surprized he's not afraid of fire, or at least this particular fire. I heat water, make hot chocolate. Drink it down. Then enter my tent to sleep. I awake, pop my head outside the tent. The new declination of the sun informs me I've been out for three hours. The raven is standing right beside the door. I feel flattered by his companionship, although I am not yet vain enough to disallow the fact that the camp food is kept in several white buckets stored by the side of my own tent.

The bird does something curious. It flies off the bluff and hides in a willow thicket beside the shore when one of my traveling companions, Jonathan Churcher, strides into the makeshift kitchen to fix a sandwich and brew a cup of coffee. I say nothing about the raven, who rejoins me within a minute of Jonathan's departure.

Immanuel Kant wrote that the human hand is the most visible aspect of the human sensibility. We are creatures of hands and fingers that long to touch and feel and caress our environment. Unfortunately, the fulfillment of this longing has developed into one of humanity's most detrimental traits. That which we touch we too often alter for our own utility. To the many species of animals that need unadulterated ecosystems to prosper, the human alteration of habitat must be viewed—in the gut if not always in the mind—as an augury of their destruction. Most animals seem to know this fact about human hands, although most humans do not seem to know it at all. Ravens apparently know it exceedingly well because my own wandering hands soon cause a major rift in the fragile relationship that is developing between the two of us.

I'm munching my way through a stack of Ak-Mak crackers. The raven coos and clicks as his way of asking for a handout. I oblige. He takes one square at a time from my palm. When the bird directs its full attention to gobbling down a square, my hand abruptly darts across the unstated boundary line between our personal spaces to affectionately stroke its hard, black, bumpy back. The raven lets loose with a piercing squawk. I yank my hand out of reach of its intimidating beak and then quickly pull myself two feet backwards. The raven stays where he is, although clearly in turmoil. He chitters and chatters, jerks his head to and fro, right and left, moving forward and back. Despite the agitation, he displays no intention to stab at me.

I speak to him in a tone of whispery supplication, much the way the little Bushman pleaded with the monkey who stole the sinister Coke bottle in the film, *The Gods Must be Crazy*. "I'm sorry, I'm truly sorry, please believe me. I won't touch you again." He does not respond, but continues to jerk his head back and forth, finally regains his composure, looks me over sideways as if he was sadly mistaken to make eye contact with such a rude person who either never learned the rules of raven protocol or, far worse, refuses to honor them. He flies off, squawking "nevermore" in the strongest raven language possible. I am devastated. How could I be so disrespectful? I'm hardly unaware that human touch is taboo, the kiss of death, among wild animals. I'm sorry. Please. Give me one more chance. The bird settles on the riverbank a hundred feet away.

It takes three hours of apparent nonchalance and unspoken conciliation between the two of us before the bird decides to venture close. But he relents, flies to my side, where he makes that strangest of all raven calls that sounds like a drummer banging on woodblock. Once, twice, three times. I feel blessed by his proximity: a raven's way of communicating that my indecent affront is forgiven.

I am no stranger to ravens. Where I live in the Pacific Northwest, the species is one of the most common birds, although my own local ravens are at least a third again larger than this underfed Arctic bird. They also produce a more varied repertoire of calls. To hear an unidentifiable animal calling in the woods near my home—even to hear what to most people's ears sounds like a rooster escaped from the coop—is to assume that it's a raven experimenting with a

new call. Where I live I have never heard of a raven openly
mingling with a human being, which seems unaccountable
considering the number of local Indian myths that focus on
human interactions with the species. Raven was traditionally considered a trickster, the northern cousin of the
Southwest's Coyote, protagonist of hundreds of folk tales
among indigenous people from Washington State to Siberia
to Greenland who portrayed the bird as a comedian and a
malefactor who often became the butt of his own jokes.
Raven possessed genius, the first shaman, a true prodigy
among animals. He put the sun in the sky, regulated the
tides, created humanity from out of a clamshell, then sealed
the bargain by bringing us culture as well. The sheer number of these myths about the human-raven bond suggests
that as late as fifty years ago, human beings and ravens
probably enjoyed some measure of a ritualized dialogue,
perhaps folded into the layers of an arcane native ceremony
revitalized each year through a secret mix of initiation and
psychotropic prodding.

Nevermore. To the local ravens, I am no more an individual than they are individuals to me. Call me *generic man*,
the meanest-spirited and most dangerous species in all of
creation. The result of this generic reputation is clear. The
local ravens treat me as the personification of evil. I occasionally try to emulate them vocalizing among their kind.
The response is immediate. They stop calling altogether and
beat a hasty retreat. It's to be expected. In the past year
alone, two raven nests in my neighborhood have been felled
by neighbors for what are labeled utilitarian reasons. In
both cases, the presence of raven nests was not considered

any good reason to keep the trees standing. Generic man did it. It's he who used the birds for target practice. Despite the fact that this generic man views his raven vocalizations as a gesture of admiration and friendship, the act gets interpreted in the context of centuries of disintegrating protocol between our species. I remain an optimist, and so, for other generic men and women who love the raven, I offer this advice. Keep squawking, rasping, hissing, knocking on wood. Something's got to give. Maybe not today. Maybe somebody's great grandchildren will notice a difference in a hundred years.

I have not seen my two campmates all day. Daniel is searching for beluga whale skulls in an abandoned Inuit hunting camp. Jonathan has paddled off in the other direction, following a moose's splayed footprints in the hope of landing a photograph of North America's tallest animal. The land basks golden-orange in the eerie light of midnight. The wind is stronger than last night. I feel sleepy, retire to take a nap. The sides of my tent roar and snap like a whip as I unzip it and climb inside. Yesterday, Daniel strung up a whole beluga whale skeleton on an old Inuit drying rack a hundred yards from my campsite. As the wind accelerates, the bones start clicking and clacking against one another. I ordinarily keep the tent tightly sealed to keep out the mosquitoes. Tonight the wind keeps them grounded better than anything I might accomplish with zippers so I open the tent a crack at the bottom in an attempt to equalize the air pressure inside and out. I lie down, must fall into a dream because I am soon awakened by a gentle jab to the shoulder. I pop open an eye and notice my friend the raven. He is glaring down at me from a perch on the metal frame of my pack. That scimitar beak, three inches long and black as coal, is just above my face. I instinctively place my hand in front of my eyes, pull my face back.

He touched me? Is that what he did? Touched me? "So, you've decided to up the ante," I remark loudly to be heard over the noise of the fierce wind buffeting the walls of the tent accompanied by the rattling of the whale bones. He is cooing while poking his beak at the pack. "A few crackers will do it, please." Is that what he wants? Is he asking me to open the top zipper to liberate the round salty crisps that we both know lie inside? I nod my head in affirmation, reach up, unzip the pack without moving it, find the cracker box with my fingers, extricate it, zip up the pack, open the lid of the box, unfold the plastic inner wrapper, and grab a handful of brown corrugated crackers. The bird reaches daintily from his perch on the frame. Selects a cracker. I feel blissful that a wild animal would honor me with such a close encounter.

At the moment of our mutual communication triumph, a substantial glob of white goo squirts from the raven's hindquarters onto the zipper of my pack. Now it's my turn to react without premeditation. I let loose with a scream so shrill that, truthfully, it would only be justified if the pack cloth were sizzling into a smoky slag from contact with the odious juices emitted by such a vile scavenger. I feel enraged, but also a bit frightened, point lividly at the mess, then at the bird who suddenly seems to have quadrupled in size. He flaps his wings. They have grown to fifty feet wide. "Get out of here! Get out! RIGHT NOW!!!" I scream, raising a hand to throw the first projectile I can grab which, in this case, is a handful of crackers. They spin across the length of the tent like a drizzle of frisbees, and thud against the screen. The bird appears mostly unfazed by my outburst. But something is communicated. He jumps lightly off his perch, waddles cross my sleeping bag-covered legs, picks up a cracker, delicately lifts the tent screen with his beak, and ducks through the hole.

I break off a piece of toilet paper, clean up the sticky mess, and then toss the soiled paper out the hole. An hour passes in the golden Arctic night. I regret my response and wonder if, indeed, there might have been any special significance to the fact that the raven defecated precisely on the zipper pull? Who's to say he doesn't interpret the sudden appearance of so many crackers as a just trade for his own murky deposit. What do I know? Defecation could be a raven's most deferential response to an offer of food, the analog to a human curtsy, a bow and a thank you very much. What if he was simply trying to tell me in his most erudite manner that, "Ah yes, my dear fellow two-legged. Allow me, your most grateful raven, to poop most fulsomely on your zipper as a gesture of my humble esteem?"

Deena Metzger has written that animals are different intelligences, each species holding and expressing a body of knowledge in its own manner, each species different in its knowing and responding to the world. Yet in so many ways the raven and I are alike. Subtle gestures enacted to display respect and friendship and ultimately meant to elevate our relationship to a new level are not understood at all by the other. Other gestures of no consequence whatsoever get interpreted by the other party as uncouth impudence. We two are bumblers, an interspecies odd couple, inadvertant perpetrators and, consequently, overreacting victims of our own species-specific behavior patterns. Yet we long to connect, both of us striving to cultivate the novel camaraderie that binds us to a middle ground of our own invention.

Apparently, both of us also know how to forgive.

When I open my eyes again, there are mosquitos on my cheeks. The wind has stopped. I dab the bugs to oblivion, zip up the bottom flap of the tent, then fall asleep again, dream, waken a bit, write, nibble, read, sleep again. The raven's black silhouette remains stooped in a submissive pose just beyond the closed-up tent screen. He sways and coos, trying to win me over with whispery supplications, seduce me to open the zipper. "Please, my good friend," I hear him cooing, "tell me what I have done to deserve this snub. You must know I meant nothing by it. Let bygones be bygones. And why not? Let me inside again. Perhaps share another cracker, have a good talk about the meaning of life."

I wonder why I haven't seen another raven since this one arrived on the scene yesterday. Is it coincidence? Or do I belong to him. His conquest. His possession. His pet. Poe felt far more vindictive about his own raven whom he depicted as a symbol of Death, a metaphor that harkens back to the Middle Ages when ravens were considered the companions of witches, like the bird who counsels the evil queen in *Snow White*. The Catholic Church, in particular, saddled the species with so much diabolical baggage because this raucus, midnight-black scavenger that picks over the bones of the dead clearly has a keen intellect.

Ornithologists tell us that ravens possess as great a variety of calls as parrots, mynahs, and mockingbirds. Their calls correlate so closely with social behavior that it suggests the rudiments of language.

Ravens are also notoriously mechanical, the engineers and physicists of the avian world. They have been observed pouring water from a pool onto dry objects to plump them up before eating them. In captivity they have been observed placing solid objects in a cup of water to raise the level to where they can get a drink.

Then there is my own raven. More than once over the past day, I have been forced to stop dead in my tracks, stare at this Other. He seems a patient friend, occasionally a teacher, trying his best to get me to understand his drift. He has continually raised the stakes of our mutual reverie.

Morning arrives. The sun sits high in the southeast quadrant. I lie in my tent fully awake, lying on my back examining the effects of bright sunlight filtered through the green ripstop nylon. Thousands of mosquito bodies bump up against the fabric. With my eyes closed it sounds like rain. I hear the sound of a food bucket being pried open, the rhythmical priming of the camp stove. Is it possible? The raven has learned how to use the stove? I rush outside to encounter Jonathan sitting on the ground staring placidly at a bowl of granola he holds like a robin's egg in the nest of his gargantuan hands. I walk around the tent. Scan the plain. The raven is gone. When I ask Jonathan if he turned into a raven last night, he peers at me quizzically, then grins broadly, "Oh yah, sure, that was me all right." I sit down on the ground to tell him of my experience.

He nods, downs a few spoonfuls of granola, then stops long enough to uncork a story he heard last winter from a local trapper from Tuyktoyuktuk named Thomasie Cowcharlie.

"Thomasie was out in the bush about two hundred miles south of here when a raven arrived in his camp. Just like your bird, this one made himself at home, kept cooing as if trying to communicate. Thomasie made no response, so the raven flew off, returning a moment later with a stick in his mouth. The strangest thing happened. The bird traced figures in the dirt, pausing every so often to stare into the man's face, as if searching for a sign of recognition." Jonathan's droopy face displays nothing. He takes another few bites. "It's a true story. But you know I always thought it was too bad that guy didn't copy the scratches down on a piece of paper. I would have liked to see what they looked like."

Jonathan looks me in the eye, and then tells me it's time we left this place. His tone implies that it's not some whim of his. We must leave. Our time is up. I don't ask him to explain, it's never been his manner to buoy up his hunches with logic. I request a few more hours. I want to take the boat a few miles offshore and look for beluga whales. He nods, although a minute later I see him disassembling his tent. I eat my oatmeal with maple syrup and dried apricots plumped up, raven-style, by letting them sit overnight in a bowl full of water. Then I grab my journal to write down the story of Thomasie Cowcharlie.

There on the last page, I discover a single sentence that, for the life of me, I cannot remember writing, although it was probably entered sometime during those long hours of half sleep, half waking:

What would this bird and I have left to talk about after ten thousand years camped in this spot.

Jim Nollman is a pioneer in the field of communication between species and is the founder of Interspecies Communication, an organization dedicated to promoting dialogue between humans and wild animals. He is the author of two books, *Spiritual Ecology* and *The Charged Border: Where Whales and Humans Meet*. He lives with his family in Friday Harbor, Washington.

Laughing Loon

SIGURD F. OLSON

*Once you've heard it you will never forget the
lonely music of the northern lakes.*

THE CANOE WAS DRIFTING OFF THE islands, and the time had come for the calling, that moment of magic in the north when all is quiet and the water still iridescent with the fading glow of the sunset. Even the shores seemed hushed and waiting for that first lone call, and when it came, a single long-drawn mournful note, the quiet was deeper than before.

Above came a swift whisper of wings, and as the loons saw us they called wildly in alarm, increased the speed of their flight, and took their laughing with them into the gathering dusk. Then came the answers we had been waiting for, and the shores echoed and re-echoed until they seemed to throb with the music. This was the symbol of the lake country, the sound that more than any other typified the rocks and waters and forests of the wilderness.

To me only one other compares with it in beauty and meaning, the howling of the husky dogs around the Indian villages in the far north. Their wild and lonely music epitomizes the far reaches of the Canadian Shield, means nights when northern lights are a blazing curtain along the horizon.

While the northern loon in startling black and white, with its necklace of silver and jet and five-foot spread of wings, is of great interest scientifically, it is the calling that all remember. Whoever has heard it during spring and summer never forgets the wild laughing tremolo of the reverberating choruses.

One such night is burned into my memory. It was moonlight, the ice had just gone out, and the spring migration was in full swing. Loons were calling everywhere, not only on Knife but on adjacent lakes, and the night was full of their music from sunset until dawn. The echoes kept the calling going until it was impossible at times to tell which was real. While I listened it seemed to me that in that confused medley of sounds was a certain harmony as though major chords were being held for periods of time. It may have been imagination, but I have heard hints of it at other times as well. On this night there was no mistake, for the calling blended with the echoes until the illusion was complete.

The weirdest call of all is the yodel somewhat similar to the break in voice and clear bugle-like note used by humans in calling across the wide valleys in the Alps. This is the danger call used when a canoe is approaching a nesting area or when invasion is imminent. It can start all the loons within hearing, and when the yodeling blends with tremolo they are really making music.

The third call is the wail often mistaken for the howl of a wolf, and of much the same quality. It rises and falls in pitch and is used when a mate is calling for relief from its brooding on the nest or when signaling the young. Just that morning we heard it among the islands. We had been watching a pair swim slowly around the little bay where they had nested, with a lone chick riding sedately upon the back of one of them. When they saw us, they gave their warning calls at once, for that lone chick riding so grandly around the bay and no more than a day or two off the nest was far too small to fend for itself. We paddled toward them while the calling grew more intense, came at last directly between the parents and their young one, which now was trying desperately to dive. A week old it would have been able to submerge and swim for fifty feet or more, but this little chap was at our mercy and the parents were aware of its danger. At times they came almost within touching distance and tried to draw us away with the old ruse of pretending to have a broken wing and thus easy to catch. How they floundered and threw themselves about. When their enticements failed to work, they approached again, rearing up on their tails and uttering loud cries as they balanced there and all but treading water before flopping forward on their breasts. The performance was repeated over and over again. They screamed and hooted and yodeled and gave the laughing call, but to no avail, while the chick, now confused and thoroughly frightened, swam hopelessly beside the canoe. Other loons in the vicinity swiftly joined the commotion, and the entire area was in turmoil.

Deciding they had been frightened too much, we turned

and paddled back to the point, but for a long time after we had gone the calling continued. It was not surprising they were alarmed, for this lone chick brought out all of their protective instincts for the season of mating and nesting. Seldom owning more than two and often only one because of predation, they found in that last chick their whole excuse for being.

Just after the ice was out we had watched that pair come into the bay, stake out their nesting area, and repel invaders whenever they approached. One day we watched the courtship. They came toward each other slowly and, as they neared, dipped their bills rapidly in the water and just as rapidly flipped them out again. This was followed by several short swift dives, exaggerated rolling preens and stretchings such as only loons seem able to do. Suddenly they broke away from such intimacy, raced off across the water, striking the surface with powerful wing beats in a long curving path that eventually led back to where they had started. All during this time they indulged in the laughing call. Sometimes in the ecstasy of display they reared high on their tails as they did when their chick was endangered, struck their snowy breasts violently on the water, then raced again around the bay. Only once did we see this, but shortly afterward the mating was over and then we found the nest in a tussock of grass on a little swampy island close to shore and facing the open water. It was placed so they could slip off swiftly and reach the deeps should danger come behind them from the shore. The two olive brown and somewhat speckled eggs were soon laid in a small shallow depression in the grass that was built up during the days of incubation until it was a concave little mound, each mate doing its share while it sat there, pecking and adding a grass blade at a time from the vegetation within reach.

A couple of weeks later one of the eggs was destroyed by some prowler, possibly a mink, a crow, or a muskrat. The remaining egg now took all of their attention, and they guarded it jealously every moment of the day and night. If this had been stolen too, it would have meant a new nest and possibly another hatching.

Scientists say that in half the nests only one hatches out, and that the low rate of survival accounts for the fact that loons are never numerous. If two individuals reproduce themselves after their third year, then things are going well. It is surprising in view of the high mortality rate that populations remain as steady as they do; in spite of predation, loons are often found on almost every lake in the north.

One afternoon we sat on the point watching a flock of them playing on the open water. They had been there as a group since midsummer, bachelor loons and pairs that had not nested or had lost their eggs. Now free of responsibilities, these thwarted birds gathered each morning and spent the day together in the open. It may have been that the fishing was good in that particular spot, but I am tempted to believe they got together for a companionship that took the place of nests and young.

Suddenly one of the group called and then all together until the channel before us was again full of sound. Excited by their own music, they chased one another madly across the water, returning always to the place they had left. Toward dusk the flock began to disband, single birds first and then pairs flying back, no doubt, to their abandoned nesting areas. Sometime in the morning they would drift back again by ones and twos to spend the day together as they do on many of the larger lakes all summer long.

A pair flew close to the point and settled in the bay off the beach, and we watched them diving there for minnows, timing them to see how long they could stay submerged. Seldom did one stay under for more than half a minute, but there are records of dives as long as two and three minutes in duration. Some have been recorded even longer than that, but such observers may have failed to see a partial emergence for air. They are wonderful divers and swimmers, can pursue and overtake the swiftest of fish, and it has been said a loon can dive at the flash of a gun and be underwater before the bullet strikes.

They can also submerge gradually, can control specific gravity possibly by a compression of feathers and explusion of air from the lungs until the body is approximately the same weight as the water. All divers have a high tolerance for carbon dioxide, and oxygen needs are met, not from free air in the lungs, but from the oxyhemoglobin and oxymyglobin stored in muscles, substances responsible for the dark color of flesh in most waterfowl. This explains the diving, the gradual sinking from sight, and the fact that they have been caught on fishermen's set lines in Lake Superior at depths of two hundred feet.

Once I sat in a canoe at Lower Basswood Falls and watched a loon fishing in the rapids not fifty feet away. Suddenly the bird dove and swam directly under the canoe not two feet below the surface. The wings were held tightly

at the sides and the legs the sole means of locomotion. When
a young chick is learning to swim beneath the surface it uses
both legs and wings, a reversion perhaps to the days of its
reptilian ancestors; a habit generally abandoned, however,
when it becomes adult.

It was now much too dark to see and we left our loons
for the light and warmth of the cabin, but in the morning
we watched them again. The pair had stayed close to the
bay during the night and now were swimming around in
the sunshine, getting ready to join the gathering flock on
the open lake. We watched them, the brilliant black-and-
white markings on their backs, saw one preen, rolling over
on its side exposing the silvery-white breast until it glit-
tered and shone in the morning sun. The other rose to its
full height, flapped its wings vigorously, and settled down
again. Then both dove with scarcely a ripple to mark their
descent and soon were far past that point, heading for the
rendezvous.

A pair flew overhead, and we heard plainly the whistle of
their wings, watched the slow and powerful beats as they
headed across the lake. As they passed the gathering flock
they gave the tremolo once and then settled down with the
rest. I had hoped they might do what I had seen them do in
the past, glide into the waiting group with wings set and
held in a motionless V above their backs. Once I had seen
them come in that way on Kekekabic, approaching the lake
like seaplanes about to land in a long unbroken glide from
the top of the ridge to the water's surface.

But, while they are strong flyers and can swim and dive
as few birds can, they are absolutely helpless on land, and

only once have I seen one more than twenty feet from the water. I was coming across a portage with a canoe on my back, and there, to my amazement, was a loon standing bolt upright in the center of the trail. I was so startled by the apparition in black and white that its scream of alarm almost made me drop the canoe. The bird turned and literally hurled itself toward the shore, half flying, swimming, and running on its ridiculously tiny legs. With a wild water-choked yelp it plunged into the shallows and out to diving depth and swiftly disappeared. That explained why nests are always close to the shore. Loons must be able to slide instantly into the water, cannot waste precious moments struggling over land. No creature is clumsier out of its element than this great diver of the north.

The sound of a whippoorwill means an orange moon coming up in the deep south; the warbling of meadowlarks the wide expanses of open prairies with the morning dew still upon them; the liquid notes of a robin before a rain the middle west and east; the screaming of Arctic terns the marshes of the far north. But when I hear the wild rollicking laugher of a loon, no matter where I happen to be, it means only one place in the world to me—the wilderness lake country and Listening Point in Minnesota.

Sigurd F. Olson was a teacher, author, philosopher, defender of the wilderness, and environemntal leader. He sought a place which typified the wild and sacred north country he loved, which he finally found at the edge of the Boundary Waters Canoe Area near his home in Ely, Minnesota. He named it Listening Point. Although he passed away in 1982 at the age of 82, his family has carried on his legacy by establishing The Listening Point Foundation, a non-profit organization designed to preserve the natural and historical integrity of Listening Point. The beauty of this place can be found in his second book, *Listening Point*, from which this story was excerpted.

Without a Ripple

AMY GREIMANN CARLSON

Ahhhh, to be like the heron
and simply wait.

BEWILDERED ABOUT MANY THINGS THESE days, I am always scurrying from here to there crossing off things on a never-ending list; like digging a hole in the sand, the deeper it gets the more unstable it becomes. As the list grows I become more and more frazzled, racing after time. There never seems to be enough of it.

Wallowing in my lack of time, I write just to get the pen started while sitting outside on a rock being buzzed by hummingbirds. I am wearing red and sitting in the flight path between elderberry bush and feeder. The male is currently perched on the feeder chirping at either his missus or me — I can't tell. Oh, how I wish I could talk to birds or at least know their thoughts. What must it be like to be able to fly in currents over a ridge top? Or make love on the wing? Or be in constant song? My racy companions this brisk afternoon can, if I sit long enough and quietly be, teach me how to better deal with my nature, my own racings, my connections to the natural world.

When I am most flummoxed, as I am today, I head outdoors to one of several favorite places to sit, sometimes with pen and paper, sometimes with little else than my thoughts, which most of the time is far from little else and quite a problem. I recently received a card from a dear friend, Jo, which vividly illustrates the all-consuming and destructive tendencies a brain can possess. A cartoon: first frame—a man sits on a chair; second frame—a bubble appears above the man's head; third frame—the word think appears in the bubble; fourth frame—suddenly there are many thinks in the bubble; fifth frame—the thinks begin to escape the bubble and devour the man's head and so on until the man has disappeared and the last frame is filled with thinks.

My mind on this very day has attacked me, aided by hormones, and I have come outside on my rock to feel the storm cresting the ridge, to be buzzed by my tiny friends who keep me company despite my racing mind. I must meditate. I must stop the attack by drinking in the rhythms of stillness and movement all around me, to remember the wisdom of the heron who taught me years ago this rhythm that I so desperately need this day.

Lopez Island in the San Juan Islands of Washington State welcomed Scott and me with a campsite within the embrace of a cove filled with sandy beach. Upon arrival, I flung off my shoes and made a mad dash down to the water's edge, plunging my big toes into frigid Puget Sound. With a yelp

I yanked them back out, beet red and stinging. Walking as though on pins and needles, I gingerly forded the expanse of sand back to the tent. Rubbing my feet back to life, I assembled the camping stove to heat water for our dinner, mouth-watering freeze-dried stroganoff. After washing this sumptuous repast down with some merlot, I grabbed a bar of dark chocolate in one hand and my friend's hand in the other.

"Lets go watch the sunset!" I bleated, waxing about missing my New England childhood and its sunrises. Sunsets were still a novel miracle to behold. I didn't give Scott a chance to respond to my monologue, pulling him down to the beach. The sand felt warmed by the afternoon sun. Each step gave the feet a massage, an *ahhhhhh* moment after every plunge of a foot. Wanting more, I plopped down on my behind and extended my legs, feeling the coarseness on the calves, hands moving arcs of warm granules beside my thighs—ecstasy. Sand up the shorts, sand in the hair, sand up the nose, and yes, sand on the chocolate—I was in my element. With a quiet beginning to the evening, water calm, the sun vanished behind the pines of a neighboring island. Dusk. We sat in kairos—timelessness—no lists, no talk, and almost no thoughts. We were ready.

And then it happened. Out of the corner of my eye I sensed motion. Three massive silhouettes glided into full view within seconds, paralleling the shore. We held our breath…herons…with wings seemingly 25 feet across. They looked as though they were going to sail right passed us when suddenly one of them broke formation, banked a perfect 90-degree corner and came straight at us. By this

time, the failing light shrouded us in semi-darkness as we sat
as still as blades of grass on a windless day. Our heron,
silently, without one flap of its "25-foot" wingspan, glided in
for a shallow water landing, coming to rest within an arm's
length of the two human statues poised on the beach and
became a heron statue. It stood in knee-deep water, frozen,
with not a pulse pounding, a feather fluttering, or an eye
roaming. It simply was. If we hadn't seen it fly in, we might
have wondered if it weren't an artist's creation commis-
sioned by the park in which we camped. People and bird,
both still. As I waded in the stillness of this moment I understood for the first time that I had finally touched the biblical
mandate, "Be still and know that I am God."

But my back ached to be freed from its locked position.
My neck pleaded with me to look in another direction, but
I instructed all body parts to remain at attention. They
screamed. I sat, and sat, and sat. I was not going to move
from this moment until the bird broke the magic. Time
passed. I was just about to give in to my body's protests
when the heron, as if he could read my thoughts, began his
dance. Never before or since have I been witness to such
grace and finesse that was displayed that evening by that
bird on that beach!

With utmost care and concentration, he lifted one leg
slowly out of the water without a wobble, without a drip,
without a ripple, without any other movement of any kind,
and dipped it back in with pointed foot so as not to cause
any water displacement. As smooth as silk, he took another
step with his other leg in the same manner as the first. In,
out, in, out, until an abrupt pause, like freeze-acting, he

stopped in the middle of his movement and turned statue once again, but this time it was different. We could feel him waiting for something; a tangible anticipation of something good; a fish.

And then: he cocked his head to the side as if to get a better look with one eye, and without hesitation, pierced the dusk with a swift and sure downward swoop of the beak, catching his flailing prey and lifting it out of the water skyward to swallow it most heartily. Every bird's *ahhhhh* moment. We continued to watch in awe as he stepped, paused, cocked, and struck seven more times, never once missing. He never was in a hurry. He never stumbled or fretted. He never made a ripple. He never gave up. He never counted the fish he caught. With his total being he lived in the moment, smoothly, without falter, feeding himself and us till our bellies were full. Together we had participated in something holy, partaking in a precious ritual, filling our souls with the wisdom of stillness and the rhythms of a creature who moves with his creator.

I want to tap that wisdom now when I am far from still and my lack of rhythm sends me reeling, causing ripples all around me. Can I sit here on a dry mountainside surrounded by balsam root and lupine and draw in this wisdom taught to me so many years ago and so far from here? Can I set free the memory of a heron with a 25-foot wingspan and rippleless steps to help me learn how to feed myself again? I need that heron! Instead I have hummingbirds dive-bombing my head, joyous, piggy little bee-wanna-bes sucking sugar water from a feeder and chirping at me from the ocean spray bush. What do they have to teach me? The lesson has yet to be learned, but I am confident it is there. I just need to be like the heron and wait.

Amy Greimann Carlson is a teacher, editor, and gardener who lives in Leavenworth, Washington, with her husband Reed, juggling many projects in between building a house.

Stop the Car

MONICA WOOD

Who needs all the fancy gear when you have the kids along?!

M Y BEST FRIEND ROBIN AND I LIKE GEAR. We're bird-watchers—"birders" to those in the know—and our bird paraphernalia makes us feel lucky. We have vests with 24 pockets. We have field guide holders and notebooks that hook to belt loops. We have bird whistles and gum boots and other needful things. Birding is a hobby that requires long, Zenlike stretches of patience. The right accoutrements—an extra spotting scope, say, or a bag of chocolate bismarcks—can turn a drizzly vigil into a festival of anticipation. Gear is good.

On this wintry Maine day, however, we're carrying a bit more gear than we bargained for: Anna and Kate, Robin's children. Anna is seven months old and oblivious, but Kate, at two and a half, is well acquainted with the art of expectation. "Where's Kate's owl?" she asks every hundred feet or so, her shoes ticking against the plastic ridge of her car seat. The owl in question is the great gray, a rare, magnificent winter visitor that Robin and I have firmly resolved to witness, babysitter or no babysitter.

During the ride, a straight shot north on Route 1 that passes frozen inlets and craggy little fishing towns (in short, all the places where there is absolutely no chance of spotting a great gray owl), the kids are perfect. Pink-cheeked and snoring, these polished little apples of our eyes have fallen asleep. Robin and I chat softly, wondering how a great gray owl might look in person. I read aloud the owl's description from the old Peterson's, the new Peterson's, the Audubon, and the National Geographic field guides. We eat a couple of chocolate bismarcks for luck.

An hour later we approach a spit of land that juts like a broken finger into the Atlantic Ocean. Robin slows down as I read the directions, and we find an ordinary country road flanked by peeling houses and fallow fields. "Start looking," I whisper, and Kate startles awake. I try a preemptive strike, lest she wake the baby. "Hi, sweetie," I croon, handing her a doughnut—backup gear that does the trick. This is Kate's first doughnut, and she is pleased. We are geniuses. We are birders extraordinaire.

We inch down the road until we spot three other gear-laden birders gathered at the edge of a field. Within seconds Robin and I are out of the car. We sidle over to these people and ask, "Is he here?"

There are two kinds of birders in this world. We are the kind who hug and dance. They are the other kind. We manage to extract the relevant information: the owl has been seen in this very field at more or less this very time for three days running. That's the good news. The bad news is that Kate's doughnut is gone. The sound emanating from Robin's car, reminiscent of screech owls I once heard in the north Maine woods, alerts us that we're about three minutes to meltdown. We retreat to the car, trying to appease the spoilsports in the backseat. One of the birders knocks tersely on the window: "Maybe if you drive around for a while they'll fall asleep." Mortified by this helpful advice, Robin starts the car. As we leave the scene, harboring just the tiniest wish to leave the kids in a snowbank—not forever, just for ten minutes, even five, long enough for us to catch the smallest glimpse—Anna falls back to sleep. It's a miracle! But Kate is not so easily duped; our adventure is cut short. "That's that," Robin sighs. "Let's go home."

A minute later, at the far end of the road near a saggy ranch house, I feel my mouth drop open. "Stop the car!" I shout. Robin stops. Kate stops. "Look," I tell them, pointing to the wintry scrub of yard. There, staring out from the naked branches of a birch, stands the great gray owl. It turns its head to leer at us with fire-yellow eyes.

We bound out of the car, pulling Kate with us and leaving all our gear, for the owl is so close—ten feet at most—that we can see the delicate parentheses of feathers that frame its massive head. We gape at the owl. We name him Frank. We hug and dance. Kate stands between us, looking up. Then, as if delivering a message only owls can comprehend, she opens her mouth and screams. Wings lifting like a velvet cape, the owl disconnects its heavy body from the spindly tree that held him.

Oh, what a day! On the way home we ponder what propels some birds to wander thousands of miles from home and other mysteries of the natural world. After a while, it strikes me: we could still be waiting in vain at the edge of that empty field. I glance into the backseat at the gear jumbled up with diapers and size one mittens. We didn't need the binoculars. We didn't need the scope. We sure didn't need a bird whistle. What we needed, as it turns out, was the kids.

Monica Wood is a fiction writer whose short stories have been widely published and anthologized. She won a 1999 Pushcart Prize for short fiction. She lives in Portland, Maine.

Short-tailed Albatrosses

DIANE ACKERMAN

The toll is high for a visit to the remote Japanese island of Torishima, the final stronghold of an endangered species.

A S EVERYONE PREPARES FOR THE HIKE ACROSS the island, we indulge in small good-luck rituals— retying our shoes, adjusting our helmets, tucking our pants into our socks as protection against scree. Then thirteen of us set out in a long caravan climbing behind the garrison, past the abandoned weather-station barracks, over a steep meadow of grasses and low, bunchy, yellow chrysanthemums. Below us, skirts of frozen lava ripple toward the coast, where they once enveloped a whole village. Making our steepest climb in the early part of the day, we cut across the mountains more obliquely, walking up a glacier of crushed lava, and over ground singed with bright yellow sulfur salts and hot black scabs. By midmorning, we reach the flattest place on the island, at the base of Sulfur Peak. There a field of lava rocks—missiles ejected from

the volcano—has turned the narrow col into a wind-
blown moonscape of starkest black and white. Moon
Desert, Hiroshi calls it. He points to emptiness at the end
of the col, where the land drops away and the entrance to
the cliffs begins.

"We'll be able to see the albatrosses from there," he says
excitedly.

Everyone else rushes on ahead, but Peter and I walk
slowly as before. At last we cannot make the moment wait
any longer. The col opens into an explosion of tall pinnacles
and wind-ripped cliffs, where rock walls spill down through
twisted chasms. There before us stands the fortress of the
ahodori. Far at the bottom, down an impassable set of inter-
locking cliffs, a small flock of brown-and-white birds dot the
grass. They look like handkerchiefs someone has dropped
onto a lawn. An invisible fist knocks the breath out of me
and I sigh out loud. There are so few of them. It is heart-
breaking to see the last remaining nesting short-tailed albatrosses on earth. Over the breeze, we can just make out their
whistles and whinnies, and their castanets, which sound like
hollow wooden pipes hitting one another. The scene throbs
with color—the bulging, oxidized orange cliffs, the green
grasses below, on which the albatrosses nest, the tan rock
face, the golden ochers, the black lava. Through binoculars,
I see the yellow crowns of the birds, so close now, but still
so inaccessible. Above them, a fantasia of albatrosses sails
across the sky. Men built a garrison at the other side of the
island, but nature built one here that is far stronger—almost
impenetrable. Because of this natural fortress, based entirely
on the bad temper of rock, the birds have survived the

onslaught of humans. Peter stands at the lip of the cliff, one hand lightly pressing his binoculars against his chest, his eyes damp with emotion.

Hiroshi joins us, and we three stand silently and behold the fortress for some minutes. It is utterly astonishing that Hiroshi has been studying the birds in such an impossible locale for the past ten years, that he has managed to bring out news of them and even on rare occasions to take the outside world down below for a closer look. That the birds are increasing in number is a great testimony to Hiroshi's work and to the support of the Japanese government. It's comforting to think that in a high-speed world, where people sometimes content themselves with shallow efforts, naturalists like Hiroshi are devoting their lives to saving one species. What a rich remembrance, to know that you preserved a miraculous form of life from disappearing forever from the planet.

"Let's go," he says at last, and we set off along the east side of the walls. Hiroshi has marked a large O in white paint on some of the more secure rocks along the way. It is a steep, slippery descent down sheer four-hundred-foot cliffs. When we come to a particularly awkward plunge of rocks near the edge, Hiroshi attaches a rope to a rock. Passing the rope behind the waist, and holding one section in the right hand, one section in the left, a strong climber can lean back against the rope and use it to slip and brake his way down without using a harness. I have never climbed with ropes before, but I like the feel of the rope as it slides and rasps through my hands. Leaning back, I try to lower myself slowly, but my foot swivels, and suddenly

I skid downhill toward the cliff edge, clinging to the rope.
Loose stones clatter below. Everyone freezes. Above me, I
see Peter, Hiroshi, and the ten other men transfixed to the
rocks, watching me suspended over a four-hundred-foot
chasm, all the emotion smashed out of their faces. There is
no point in looking down. My mind fills with a single
thought: *Don't let go of the rope.* Hanging on with my left
hand, I bring my right hand around, find a handhold, and
pull myself back up. Once I find my footing, I continue
across a rocky bridge and let the rope loose for the next
person. Above me, people begin to move normally again.
The next climber takes the rope, becomes confused, freezes
midway across, and will not go on. Peter climbs down after
him, at last coaxing him along. Despite their knapsacks full
of photographic and surveying equipment, the rest of the
team gradually work their way down the first section of
cliff, and then we angle across to a more severe plunge.
Here Hiroshi has hammered four pitons into a rock at the
top, from which he has hung a rope. Peter and Hiroshi
have both been rock climbing for many years, and I understand at once how seductive it can be. At each station along
the way, you feel hawklike, perching high in towering freedom to pause and look out over the valley below and the
ocean beyond. But I especially like the puzzle of figuring
out which rock will make a handhold; what tablet, pyra-
mid, or silo of earth to cling to; on what slender ledge to
place my foot. At times, you are violently gripping the
bones of the planet, and at others tiptoeing down the shal-
lowest stairway. It is a strange, tentative searching with all
your limbs that unites you, as nothing else could, to the

core of the planet, to the violence that forged it, to the
thrust and fall of the rock frozen forever in the memory of
a mountain. Rocks have veins and faces. And there is a tex-
ture of rock—in one moment raspy, spiky, and brutal; in
the next gentle, forgiving, and smooth. There are the colors of blood, midnight, and autumn. There is the steep per-
suasion of gravity, drawing you down its rocky spine.
Again I misstep and, holding on to the rope, slide back into
a ledge, collect myself, and continue down to where
Hiroshi, seeing that I'm all right, leaps into a hill of deep
sandy lava and cascades with it clear down to the bottom.
Peter does the same, and I follow. Then we scramble up a
small dune and suddenly find ourselves staring straight
across a plateau at two bustling colonies of short-tailed
albatrosses.

Nesting, yawning their wings, romancing, tending their
eggs, bickering, they go about their normal ways, only two
hundred yards from us, far enough not to be frightened by
our presence. Vibrant white, with radiant yellow heads and
coral-pink bills tipped in blue, the adults are unbelievably
beautiful. A subtle wake of shadow runs behind each dark
eye. Glossy, elegant, smooth as wax, they stretch their airy
wings and, even while sitting, embrace the wind. The ado-
lescent birds are brown or have mottled plumage of brown
and white, some with striking white epaulets. All wear
small, discreet colored bands around their legs—a present
from Hiroshi so that he can identify them. Each color
denotes a different year. A white band, for example, was
put on the right leg of each of the forty-seven birds hatched
in 1986. The two colonies of birds are separated by a black,

swirling drape of lava, which is narrow enough for the birds to walk across. Young birds sometimes take a mate in the other village and settle there. Depending on the wind, a bird may land in the lower village and climb up to the higher one. The older birds (with whiter plumage) prefer to nest in the center of the colonies, the younger birds near the edges. Some are sitting on eggs. Occasionally a bird will stand, rearrange its feather petticoats so that the egg nestles tightly against the warm brood patch, and then, with a twitch or two, settle down deep into its soft haunches again. Two eggs lie outside of nests, which means the chicks within will have died. In a species as rare as this, where every newborn counts, that is a tragic sight.

A particularly lovely female with a bill the sultry coral of the Bahamian sunset opens up her downy wings and preens them gently. Every single feather has a nerve ending she can use. I try to imagine what it would be like if I could put my arm out and twitch each hair separately. A male approaches her, and suddenly she spreads out the white skirts of her wings and curtseys to him. He curtseys back. Then he reaches with his bill and brushes up a few feathers on her breast. This drives her wild. She slides her bill down along the side of his and starts delicately kissing the small feathers at the base of it. He does the same to her, and they pull back a few inches and start a crescendo of clacking that sounds like a spoon hitting hollow wood—castanets. They roll their heads together from side to side, as if packing an imaginary snowball. He rocks forward onto his toes, aching toward her, and presses his chest out like a sail in a strong blow; she does the same. Suddenly they toss their heads skyward, stretch their necks long in mutual yearning, quiver and flap and trumpet to high heavens.

Their wild, otherworldly music drifts across the grass, half whinny, half moo, like "surrealistic lowing of cattle," as Peter describes it. Next they do a "Groucho walk" around each other—a low-down strut with their shoulders hunched—and then they face each other and start to curtsey again. While this erotic minuet continues, dozens of black-footed albatrosses, a darker and less extravagant-looking species nesting nearby, engage in more modest courtship dances of their own, in which they sound like speeding cars screeching around tight curves.

All at once, a white short-tailed albatross sails in off the ocean, flies a wide spiral around the colonies, banks and tilts with fluent grace, and begins what's called reefing. Arching its chest, it pulls the huge sails of its wings in halfway, lets its big feet hang down like a plane's undercarriage, ruffles up its tail feathers as a sort of air brake, and tries to slow down enough to land. Round and round it flies, soaring and reefing, swooping low and funneling high, with an eloquence that leaves us gaping, not quite sure on which pass it will lose flying speed and touch down at last. The sunlight shines through its yellow feet, as if through the paper panes on a sliding door in a Japanese house.

"*Kirei*," I say, more an exhalation than a word. It is Japanese for "beautiful." And I mean all of it: the heat mirage, like a transparent curtain of shop silk between us and the colonies; the nesting birds, perfect as alabaster statues; the ceremonial square dance of the courting pairs; the incoming bird whirling low and then climbing into steep registers of sky, where it half-swoons like the high notes of a saxophone solo.

"*Kirei*," Hiroshi says quietly, his eyes also following the hypnotic flight of the albatross, which twitches its tail a few times.

"Why are they called short-tailed albatrosses?" I ask. "Their tails don't look unreasonably short." Without shifting their gaze, Hiroshi and Peter smile.

"It's because of the way their feet stick out," Peter explains. "A large bird needs long legs and big feet for take-offs from water. In fact, sometimes, if the wind isn't quite right, they'll run for about fifty yards or so and give up. The tail appears smaller than it really is, but that's an illusion. They could just as well be called the long-legged albatross."

"It would perhaps be better to call them by their other name—Steller's albatross," Hiroshi says. "Especially since a number of the animals named by Steller—who was a great naturalist—have now become extinct." Pulling a notebook from his pocket, Hiroshi begins taking the year's census of birds, eggs, mated pairs. Peter takes a sketchbook and soon fills two pages with courting pairs of albatrosses caught in the midst of telltale gestures. An albatross passes over our heads, and the wind rushing loudly through its feathers sounds like the distant roar of a 747. At last it reefs in low over the high village, stretches its feet down even farther, as if somehow to telescope them to the ground, does a head-to-toe twitch arpeggio with umbrellaed wings, and lands in a series of recovered falls, which ends only when it somersaults into a back flop. We laugh. Albatrosses are great courtiers, great aerobats, but also great buffoons.

By midafternoon, the birds who spent the morning feeding at sea return to their colonies. One by one, they enter the fortress skies to form a giant "kettle" overhead—a bubbling of birds. As one dives down, finds a clam, drops anchor, and lands, another slips in on top of the thick stew of albatrosses now circling, angling, diving, wheeling, sliding across the sky. Wings spread, they make black crosses against the silver sea. An albatross sails in low over our heads, drops its feet, reefs in its wings, cuts close to the ground, only to be lifted again by an updraft. It spreads its wings and sails around for another try, misses again, sails around once more, braking with its feet, swooping and turning, in desperation heading in close to the cliff face to get a stall effect, which finally works. In twenty attempts at landing, it did not flap its wings even once.

The albatrosses seem so safe and at ease in this rocky cloister. Every one of them is descended from a few who were at sea when their brethren were killed. Once young birds are fledged, they go to sea and will remain there from three to five years. Some young birds that had left the island, escaping both the bludgeoning by the feather hunters and the volcanic eruptions, were the progenitors of all the birds we see today. If, unlike other albatrosses, these birds are wary of humans, it's understandable. Fowlers started coming to Torishima in 1897 to harvest the feathers, and by 1900 there was a thriving settlement of 300 people. When the volcano erupted in 1902, there were 125 people in the village, and all of them died under a boiling mantle of lava. But other fowlers came to replace them, and continued arriving until the 1920s, when there were no

longer enough albatrosses to make a permanent village
worthwhile. In 1933, a Japanese edict declared Torishima
off-limits. But in 1932 the fowlers, knowing that they were
soon going to lose a favorite hunting ground, set out for one
final slaughter. This massacre reduced the number of birds
from a workable breeding stock of about two thousand to
only thirty to fifty individuals. In 1939, the volcano erupted
again for the second time in this century. The Moon Desert,
which had once been a favorite nesting ground of the short-
tailed albatross, was charred to blowing cinders. During
World War II, the government built a garrison on the island,
and the men reported sighting only one albatross. In 1949,
Oliver Austin, an American ornithologist, circumnavigated
the island in a Japanese whaler but did not see any albatrosses at all, and he believed the bird to be extinct. In fact,
there must have been a few hidden nests, perhaps no more
than four or five. A few birds were spotted in 1950. In the
autumn of 1965 there were many earthquakes, and the per-
sonnel from the weather station were evacuated.

Alone at last in their stone citadel, the impoverished
family of short-tailed albatrosses gradually began to rally.
Conservationists made sure the species was internationally
recognized as endangered by the International Council for
Bird Preservation, which held a congress in Tokyo in 1960.
This led the Japanese government to designate the short-
tailed albatross a national monument in 1962. When Hiroshi
became involved with the project, he threw himself into it
like a dynamo. On November 17, 1976, he made his first
trip to Torishima, and he has returned at least twice a year
ever since, to study the birds, monitor their progress, and

do what he can to help them recover. In 1956, there were just twelve reported nests. But in 1988, eighty-nine eggs were laid.

This may sound like a success story. But short-tailed albatrosses are still desperately endangered. If the volcano should erupt again, as it could at any time, and the area where we now sit should be destroyed, it is unlikely that the albatrosses would be able to nest anywhere else on the island. Breeding would stop. So it is crucial that the albatrosses be attracted to as many other sites as possible. Hiroshi hopes that if the birds can be persuaded to multiply well on Torishima, they will seek nesting colonies on other islands, too. On the leeward Hawaiian islands, short-tailed albatrosses have been spotted sitting alongside black-footed and Laysan albatrosses; and they have been seen on Minami-Kojima in the Senkaku Islands. But they haven't been seen nesting in either locale.

Although Hiroshi has been their knight errant and keen observer, the short-tailed albatrosses remain a feathered mystery. Because there are so few birds, it's difficult even to chart their seasonal movements. But we do have a few scraps of information about their habits, in particular, and much more is known about the habits of albatrosses in general. In early October, the short-tailed albatrosses return to Torishima and congregate offshore for a few days, and then start landing on this small platform at the base of the cliffs. Albatrosses live long lives—on the average, from forty to sixty years. Each bird one sees is a long-term inhabitant of the planet. They are monogamous, and a pair will rendezvous at the previous year's nest site. A young bird will return to the island after two or three years at sea and begin the baroque courtship display that ensures a tight pair bonding. Young birds may not understand how to copulate, but they often try it anyway, even if it means sitting on the head instead of the tail by mistake. What they're doing in their early years is practicing romance and learning how to set up a home. The courtship display—which they must perfect to such a razor-fine finesse that they can dance in unison as one rapture, one yearning—is necessary to bring the pair to a pitch of arousal where copulation can occur. Intercourse itself lasts only about thirty or forty seconds in albatrosses. The extravagant buildup is everything....

When the light starts to fail at day's end, we reluctantly pack up to leave. Soon the cliffs will be full of nesting shadows, and climbing back up to the land of humans will be too difficult. We must go, but we would prefer to stay, camped out at the edge of this natural stage, watching albatrosses coast among the Gothic spires of rock. Being close to albatrosses is an experience somewhere between the spiritual and the sexual. As their whinnying cries fill the air behind us, we hoist our burdens and start the long climb.

When we return to camp, we find the government team is back and busy with dinner, so we unpack and take seats around the low table. We laugh when we see the banquet being spread before us; expeditions usually mean canned goods and stale bread. Tonight there is pepper steak, rice, barbecued fish, freshly prepared sushi, and fresh vegetables. Then the cook brings round a platter of cooked limpets. A delicacy, they are dense and gristly, reminding me of the inside of a horse's hoof—including the stones. Mandarin oranges and beer and strong Japanese spirits follow. Overhead, five bird constellations watch us in silence—the Crane, the Swan, the Phoenix, the Peacock, the Eagle— from their stone-cold aviary among the stars. Peering into the well of night, my gaze tumbles toward deep space, and back in time, toward the first feathery tantrums of the universe. My craft is so small, I think, and the ocean is so wide. Exhausted, at last, from the long day's rigors, everyone wanders into the bunker, crawls into a sleeping bag, and waits with eyes closed for the generator out back to run down, so that the lightbulb inside the bunker will fade for the night.

No alarm sounds, but at precisely three minutes to six, all of the men wake up, stretch their arms wide, and then, one by one, drift lazily out of the bunker. The cook yawns, tucks in his shirt, puts a large kettle on the gas burner. We eat breakfast quickly, excited to be heading back to the fortress. Though Hiroshi's backpack looks even heavier today, he somehow manages to carry it cheerfully, even taking the short, slow steps of a man on a long journey with a heavy load. Once more, we climb up past the abandoned weather-station barracks. The haunting notes of a plover drift across the morning as we hike over the lava lakes and through the fields of yellow chrysanthemums. Today the walk is faster and easier. The journey up is different from the journey down. While we're fresh, we climb steeply at first, then continue across the lava fields to the lap of Sulfur Peak, where the ground is hot to the touch and sulfur fumes dance in the lengthening light of dawn. Some areas of the Earth look raw. Without the volcano, there would be no Torishima, and no refuge for the albatrosses. Throughout the oceans of the world, magma from the molten core of the Earth pushes up to form volcanic islands like this one. The molten lava solidifies, becomes more stable, and slowly drifts, while other hot spots produce more volcanic islands, and soon there is a steaming archipelago. This is my first volcano, and I love watching the sulfur fumes dance like *djinns*.

As we climb across the pungent fields, I feel the warmth of the island's molten heart through my boots. Steam, like a dragon's breath, rises all around us. In the Moon Desert, where the lava sand blows, each footstep leaves a cloud, as if one's life force were burning right through the soles of one's feet. Yesterday we left pouches of water at this spot, and I fall to my knees and hold one of them overhead, pour a long gush of water down my throat, and wash the black dust deeper inside me. Then we continue on through the narrow col. Soon we are at the edge of the fortress and begin climbing down. More tentative than yesterday, I find the first rope easier today. At the second, searching out good footholds, I slide down a rock with one foot, carry the second foot around, slide down to another ledge. The next toehold waits below. Stretching, I give the rope a little slack, stretch farther, lower myself, feel toward the spot, then —*bang!*— the floor shoots away underneath me, and spinning around, I fall backward, my left hand gripping the rope as I smash against sharp rock. Pain butts deep into my back. Below me, Hiroshi has already climbed out of sight. Peter, vigilant nearby, looks calm but ready to spring.

"I'm hurt," I call, and the words come out as a long moaning.

He rushes to me, where, in mid-cliff, I am wedged in a colander of rocks, and he says, "Breath deeply. That's better. Get some air in."

"I think I've cracked a rib." Looking down at the cliff below, then up at the cliff above, I wonder, How will I get out of here?

Perched below me, Peter checks the best route down. Although I know it's going to be painful, I must somehow turn around and hold on to the rope tightly with my left hand. My hands are what will save me. I turn and grasp the rope. That small movement sends lightning forks through my chest and back. Peter calls out footholds.

"Stretch your right foot down to where my feet are," he says. I do. "Now move your left foot below you to an open space beside those two narrow rocks." He steps down six inches. "Right foot just above where my right foot is..." And so we climb down to where the rock face quits and the lava hill begins. There, struggling to keep my torso straight, I put my hands on his backpack and follow him slowly down to the bottom of the dune.

Hiroshi runs forward, anxious and sympathetic. The two men try to pinpoint the pain bleating low on my left side, which has made it impossible to bend at the waist — or cough, speak loudly, sneeze, or laugh, as I soon discover. I will be doomed to a life of shallow breaths for some weeks. Guiding me up onto the crest of the lava dune which is our lookout point, they dig a pit, brace it with knapsacks, and settle me into the hold. Later I will learn that I have broken three ribs—complete breaks, with the rib spars lying parallel to one another. For months, I will not be able to lie down or stand up by myself, and pain will be my constant companion. But when I watch the albatrosses coast overhead, holding the sky upon their wings, filled with the restless ongoing of their flight, I would not trade my lot for anyone's. Life is too full of easy entrances and exits. The birds need their fortress, which is all that has saved them. I do not welcome this pain, gnawing like a wolf pack, but if that is the toll that must be paid, then it is well spent. Taking a breath, I laugh quietly to myself. No wonder they have survived here. I am proof that their fortress works.

At twilight, when like monks we finish our silent beholding, which for me is a form of prayer, we gather up our knapsacks and consider the ascent. Hampered by a tight straitjacket of pain, I cannot move the left side of my body; yet somehow we must climb back up the cliffs. Hiroshi loops a guide rope high around my shoulders, and Peter lifts me bodily. We are a good team, in calm and in distress. Working together, the three of us finally emerge from the fortress and climb wearily back down toward camp.

"A great day, despite everything," I tell them, and I mean it. "Who would drink from a cup when they can drink from the source?"

The next morning, Peter and Hiroshi set off by themselves, the government men prepare to leave on a chartered boat, and I spend the day in camp. The pain has gotten much worse, and I can feel bones shifting like mah-jongg tiles when I inhale. Soon a fever begins, and will not relent under an assault of aspirin, acetaminophen, and antibiotics. The closest hospital is eighteen hours away by fishing boat. I know breaking your ribs can swiftly lead to pneumonia, and as my fever soars, I drift in and out of consciousness. In lucid moments, I consider grim possibilities. I may die on this remote island, alone in a stone bunker, far from home and loved ones. When one of the engineers returns for his gear, I whisper the Japanese for "Help." Using pantomime and a few words from a Japanese phrase book, I tell him, "Sick. Broken inside. Please, find Hiroshi and Peter. With albatrosses. Please go fast, fast." I give him a short note to deliver. When the runner leaves, I wrap myself in a heap of clothing and blankets and wait. A young Japanese woman arrives—I do not know if she is real or a hallucination. She feels my burning head, takes off her white shirt and washes my face with it, fills the shirt with ice—Where did the ice come from?—and lays it across my forehead. Then she disappears. Deep within the bunker, I watch a few rays of sunlight construe the narrow room. The outside world trembles with light. I dream of blinding-white albatrosses, whose yellow heads sparkle as they whirl in the twilight like an unnamed constellation. Suddenly a shape appears at the door. Panting, sweat pouring off him, his hair slicked back like a steel helmet, Peter looks as if he had just fallen down a birth canal. Taking off his pack, he sits down, and we discuss the various ways off the island. The safest is to go on the government charter boat, which will be leaving soon. The fever is steep and mysterious, and we must act quickly. He has already said good-bye to Hiroshi, who stayed

behind at the fortress, at his post with the albatrosses, where
he belongs.

An hour later, we climb aboard a boat three times as
large as the one that ferried us to Torishima. This one, only
two months old, gleams with stainless-steel fittings, pile car-
pets, and sleeping bunks. A charter boat, it cruises the
islands to the north, mainly on scuba-diving and fishing
trips. The mystery woman who bathed me with her shirt is
a crewmember, and the captain has radioed ahead for an
ambulance to meet us at dockside. Before heading north, the
captain circumnavigates the island, which gives us a fine
view of the bolts of lava where the village was washed into
the sea. Sulfur Peak stretches up raggedly, as if to pipette
the blue sky. At last, the fortress of the *ahodori* drifts into
view, with its cantilevered walls, amphitheater of jagged
rock, and small green apron dotted with white. Surrounded
by the frozen cascades of rock, the birds look delicate
and fragile.

"The world's entire population of nesting short-tailed
albatrosses," Peter says sadly. A moment later, he grins
broadly. We both do, feeling the same indelible thrill at
having seen them. "Look, there's Hiroshi!" He points to a
lone figure sitting on a dune of lava underneath a snowstorm
of soaring birds. We wave to him, and Hiroshi lifts his hat
and waves back. As the boat turns north, and the sun begins
to set in a thick welter of clouds, a recording of "Auld Lang
Syne" gushes from the loudspeaker. Short-tailed albatrosses
swoop and slide across the wave crests. One dives just off
the bow of the boat, picking up speed as it enters the realm
of calm air. Now it turns across the wind, skates behind a

wave, and then tips its wing, turns up, and rises fast, almost vertically, behind the wave crest, tilts around, and then starts across the wind again, zigzagging at colossal speed. For some time, we stand in the glow of the setting sun and watch the albatross cartwheel over the waves, changing from white when it's framed by the dark water to black when it's framed by the paler sky. Positive and negative, it dives from the transparent air down to the thick gelid water and up again, lacing the sea and sky together with its swooping flight. It is the wind's way of thinking about itself. At last, it flies straight down the sun street and out toward the horizon, under a tumultuous bruise of sky, where shadow haikus dance on the water, and disappears into a bright kingdom of clouds.

Diane Ackerman is the award-winning author of several books including *A Natural History of the Senses*, *A Natural History of Love*, *The Moon by Whale Light*, and *The Rarest of the Rare: Vanishing Animals, Timeless Worlds*, from which this story was excerpted. Her work has also appeared in *The New Yorker*, *National Geographic*, *Parade*, and *Condé Nast Traveler*. She lives in upstate New York.

II

Kindred
Spirits

Crazy Courage

LOUISE ERDRICH

*An unlikely stand-off gives testimony
to a greater reality.*

THE HAWK SWEEPS OVER, LIGHT SHINING through her rust red tail. She makes an immaculate cross in flight, her shadow running along the ground behind her as I'm walking below. Our shadows join, momentarily, and then separate, both to our appointed rounds. Always she hunts flying into the cast of the sun, making a pass east to west. Once inside, I settle baby, resettle baby, settle and resettle myself, and have just lowered my head into my hands to proofread a page when a blur outside my vision causes me to look up.

The hawk drops headfirst out of a cloud. She folds her wings hard against her and plunges into the low branches of the apple tree, moving at such dazzling speed I can barely follow. She strikes at one of the seven blue jays who make up the raucous gang, and it tumbles before her, head over feet, end over end. She plunges after it from the branches, flops in the sun. They both light on the ground and square off, about a foot apart in the snow.

The struck jay thrusts out its head, screams, raises its wings, and dances *toward* the gray hawk. The plain of snow must seem endless, an arena without shelter, and the bird gets no help from the other six jays except loud encouragement at a safe distance. I hardly breathe. The hawk, on the ground, its wings clattering against the packed crust, is so much larger than its shadow, which has long brushed in and out of mine. It screams back, eyes filled with yellow light. Its hooked beak opens and it feints with its neck. Yet the jay, ridiculous, continues to dance, hopping forward, hornpiping up and down with tiny leaps, all of its feathers on end to increase its size. Its crest is sharp, its beak open in a continual shriek, its eye mask fierce. It pedals its feet in the air. The hawk steps backward. She seems confused, cocks her head, and does not snap the blue jay's neck. She watches. Although I know nothing of the hawk and cannot imagine what moves her, it does seem to me that she is fascinated, that she puzzles at the absurd display before she raises her wings and lifts off.

Past the gray moralizing and the fierce Roman Catholic embrace of suffering and fate that so often clouds the subject of suicide, there is the blue jay's dance. Beyond the impossible corners, stark cliffs, dark wells of trapped longing, there is that manic, successful jog—cocky, exuberant, entirely a bluff, a joke. That dance makes me clench down hard on life. But it is also a dance that in other circumstances might lead me, you, anyone, to choose a voluntary

death. I see in that small bird's crazy courage some of what
it took for my grandparents to live out the tough times. I
peer around me, stroke my own skin, look into this baby's
eyes that register me as a blurred self-extension, as a function of her will. I have made a pact with life: if I were to die
now it would be a form of suicide for her. Since the two of
us are still in the process of differentiating, since my acts are
hers and I do not even think, yet, where I stop for her or
where her needs, exactly, begin, I must dance for her. I
must be the one to dip and twirl in the cold glare and I must
teach her, as she grows, the unlikely steps.

Louise Erdrich grew up in North Dakota and is of Chippewa and German-
American descent. She is an award-winning writer whose books include *Love
Medicine*, *The Beet Queen*, *Tracks*, *The Bingo Palace*, and *The Blue Jay's Dance: A
Birth Year*, from which this story was excerpted.

Sweet Hope Waiting

BARBARA EARL THOMAS

*There is no greater thrill than watching
your young ones take flight.*

THE BIRDS WERE PLENTIFUL THAT SPRING. The air thick with sparrows, starlings, low-flying crows, and fabulously fat robins. Since the vines around my porch had finally started to thicken, it seemed that the birds approached ever more closely, swirling, dipping, and then lighting to pick at invisible insects or to drink from the moisture trapped on the leaves. One morning after I turned to enter the house, after inspecting my seeding flower bed, a robin squawked as I opened the screen door. Startled, I looked up to find her aloft in the corner, perched on the edge of my hanging fuchsia basket. Amidst the foliage I could make out her profile, a solid inflated form out of which stared one piercing black eye. For some moments I stood transfixed by her. But I could see no evidence for her to protest. I broke our gaze, went in, and gave it no further thought.

In the week that followed, I noticed her again and again. She squawked upon my entrance or exit. With each squawk her glare intensified. I just stared back. The longer I held her defiant gaze, the more she puffed up. I began to anticipate her presence and that annoying commotion. Like an official announcement, it heralded my comings and goings, and affirmed my presence. When she was away from the basket, I wondered, I'm here, so where are you? Come announce me, pierce me with your black eye.

I took to watching and waiting for the bird. Once I was able to pick her out from among the several in the yard, I noticed that she was not always alone. At times she was accompanied in her daily activities by another smaller robin. I watched them come and go in and out of the vine, rustling it as they went. They appeared content to have me there as long as I remained still. They never flew directly into the vine. One or the other might stop first on the telephone wire, then cautiously move to the magnolia just south of the porch, then on to the rosebush and then furtively move onto the vine. They came carrying in their beaks twigs and other bits of debris. By now, I knew their secret: they were building a nest somewhere in the upper corner of my vine. I looked for it, at first casually and then with determination. For days its location eluded me until, while watering my hanging fuchsia basket, I spied an unusual formation at the base of the plant's branch structure. It was a weaving in and out, a soft scooped-out cup, a construction in progress.

After a brief moment of triumph, panic set in. What was wrong with these birds? Where were their instincts? Why did they pick this hanging basket, and not a tree, on a porch within eye and earshot of humans? I could only imagine that these birds are just like us, pushed by the pressures of an ever-speeding world until they had lost their intuition. I surmised they had picked the porch because the overhang provided protection from low-swooping crows, and the plant because it offered so much foliage and the branches formed a perfect warp for weaving a nest. But without water it would soon not be an ideal hiding space. If the nest was going to be there I had to somehow figure out how to water the plant. And furthermore, if we were all going to be out there on the porch together, the bird was going to have to stop all that squawking every time I walked in and out of the door. After all, it was my porch first.

With the construction of the nest completed, the two birds' flights in and out of the vine waned, and the job of tending it fell, at last, to the one that had so abruptly caught my eye some weeks ago. If my fat bird friend, whom I had taken to calling Mama Bird, squawked when I was outside, I'd talk to her out loud. I'd say, "Hey pipe down, no one's done anything to you yet and you've been here for weeks. And besides, you made this decision, so live with it!" This must have seemed reasonable, for she soon quieted down and just sat in motionless profile when I appeared. She even let me water the plant on the side away from the nest with my long-spouted watering can, but she always kept that one black eye trained on me.

On a day when Mama Bird happened to be away, I ventured carefully up on the ledge of the porch to peer down into the hanging basket. While I knew that the eggs would be there, I was surprised and touched to actually see them. There they were, three tiny eggs of the most delicate translucent blue I had ever seen. They glowed and in their translucence appeared to be floating just above the nest that held them. I moved quietly away and down. It was too much. I began to wish again that she had done it in a tree.

In the days that followed, Mama Bird and I fashioned a set of rules that allowed us to be on the porch together. I agreed not to bustle too near her nesting station and she came to understand the futility of her wild squawking. But that eye of hers, to which I had now grown accustomed, maintained its strict surveillance, keeping me in line lest I forget myself and somehow offend. It grew hard to imagine what a fuchsia could look like without a fat robin burrowed in amongst its branches. I began to think that hanging pots should come with birds to nest in them.

I must admit I wasn't actually looking forward to these pink-eyed, naked chicks chirping for worms. I'm a worrier. I worry about everything. I was just at the point of hyper-ventilation when I heard her trill, and caught sight of her circuitous approach. From treetop, to rosebush, to vine, Mama Bird traveled back with her beak full of a dark, wiggling mass. The pink ones met her return with jubilation and a bobbing-headed joy. I could see them there, all three of them with their beaks stretched open, instinctively begging. So this is how it's done. I thought I should water the lawn and even open the compost bin that was always full of worms. Maybe I could even scoop out a few rich shovelfuls and bring them around so she wouldn't have to fly so far.

When Mama Bird was not feeding the chicks, she was

sitting on top of her brood to keep them warm. They grew fast. At feeding time I could easily see their heads above the ridge of the nest. I was now in the habit of checking each morning and night to see if my fat robin was there at her station. In the evening before bed I viewed it as good omen when I was able to make out her profile, sitting steady and solid on her nest, ready to pass the night.

On one of these nights I was awakened by the most piercing, mournful shrill I had ever heard. It was the sound of terror. It surrounded me, filling the room. It entered my bones and I bolted upright, I knew in an instant that it was the bird. She was there, just beyond my bedroom window, beating her wings furiously against the gutter, which echoed her shrieking. Like a shot I was up and out of the bed with my husband close on my heels.

In an instant I was on the porch. To my horror I found a big, yellow, thick-necked tomcat seated snugly in the middle of the fuchsia basket. He had one bird in his mouth. The two others had fallen down onto the porch floor and were there stumbling about. In shock and disbelief, I waved my arms wildly and screamed at the cat to get out! Get out! In response the cat just turned its head calmly and eyed me as if I was the most absurd creature it had ever encountered.

Seeing the predicament, my husband quickly jumped up onto the ledge and forcibly extracted the cat by the scruff of the neck, flinging him to the porch. Upon hitting the ground, the cat shook its head, dropped its prey and shot me one last confused glance before retreating into the night with baby bird on his breath.

By this time the neighbors on either side were out in their

yards wondering who had been burglarized, or worse, murdered. I remember only briefly acknowledging their presence before my attention trained on the calamity at hand. Two birds were still wobbling around while the mama bird moaned somewhere not far off. The carcass of the third lay lifeless on the edge of the stair leading out to the yard. I thought I saw my husband make a motion as if he were going to pick up one of the birds. Now I was shrieking. Don't touch them! Somewhere in my bungled brain I remembered hearing that parent birds wouldn't care for their young if they were touched by human hands.

My first thought was to take down the plant holding the nest to see if I might coerce the chicks to jump up into it. Upon looking again at the terrified, weary little creatures, I immediately thought better of that plan. In a flash I found myself in the kitchen, looking around for some helpful tool. What I chose was a large ladle-like soup spoon. Back out on the porch, instrument in hand, I swooped down and pre-sented the spoon at the feet of one of the little birds. Without hesitation, to my amazement, it jumped right into the spoon as if it were the elevator it had been waiting for all of its little bird life. I lifted it quickly and carefully back up into the nest. The second baby followed suit.

I anxiously awaited Mama Bird's return the next day. I watched and worried. Several times I found myself just standing in front of the window or out on the porch, willing myself to see her familiar shape. The waiting was long and painful. It was unbearable to consider that I might have saved the chicks from the cat only to have them die of expo-sure and hunger. I imagined Mama Bird on some nearby branch weighing her options and watching me with those black robin eyes.

I, too, was weighing my options, none of which seemed the least bit reasonable. While not impossible, the idea of climbing up to the nest several times a day with worms had absolutely no appeal. I vacillated between being desperate and morose. When I finally could stand it no longer I went out onto the porch and called to her in a high-pitched singsong voice, chanting, Mama Birdie, Mama Birdie, over and over—willing her to take up her place once more in the fuchsia.

As the day wore on I resigned myself to the difficult task ahead and the reality of the poor prospects for my brood. I scolded myself for not having anticipated the possible dangers.

With dusk at hand, I was at the point of conceding when I heard a movement and bustle from the basket. It was too much to hope for, I thought. I feared that my wanting had finally driven me to hallucination, a conjuring of phantom birds. But no, it was true. It was her solid robin-self, briskly surveying the damage and checking the babies. She was back! Like a condemned man reprieved, I was filled with such joy I could barely contain myself.

This was a second chance, rarely granted, and with it I would not fail or be caught off guard by natural, or any other, predators. I staked out the porch. What we needed was a gentle but effective barrier, an early warning system, or a moat perhaps filled with water. My solution was to gather up all the available buckets and jars, fill them with water and place them all around the porch and along the ledge leading up to the nest. This obstacle course was meant to impede and confuse any predatory approach. Cats trying to make their way up to the nest would either fall into the pails, which would make them so crazy they would leave, or knock over the jars, in which case I would hear them and come running.

The next step was to move my sleeping quarters from the second to the first floor. I convinced my husband that we should sleep on the sofa bed with the front door ajar until the birds completed their nesting. After all, one could hardly maintain a vigil sleeping upstairs a floor away. The final piece of the plan called for one of us to be at the house at all times. It was too stressful to leave the house thinking I might find dead birds upon returning.

Who can guess what Mama Bird made of it all. But in truth I sensed that she went about raising the two remaining chicks with a renewed energy. Perhaps she, too, was joyously living her second chance, having escaped nature's odds. And, while she continued to keep close watch on me and all else surrounding her porch, I swear that black eye of hers had lost its opaque darkness. It had become instead a dark liquid pool that shone. It no longer nailed me or shut me out. Now, when she held my gaze, it included me in its reflection as something necessary and natural to her home on the porch.

Mama Bird chirped and sang as she flew in and out to the chicks who were no longer the pink-beige things I had spied only weeks before. They were now gawky preteen downy birds, starting to show their first signs of feathers. Although Mama Bird continued to bring food in, she seemed to do so less frequently, and at times she would sit in the little tree just across from the porch in full sight of the nest and sing to the young ones, who grew excited and implored her to feed them.

Around this time I rarely left the house. I knew that soon I would see their first flight. Now and then she would arrive without worms, and the teen birds would flap their wings and move about in great agitation. She would groom them and fly to her perch in the tree just across from the nest. As she sat in the tree watching her brood and they watching her, I heard a distinctly different ring to her song. It was a low, resonant, melodious coo that seemed to come from some place deep inside her chest. It was cajoling, and it drew the birds up onto the edge of the nest, flapping their wings.

One and then the other would take its place at the edge of the nest. Testing for flight, they would jump up, teeter, flap their wings awkwardly, and eventually fall back into the nest, seemingly exhausted or hoping that Mama Bird would see their difficulty and just bring them their food. But she just continued her song, low and sweetly, "It is your time, it is your time, you must come, you must come."

All of this I watched for hours from my station out beyond the porch, beyond the driveway, crouched low, sitting, watching and waiting. Each new attempt drew my silent urging in consort with Mama Bird for them to go up and out. I dared not even go to the bathroom.

Finally the bigger of the two birds made his most courageous effort. He unfolded his wings, and stretching them, he went even further than before. He pulled himself up and out as if unwrapping to become a larger bird. It was as though the timer of his instinct had just gone off, and he knew something now that only moments before he hadn't. Once more he mounted the edge of the nest. With wings in motion, he chirped to Mama Bird. She, in return, cooed low and soft, steadily imploring, imploring. In measured response, a loosened grip, an edging forward in one last tilt that almost looked like falling, the bird flew off.

Having held my breath, for how long I could not say, I gasped and lunged slightly forward. With my heart pumping the sound of oceans through my ears, time stood still, all was silent witness, and one flight stood out from among countless first flights taken.

Barbara Earl Thomas's porch can be found in Seattle where she writes and paints. An artist of some reknown, she also is the author of *Storm Watch*, a book of her paintings and writings.

Bird-Watching as a Blood Sport

DAVID JAMES DUNCAN

*The spirit in which we see can be the
difference between life and death.*

ON CERTAIN NIGHTS WHEN I WAS A BOY, I used to lie in bed in the dark, unable to sleep, because of eyes—staring, glowing eyes, arrayed in a sphere all around me. The eyes seemed to be alive, though they were not visibly attached to bodies or to faces. They were not, so to speak, attached to emotions either: they conveyed no menace, no affection, no curiosity, no consternation. They simply watched me with a vigilance as steady and beautiful as the shining of stars at night.

Because their beauty was so evident, the eyes would not have troubled me were it not for this: I could not escape them. They had the ability to go on staring whether my own eyes were open or shut; they could, in other words, move with me from the real into the imaginary world. I was in awe of this power. My mother and father, the moon and the sun, the entire world, would vanish when I closed my eyes. But the eyes in the sphere would not. And I didn't even know whose eyes they were! I wanted very much to find out.

I told my big brother about the sphere and asked if he'd ever seen such a thing. His reply was confident but not too consoling: he laughed and told me I'd flipped my lid. I tried my mother. She, too, laughed. "What an imagination!" she said. I let her know, with reluctance, that I did not consider the eyes imaginary. "If they're not imaginary," she said, laughing no longer, "you should ask Jesus to make them go away."

I did ask Jesus. But the eyes went right on staring. And although I spoke of them no more, I was glad that this was Christ's response to my prayer. The sphere of eyes had never threatened or damaged me. It was intense. It was beautiful. Why should I want it to go away? That no one but I seemed to see such things—this was a worry. But the sphere's sudden appearance in bedtime darkness felt like a wonder out of some old myth or fairy tale, and I *wanted* my life to feel like that. So, much as I wanted to know more about the eyes—who they belonged to, what they wanted of me—I quit worrying and let them blaze away. I really had no choice. And in ancient tales the young heroes are patient. I tried to be the same.

In late winter, when I was ten, I made perhaps my first conscious connection between the mysteries of the inner life and those of the outer world. It happened on a long hike through a doomed suburban forest, when I spotted the largest nest I'd ever seen in the top of a towering, seemingly

unclimbable cottonwood tree. Partly to dumbfound the older
boys I was with, partly out of incomprehensible yearning, I
began shinnying up the limbless lower trunk. Ninety or so
feet later, I was clinging to tiny branches just under the massive nest and two magnificent great horned owls were circling the treetop within twenty feet of me. Circling and staring—till somewhere inside I felt it: *the sense of a sphere.
Vigilant, unreadable eyes, watching. Me at the center…*

The nest was so wide that there was no way to climb, or
even to see, up into it, so I reached into it with a bare hand.
I learned later that had it contained owlets I would have
been attacked, and possibly killed, when the adults knocked
me out of my precarious perch. But though their orbit of the
tree became tighter and they began to let out quiet cries, the
owls did not attack: as luck would have it, my groping hand
found not owlets but two large, warm eggs. Again out of
mixed motives—bravado, yearning, a pagan fantasy to possess my own magnificent bird—I stuck one egg in my coat
pocket, then shinnied back down the tree.

The boys below greeted me with everything a conquer-
ing hero could hope for: praise for my climbing, awe of my
defiance of the adult owls, envy of my prize. "You crazy
asshole!" one of them kept saying, in a way that made clear
his desire to be thought the same. But seeing the mother
owl return to the nest, knowing the egg beneath her was
now destined to be raised alone, the word "crazy" struck
me as too kind. I was just a garden-variety asshole. I'd
done something stupid, knew it, and knew I lacked the
strength and courage to climb the tree again and undo what
I'd done.

I tried to make amends in a more arcane way: leaving my friends and their embarrassing praise, I trudged home through the woods, keeping a warm hand around the egg the entire way, then fetched a shoebox, a soft towel, and a lamp with a flexible neck, wrapped the egg in the towel, bent the lamp over it, and began trying to convince myself that I had created a viable nest.

To my amazement, the egg was convinced: that night it began to hatch. And the next morning my mother, knowing real education when she saw it, let me stay home from school to watch. It was a surprisingly arduous process. From first crack to full emergence took twenty hours: eggs, to judge by this one, are no easier to escape than wombs. The owlet was four inches long, naked and exhausted, its pink flesh blurred by an outlandish aura of slush-colored fuzz. Its eyes were enormous but covered with bluish skin: no staring, no sense of the mysterious sphere this time. In fact, I'd never seen a pair of eyes look less likely to open or to see—for I was their adoptive mother.

The owlet rested briefly after breaking free, then commenced a ceaseless, open-beaked, wobbly begging. Panicked by the conviction in its body language, I telephoned the zoo, reached its bird keeper, received a scolding for my nest robbing, and a prediction of doom, but still proffered the tweezered egg and hamburger and eye-droppered milk that the keeper recommended. And again, to my amazement, the owlet responded. It enjoyed my cooking, it suffered my touch, it responded to my mothering precisely long enough to make me love it. Only then did it proceed to die. Even at birth, horned owls are tough: it took a full day to stop eating, two days to stop begging, another half day to stop writhing and die.

What did not die, what lives on in me even now, are the circling, vigilant eyes of the parent owls. The eyes that I betrayed.

Vigilant, glowing eyes, arrayed in a sphere all around me… Even to mention such a thing puts me—both as a story-teller and as a character in my own story—in way over my head. Yet if deeper truths do indeed dwell in depths, there would seem to be no way to reach them without some risk of drowning.

There I'd lie, then, once in an unpredictable while, year after boyhood year, surrounded by eyes. Eyes that always appeared after the room was dark, the house quiet, and I lay still, yet far from sleep. They did not appear by opening; they simply eased into visibility the way stars do at dusk. They never blinked, never retreated, never glanced to either side. They watched me, period. By no other eyes have I ever felt so purely perceived.

In appearance they were distinctly nonhuman. They reminded me a little of angels, a little of owls, and a little of wild animals whose eyes are suddenly lit by the headlights of passing cars. They varied in size—or else stared at me from varying distances. They varied in color too. I recall shades of green, yellow, orange, all of which seemed wrong for angels. It also seemed angelically wrong, but beautifully so, that these colors glowed.

Another over-my-head mystery: the eyes in the sphere would array themselves not just in front of me but above, below, and behind me. What I mean to imply is a physical impossibility. The sphere of eyes was visible in *all* directions. In its thousandfold presence I became a point of pure perception suspended inside an encompassing globe. For a long time I drew no conclusions from this; I merely basked in it. As I grew older, though, I realized that I must see the sphere not through physical eyes, or even through my mind's eye, but through an eye that I hadn't been aware of possessing—an eye that could see in all directions at once.

Nothing else on earth had enabled me to see in this way. Nothing else had ever watched me in this way. So no matter how many times the sphere came, I felt awestruck by its arrival. Awestruck and compelled, no matter how late the hour, to stare back. But to be surrounded and stared at creates an air of huge expectation. In the eyes' presence, something enormously good or bad always seemed about to happen. And suspense is exhausting. So it was always I who lost consciousness and left the eyes staring at no one. Until, one winter not long before adolescence, I realized that for weeks now, or perhaps months, the vigilant sphere had ceased to visit.

I've seen nothing like the sphere of eyes since boyhood. But I've described my recurring vision (or pathosis) for a reason: I have continued now and then to encounter actual bird eyes—like those of the circling great horned owls—that have suddenly struck me as living refugees of that mysterious childhood sphere. I've even begun, thanks to these ongoing encounters, to suspect that the sphere, though unseen, might in some way still surround me...

In 1968, just days after receiving my first driver's license, I am driving through a small town in a nighttime line of commuter traffic when I see, in the headlight beams of the car ahead of me, a small brown ball rolling in the street. The car does not slow as it drives over the ball. Seeing no kids at the curb, I, too, choose not to slow. Then the ball rolls out from under the car in front, appears in my own headlights, and I see that it is not a ball but a balled-up screech owl.

It is uninjured but blown off its feet. And having failed to slow, I now have no choice but to straddle it. It stares straight into my headlights, eyes glowing as I take aim — and I feel myself fall, once again, into a watched center, feel something very good or bad about to happen. Then it does. Just as I pass over, the owl catches its balance, gathers itself for a leap into flight, and I feel — in the soles of my feet, in my legs, and all the way up my spine — the fatal thud of its head against the bottom of my car. I see, in the rearview mirror, the epileptic thrashing and the cloud of feathers, see the next car, too, run it over, and the next, and the next. I do not go back. I already know that I can revere a creature, mother a creature, want nothing but to love a creature, yet still kill it. I also know that what can't be killed — what will remain inside — is that moment's glowing contact with its eyes.

Highway 101, Tillamook County, Oregon. Again alone in a car, on the bridge over Beaver Creek, I turn toward the railing and see a solitary snipe (*Gallinago gallinago*). My field guide calls the snipe "a secretive bird of…marshes, and sodden fields." But this one is standing, calm and incongruous as a would-be bus passenger, right on the bridge's concrete

sidewalk. I immediately brake—having learned the necessity of this from a brown ball years before. But as I pass by
the snipe doesn't fly, doesn't even flinch. Knowing that
something isn't right, I pull over, walk back to the bridge,
and creep up on the bird, hoping it won't flush out in front
of a passing car. It watches me. I move in close, cup it in my
hands. No struggle. The snipe just stares. I stand it in my
palm. Free to fly, the bird stays, a child's dream—the wild
creature you can pet—come true. I stare at it. It stares at
me. Cars come and go. The bird radiates warmth. My hand
returns it. The sphere closes around us. It is the peace of the
sphere itself, I believe, that keeps me from seeing for so long
that the entire top of the bird's skull is gone.

I carry the snipe under the bridge, sit cross-legged by
the creek where no one can see me, and stand it again in my
palm. I then begin trying to concoct a rite that will remove
the treachery from a mercy killing. I start with simple
admiration: the camouflage plumage, sabre-shaped tail
feathers, earth-probe bill, black pearl eyes. I then try memory: fishing alone on the wide-open estuaries, I have come
upon many a *Gallinago gallinago*, and the memorable
encounters have all been the same. Silent and unseen, from
very high in the sky, a lone snipe drops into a dive, builds
up great speed, and, as it nears the ground, veers. This
veering is their magic: it turns the tail feathers into drum-
sticks and the sky into a taut skin that explodes in an
impossibly loud sound known as "winnowing." A nine-
teenth-century ornithologist likened the snipe's winnowing
sound to "the cantering of a horse… over a hard hollow
road." An accurate description, as far as it goes. But the

terror of these horses, when you're alone on a misty estu-
ary, is that you've no hint of their existence till they're suddenly riding down on you out of empty grayness.

I congratulate my snipe, as part of our death rite, on its
ability to terrify. I sing to it, stroke it, beg its forgiveness. It
stands in my palm, pulse bubbling in the hopeless wound,
watches me serenely, lets me say or do as I please. All in all,
though, I feel our preparatory rite is a near-perfect failure,
for in admiring and stroking and singing to such a bird,
love begins. It is love, therefore, that I must crush with a
rock, and love that I entomb, still warm, in a little stone
cairn. It is love whose two black pearls join my growing
sphere. So it is love that still watches me. Never blinking.
Never closing.

There is a passage in Plato that won't leave me in peace.
"The natural property of a wing is to raise that which is
heavy and carry it aloft to the region where the gods dwell,"
Socrates notes in the *Phaedrus*. Later, he says that "all are
eager to reach the heights…[but as most souls] travel they
trample and tread upon one another, this one striving to out-
strip that. Thus confusion ensues, and conflict and grievous
sweat. Whereupon…many are lamed, and many have their
wings all broken, and for all their toiling they are balked,
every one, of the full vision of being, and departing there-
from, they feed upon the food of semblance."

In this speech, Socrates takes for granted two things I've
always felt but have never heard a salaried American
teacher mention. One is the idea that all of us in a sense
"eat" with our eyes but that what we eat, thanks to our col-

lective trampling and treading, are illusions: "the food of semblance." The other is the powerful link between spiritual life and bird life. The natural property of a wing is indeed to carry that which is heavy aloft, literally and spiritually. And the American relationship with the wing is characterized by the shotgun, the drained wetland, and the oblivious speeding car.

A second Platonic passage that haunts me, this one from the *Timaeus*, is an account of the origin of vision. When the gods put together the human body, Plato writes, they placed "in the vessel of the head,...a face in which they inserted organs to minister in all things to the providence of the soul.... And of the organs they first contrived the eyes to give light...." Not to receive light: to *give* it. As the *Timaeus* has it, the gods made "the pure fire which is within us...to flow through the eyes in a stream smooth and dense...." When the outer light of day meets this inner light that proceeds from us and the two lights "coalesce" upon an external object, the result is "that perception which we call sight."

This passage resonates beautifully with Christ's "The light of the body is the eye." And with Walt Whitman's "From the eyesight proceeds another eyesight...." And Rumi's "Close both eyes/to see with the other eye." And Lao Tzu's "He who, having used the outer-light, returns to the inner-light, is preserved from all harm." Yet we discussed no such theories of vision in any church, school, or science camp I ever attended. The older I get, the more serious this omission feels.

I was raised, like most pop-science-and-Kodak-educated Americans, to believe that the eye works like a camera: an external light falls on an external object, glances off that object, enters the pupil (aperture), alights upon the retina (film), is delivered by the nerves (mailed) to the brain (darkroom), processed instantly (just the way we Americans like it), then stored in the memory (photo album) as an image (snapshot). This metaphor works well enough as a mechanistic description of the eyeball. What we Kodak customers tend to forget is that the eye is only the instrument of sight, not the sense of it.

If we focus not on how the eyeball works but on how we experience our sense of sight in action, the camera becomes a hopelessly inept model. We all live, at all times, in the center of an extremely complex, perfectly visible sphere. There is at all times a visible ceiling or sky above us, a visible floor or ground below, and an almost infinite number of visible objects occupying a 360-degree surround. What we see of this up, down, and surround is, almost literally, nothing. Human vision is as remarkable for what it screens out, or simply fails to see, as for what it actually perceives. Our sight zooms in constantly on details, blinding us to the surround; it pans, constantly, over the surround's surface, giving us "the view" but no detail; it is sidetracked, constantly, by thought, desire, fatigue, daydreams, moods, fantasies, during which we see outward objects yet perceive them not at all. This is hardly the performance of a Kodak product. If our eyes were intended to be cameras, we all deserve our money back.

Human vision in action reminds me of many things more

than cameras. A fiberscope, for one. The various forms of fiberscope (arthroscope, proctoscope, etc.) consist of a bundle of transparent fibers through which images can be transmitted, enabling surgeons to probe the human body, focus on minuscule bits of tissue, enlarge and project these bits on a monitor, and operate on this "technologically enhanced" tissue with previously impossible accuracy. Vision, as I experience my own, is a similarly abstract, selective, and often surgical procedure—a procedure I perform involuntarily on the body of my world, with sometimes joyous, and sometimes deadly, results.

Another analogy between vision and fiber-optic surgery: any fiber-optic surgical device does not merely transmit images of tissue; it also illuminates tissue. The interior of our bodies cannot be lit from outside: what a surgeon perceives through an arthroscope is therefore dependent not on external lights but on a tiny light inside the device itself. In a similar way, our perceptions of the world depend not only on exterior lights that bounce "camera-style" off objects and into our eyes but on an internal light or energy that proceeds "arthroscope-style" from within, outward, illuminating the few objects we choose to perceive.

If this sounds too wild or metaphysical to describe plain day-to-day seeing, it's a metaphysics that we all practice constantly, in perfectly mundane ways. While writing the preceding paragraph, for instance, I swiveled my eyes from the page to grab a blue ceramic coffee cup from a shelf directly behind me. En route to and from this cup my eyes moved across dozens of plainly lit objects. Yet I perceived none of them. By retracing, slowly, my eyes' route to the cup, I see that they swept across a brass banker's lamp, a Japanese painting of Ebisu playing a red fish on a cane pole, a photo of Meher Baba feeding a monkey, an old L. C. Smith & Bros. typewriter, a bunny-ears cactus, an almost life-size figurative sculpture, two jars full of pens and pencils, fifty or so books, and a large window. Yet I saw none of this. Something in me sought an object it knew to be blue, behind me, and full of hot caffeine—sought it so decisively that I turned 180 degrees, "filming" all the way, yet made an essentially blind turn.

This "seeing blindness" is the great contradiction of human eyesight. Why, with our eyes open, don't we simply see every well-lit object? "[C]onfusion ensues, and conflict and grievous sweat." For we are "balked...of the full vision of being" and do indeed "feed upon the food of semblance." Vision is a form of reception. But to an even greater extent it is a form of selection and projection. And what concerns me, what scares me at times, is the extent to which my selections and projections are at my command.

How to see more? How to see more clearly? Light is a form of energy. Humans possess energy and to some extent control its ebbs and flows. Can we then aspire to control our inner light? Can we direct the eyes' arthroscopic procedures? How sure are we, lacking such direction, of the surgeon's integrity, or even of his identity? We know so little of inner light sources, speak so little of them, sound so flaky when we do, yet our seeing illuminates so little of our world! I want to know how to aim my inner light, how to clean its lenses, how to recharge its battery. I want access to the control panel, to the joystick, or at least to the bloody on/off

switch. I want hours, *innocuous* hours, in which to fool with
my light till I know just how and just when to aim it, and
how far, high, and deep it can shine. Because without such
control—without a reliable, directable inner light source—
I frighten myself. For I have sometimes looked at a living
object, even a beloved object, and have seen illusions, shadows, nothing at all.

And still I have performed the surgery....

I am haunted by a grebe. A grebe encountered and arthro-
scopically operated upon by my own two eyes, in the mid-
1980s, at the height of the Reagan-Watt-Crowell-Bush-
Luhan-Hodell-Hatfield-Packwood rape and pillage of my
homeland, the Oregon Cascades and Coast Ranges; height
of the destruction of the world I had grown up in and loved
and given my writing life to; height of an eight-year spate of
Pacific Northwest deforestation that outpaced the rate in
Brazil; height of the war on rivers, birds, wildlife, small
towns, biological diversity, tolerance, mercy, and beauty;
height of my personal rage; depth of my despair; height of
my need for light.

Far from aware of this need, I took a long walk, on the
first clear afternoon following a tremendous November
storm, on a deserted Pacific beach—a beach beautifully
wed, in the entire 360-degree surround, to my mood. The
storm surf and swell were enormous. The air was a constant, crushing roar. Spindrift was everywhere. So were
sand dollars, washed up by the storm as if even the ocean,
in that self-absorbed era, were liquidating its inventory in
the name of quick currency. The hills to the east were

logged bald. The sun, as it sank, grew enormous and red. The stumps and my skin turned the same angry orange. My shadow grew a hundred feet long, fell clear to the high-tide line, which to my half-crazed King Learian satisfaction was a graveyard: storm-killed murres, oil-killed puffins, carcasses of gulls tangled in washed-up shreds of net, the carcass of a sea lion shot, most likely, by a fisherman who blamed it for the salmon no longer returning from a drift-netted, trawler-raked ocean to rivers mud-choked by logging.

As a lifelong Oregon coast fisherman, I had a few beautiful secrets. I could, right up until that autumn, still sneak into one stream in a virgin cedar- and hemlock-lined canyon, find big, wild steelhead and salmon in a place that felt primordial, and have them all to myself. That year, however, the elk from the vast surrounding clearcuts—hundreds of cuts, hence hundreds of elk—had been squeezed from their once vast range into that last intact canyon. And having nowhere else to go they crossed and recrossed the stream every day, right in the gravel tail-outs where the salmon and steelhead spawn, till they obliterated the redds, pulverized eggs and alevin, turned my secret stream's banks into an elk-made quagmire reminiscent of the worst riparian cattle damage I'd ever seen—a quagmire that sloughed into the little river with every rain, suffocating the salmon fry that had escaped the countless hooves.

When native elk, to remain alive, are forced to wipe out native salmon, it is time, in my book, to get sad. I quit fishing, exercised my rights as a citizen, and wrote "my" Republican senators the usual letters of distress. They answered with more loads of three- and four- and five-hundred-year-old logs shipped away to Japan as if they were nosegays the senators had grown in their own D.C. flower boxes. Meanwhile, robbed of food and habitat by the same vast clearcuts, the black bears came down out of my home forest, moved into a marsh near town, and lived by raiding garbage cans and dog food bowls at night. Since this posed a danger to humans, the Fish and Wildlife people came in and shot them all, six in a week. And the owl that used to sing to me mornings, attracted by the lights after I'd written all night—the owl that scared me worse than winnowing snipes, actually, because it happened to be a northern spotted, which has an insane guffaw of a morning cry—was now a silence, a nonexistent pawn, a hated cartoon on some poor dumb logger's cap. And in its stead, as if even the Pentagon grieved its passing, we'd built a forest-funded graphite bomber whose stealth in flight was as perfect as an owl's.

So down the storm-smashed beach I strolled that bleak November, kicking at dead birds and drowned logging dreck, wondering what reason I still had to be grateful to live on the "scenic" Oregon coast, wondering what possible definition of "democracy" I represented through my freedom to write, without persecution or incarceration, such words as:

Dear Senator Packwood,
I know you've got huge personal problems, but please! Our home here is dying, the only home we have, and we're bound by a political system in which none of the forces killing us can be stopped except

through you. So please don't get mad, don't think this
is political or personal, please know I'm only begging
for our lives when I say that our last few trees are still
falling and our mills have closed and our people are
sad and broke and lied to. And our schools are in
ruins, our totem owl dead, and our elk jammed in a
last few canyons, pulverizing our last spawning beds
with hooves they've no other place to set down, so
that the salmon we cherish, salmon our whole Chain
of Being needs to remain unbroken, salmon that have
forever climbed these rivers, nailing their shining
bodies to lonely beds of gravel that tiny silver offspring may live, they no longer come. And our bears,
old honeypaws, the joy their tracks alone gave our
children, they, too, gone, and skinned, their bodies, so
human! And our kids, our voteless kids, their large
clear eyes now squinting at stumps and at slash burns
and at sunlight that shouldn't be there, squinting at
Game Boys and TVs and anti-queer ads, squinting at
anything rather than turn open-eyed to windows and
see places so ancient and so recently loved, huge
groves and holy salmon, clouds of birds and dream-
sized animals, a whole green world so utterly gone
that already they begin to believe that they only
dreamed, they never really knew, any such blessings…

What I knew, there on the beach, was that I'd be writing no
such letter. My politics had become raw pleas for mercy.
Prayers, really. And I pray to God, thank you, not to men
like Bob Packwood.

I turned, tired, back to the dunes, to my car, and to the road through the clearcuts to a cold house I'd once wept with joy to call home. But just shy of the first dune—eyes red as fury, red as the fast-sinking sun—sat a solitary, male western grebe.

And I was back in the mysterious sphere.

The grebe was sitting in a curl of kelp weed at the storm's high-water mark. His eyes, in the evening sunlight, were fire. In the center of each blaze, a black point: punctuation; hot lava spinning round a period. A stillness, deep contact, was instantaneous. A life-and-death contract should have been, too. But—sick of humans, sick of my own impotence, sick with the knowledge of how much had been destroyed—I gazed out at the grebe through my sickness. That its body was beautiful I saw as tragedy. That it seemed uninjured I saw as irony. From studying wildlife-care books and visiting wildlife-care centers, from firsthand experience with scaups and gulls and murres, I knew that seldom do humans make a difference once a seabird washes ashore. God knew what brought this bird to this beach—hidden damage from a net, spilled oil, hidden disease, weakness from lack of food in a dying sea. *But it wouldn't be here at all,* I thought, *if it weren't too late already.*

Yet, in perfect contradiction to this pessimism, I felt fear. The molten eyes, the bird's very health and size, intimidated me. Its beak was a dagger. When I'd move close, its neck would draw the dagger back, ready to stab. To capture the grebe I'd have to take off my coat and smother it. The beach was cold; the walk back would be long. Once I got it in my car it might fight its way free. Once I got it home, then what?

Light is a form of energy that flows in waves. When a healthy wave strikes an object, we see that object in what we call its "true colors." When a lesser wave strikes the same object, we see even the truest colors as shades of gray. The sun striking that November beach was brilliant. The grebe's eyes were two brilliances. The world was doing its part. It was a wave, a light that failed to come from me, that allowed me to leave that beautiful bird where it lay.

A premonition, or maybe a desire to return to the scene of the crime, brought me to the same beach three days later. I found the grebe in the same curl of kelp, very recently dead, its body, wings, and plumage still perfect, its burning eyes plucked out by gulls. This was bad enough. But months later, when I dredged up my sad tale for a bird-loving friend, he hit the ceiling. When a grebe, he told me, any grebe, is washed up on a beach like that, *all it needs is to be set back in the water*. Grebes require a runway of flat water to take off flying, but they don't need to fly in order to live: even in storm surf they can swim like seals and hunt like little sharks. The grebe I'd found was a fisherman, like me. Just as I can't walk on water, he couldn't walk on land. "He was a hitchhiker," my friend told me. "Needed a lift of a hundred yards or so. And you refused to pick him up."

Years passed, storms came and went, I walked mile upon penitent mile on those same beaches. I never saw another grebe. I only added two molten eyes to my sphere.

Yet once those crimson eyes became part of me, something changed. Perception, that grebe taught me, is a blood sport. Life itself sometimes hangs by a thread made of nothing but the spirit in which we see. And with life itself at stake, I grew suspicious of my eyes' many easy, dark conclusions. Even the most warranted pessimism began to feel unwarranted. I began to see that hope, however feeble its apparent foundation, bespeaks allegiance to every unlikely beauty that remains intact on earth. And with this inward change, outward things began to change, too.

Hurrying home in my pickup, late (as usual) from a fishing trip, I rounded a blind curve on a coastal byway, noticed a scatter of loose gravel on the asphalt in front of me, and felt an impulse. There was a steep, logged-off slope above this curve. A solitary elk could have kicked such gravel onto the road while crossing. I'm a hell-bent driver when I'm late; I go barreling through mud and gravel, even dodge fallen trees without thinking twice. But this time, though I saw nothing, I had that sudden sense of something good or bad impending, slammed on the brakes, and as my truck slowed from fifty to thirty to ten I was amazed, then elated, to see the gravel turn into birds.

Pine siskins—a whole flock, parked right on the two-lane asphalt. I crept my bumper up next to them. They didn't fly. Maybe thirty siskins, refusing to budge from the road. Reminded me of late-Sixties college students. I got out of my truck, walked up, and joined them. I liked the late Sixties. Such easy excitement! Now I, too, could be killed by the next vehicle to come barreling round the curve!

All but one siskin flew as I sat down next to them. The flock then circled back overhead, chirping vehemently, begging the flightless bird to join them. The siskin in the road, a little male, had been nicked by a previous car, had a small wound above his eye, was in shock. Were it not for my strange impulse, I would have massacred an entire flock of avian altruists as they huddled in sympathy around a helpless comrade. Something inside me, I realized, was wildly more aware of things than I am—two imperceptible points of molten red, perhaps. I took the wounded siskin home, kept him in my bird box overnight, drove him the following morning back to the curve where I'd found him, and released him in perfect health. I was a happy man.

That was just the beginning. I remain haunted by the grebe, but it's been a wondrous haunting, for with the accompanying refusal to despair, a new energy began to flow. Not dependably; it's something to pray for, not something to be smug about. But I began, especially when driving, to feel a simple alertness and an occasional intuition: thousands of road miles, thousands of glimpsed roadside movements, and thousands of half-glimpsed roadside eyes began to work in concert to help me avoid killing, and occasionally even to save, a few animals and birds. I am not laying claim to supernatural skills. I still sometimes kill by accident, and the intuitions that save lives are almost all purchased, like so many mercies, with an earlier being's innocent blood. But this is not to say that, upon descending, my visual intuitions are not a joy.

Exactly a year after I abandoned the grebe, I was driving home down Oregon Coast Highway 101 in a torrential November rain. It was a Sunday night. A steady line of weekend storm watchers was returning to Portland in the pitch dark. The road looked like a narrow black river topped by two endless rows of insanely speeding boats. Because of the terrible visibility, I was watching the road lit not just by my own headlights but by those of the pickup in front of me. It was in the pickup's lights that I happened to glimpse a brown ball rolling along the streaming road.

I hit my brakes instantly, certain of what it was. I was also certain, because it was rolling when I glimpsed it, that it had been run over at least once, already, and that the pickup would run it over again. There was time, before the truck did so, for a one-syllable prayer: I shouted, "Please!" —terrifying my two passengers. But as I braked and pulled hard toward the highway's right shoulder, the ball rolled out, unscathed, in the pickup's tailwind and tailwater, then righted itself on the road as I shot past. It was an adult pygmy owl.

I knew by its ability to regain its feet that the owl was not hopelessly injured. But it was too disoriented to escape the road. And in my rearview mirror, approaching at fifty or so miles an hour, I saw its doom in the form of at least ten cars. Though I'd braked as fast as I could, momentum had carried me perhaps two hundred feet past the owl. I pulled on the parking brake before my truck stopped rolling, jumped out without a word to my stunned companions.

The approaching line of headlights was maybe two hundred yards away. I couldn't see the tiny owl in the dark and distance. Ten cars doing fifty, me on foot doing maybe sixteen, a living bird somewhere in between. I didn't do the math. I just ran. And how right it felt, no matter what! How good it felt to tear eyes-first into another November gale, straight down the lane in which a helpless bird huddled, straight into the headlights of ten city-bound cars—for in this running I'd found a penance that might let me again meet, without shame, the crimson gaze of a grebe.

I've played enough ball to have a good sense of trajectories and distances. I knew, the instant I spotted the fist-size silhouette in the lead car's high beams, that my hands would never reach it in time. I also knew that the lead car's driver wouldn't see me or the tiny owl till he or she was upon us, and so wouldn't slow for either of us. I still couldn't stop running. It still felt wonderful. To be an American, a lifelong motorist, and a bird lover is to carry a piano's worth of guilt on your back. I was outrunning my piano.

The owl had been staring, stupefied, at the approaching cars. When it heard my pounding feet, it swiveled its gaze at me. Instant sphere. Great good or ill impending. I heard cars in the opposite lane coming up behind me and realized that if the cars in my lane did see me, they might be frightened into swerving into a head-on crash. I was risking lives besides my own. I had succumbed to a kind of madness. Yet as I sprinted toward the cars I had an unaccountably calm vision of a conceivable, beautiful outcome.

The lead car saw me and hit its horn just as I reached the owl. I swung my right foot in the gentlest possible kick, chipping the bird like a soccer ball toward the road's shoulder. I followed the bird instantly, not quite needing to dive as the lead car shot past, outraged horn blaring. All ten cars shot past. I ignored them, searching the rain gusts and night air. And at the edge of the many headlight beams I suddenly saw my tiny owl in uninjured, earnest flight, *circling straight back toward the traffic-filled highway.*

I don't know what my body did in that moment, whether my heart stopped or my eyes sent out energy, whether my lips and lungs actually uttered the "Please!" When your whole being yearns for one simple thing, it may not be necessary to add the words. All I know is that a gust of sideways rain blasted my owl, its wings twisted in response, and it rose inches over the crisscrossing headlights and car roofs, crossed both lanes, left the highway, and vanished, without once looking back, into the forest and the night.

The eyes, it has been said, are the "windows of the soul." Since the soul is not a literal object but a spiritual one, eyes cannot be the soul's literal windows. But they are openings into and out of living human beings. When our eyes are open, they become not one of our many walls but one of our very few doors. The mouth is another such door. Through it we inhale air that is not ownable, air that we share with every being on earth. And out of our mouths we send words—our personal reshaping of that same communal air.

Seeing, I have come to feel, is the very same kind of process. Through our eyes we inhale light and images we cannot own—light and images shared with every being on earth. And out of our eyes we exhale a light or a darkness that is the spirit in which we perceive. This visual exhalation, this personal energizing and aiming of perception, is the eyes' speech. It is a reshaping of light as surely as words are a reshaping of air. I therefore feel responsible for my vision. My eye-speech changes the world. Seeing *is* a blood sport.

I'm still in way over my head. I believe that this is my Maker's intention. I'm in so far over my head that I believe I'll need wings to get out. But even over my head I sense that if all souls are one and the eyes are its windows, then those siskin, owl, snipe, and grebe eyes must all, in a realm outside of time, be my very own. So in killing or saving those eyes, in abandoning or loving them, I kill, save, abandon, or love what is outside of time—that is, what is eternal—in myself. This is Buddhist platitude, Christian and Islamic platitude, Native American platitude too, and platitudes don't make very good literature. But they make excellent aids to memory. And in a world in which one's living eyes and body must fly into split-second meetings with the eyes and bodies of others on wet night roads, storm-smashed beaches, in treetops or on blind curves, one needs all the aids to memory one can get.

The God of the Bible commences creation with an exhalation of light from spirit. Shiva is said to be capable of destroying creation by simply opening an eye. Through a life spent looking, or refusing to look, at an endless stream of other creatures, I've learned that by merely opening my eyes, I, too, take part in the creation and destruction of the world. By abandoning a grebe that entered my sphere of vision, I closed two beautiful molten windows through which I might have gazed upon a real salvation. By kicking a twice-run-over owl skyward, I opened two wondrous dark windows upon the same. One of the terrors of being human, and one of the joys, is that for all our limitations and confessions we have been given power. The life that terrifies me and the life that I adore are one life.

David James Duncan is the author of *The River Why*, *The Brothers K*, and *River Teeth*. He lives with his fmaily on a Montana trout stream, where he's at work on a "diptych" (hinged pair) of contemporary metaphysical comedy novels called *Mahatma Gandhi's Magic Word* and *Letters from God*.

The Balinese Chicken

ALICE WALKER

*An unlikely solidarity offers a
glimpse of the other side.*

"WHY DO YOU KEEP PUTTING OFF WRITING about me?" It is the voice of a chicken that asks this. Depending on where you are, you will laugh, or not laugh. Either response is appropriate. The longer I am a writer—so long now that my writing finger is periodically numb—the better I understand what writing is; what its function is; what it is supposed to do. I learn that the writer's pen is a microphone held up to the mouths of ancestors and even stones of long ago. That once given permission by the writer—a fool, and so why should one fear?—horses, dogs, rivers, and, yes, chickens can step forward and expound on their lives. The magic of this is not so much in the power of the microphone as in the ability of the nonhuman object or animal to be and the human animal to perceive its being.

This then is about a chicken I knew in Bali. I do not know her name or that of her parents and grandparents. I do not know where she was from originally. Suddenly on a day whose morning had been rainy, there she was, on the path in front of us (my own family, on our way back to our temporary shelter), trying to look for worms, trying to point out other possible food items to her three chicks, and trying at the same time to get herself and her young ones across the road.

It is one of those moments that will be engraved on my brain forever. For I really saw her. She was small and gray, flecked with black; so were her chicks. She had a healthy red comb and quick, light-brown eyes. She was that proud, chunky chicken shape that makes one feel always that chickens, and hens especially, have personality and will. Her steps were neat and quick and authoritative; and though she never touched her chicks, it was obvious she was shepherding them along. She clucked impatiently when, our feet falling ever nearer, one of them, especially self-absorbed and perhaps hard-headed, ceased to respond.

When my friend Joanne—also one of my editors at *Ms.* magazine for nearly fifteen years—knew I was going to Bali, she asked if I would consider writing about it. There was so much there to write about, after all: the beautiful Balinese, the spectacular countryside, the ancient myths, dances, and rituals; the food, the flowers, the fauna, too. When I returned, with no word on Bali, she asked again. I did not know how to tell her that my strongest experience on Bali had been to really be able to see, and identify with, a chicken. Joanne probably eats chicken, I thought.

I did , too.

In fact, just before going to Bali I had been fasting, drinking juices only, and wondering if I could give up the eating of meat. I had even been looking about San Francisco for an animal rights organization to join (although it is the animal liberationists, who set animals free, who actually take my heart); in that way I hoped to meet others of my kind, i.e., those who are beginning to feel, or have always felt, that eating meat is cannibalism. On the day my companion pointed out such an organization, in an Australian magazine we found at a restaurant in Ubud, I was slow to speak, because I had a delicious piece of Balinese-style chicken satay in my mouth.

I have faced the distressing possibility that I may never be a "pure" vegetarian. There is the occasional stray drumstick or slice of prosciutto that somehow finds its way into my mouth, even though purchased meat no longer appears in my kitchen. Since Bali, nearly a year ago, I have eaten several large pieces of Georgia ham (a cherished delicacy from my childhood, as is fried chicken; it is hard to consider oneself Southern without it!) and several pieces of chicken prepared by a long-lost African friend from twenty years ago who, while visiting, tired of my incessant chopping of vegetables to stir-fry and eat over rice and therefore cooked a chicken and served it in protest. There have been three crab dinners and even one of shrimp.

I console myself by recognizing that this diet, in which 90 percent of what I eat is nonmeat and nondairy, though not pristinely vegetarian, is still completely different from and less barbarous than the one I was raised on — in which meat was a mainstay—and that perhaps if they knew or cared (and somehow I know they know and care), my chicken and fish sister/fellow travelers on the planet might give me credit for effort.

I wonder.

Perhaps I will win this struggle, too, though. I can never not know that the chicken I absolutely saw is a sister (this recognition gives a whole different meaning to the expression "you chicks"), and that her love of her children definitely resembles my love of mine. Sometimes I cast my quandary about it all in the form of a philosophical chicken joke: Why did the Balinese chicken cross the road? I know the answer is, To try to get both of us to the other side.

It is not so much a question of whether the lion will one day lie down with the lamb, but whether human beings will ever be able to lie down with any creature or being at all.

Alice Walker won a National Book Award and the Pulitzer Prize for *The Color Purple*. Her other books include *The Third Life of Grange Copeland*, *Meridian*, *Possessing the Secret Joy*, *The Temple of My Familiar*, and *Anything We Love Can Be Saved*, as well as numerous collections of short stories, poetry, and essays.

The Parrots of Telegraph Hill

MARK BITTNER

*How one man became the unexpected tender
of a remarkable urban flock.*

T HEY WERE A SCREAM — A WILD, LOUD, exotic scream. I was standing on the sidewalk in front of my home and staring up, dumbfounded, at four green and red parrots crawling around the bushy limbs of a juniper. *What were wild parrots doing in San Francisco?* They were only ten feet away, and from that distance I could see their eyes clearly. They were personable and intelligent eyes that, at the same time, looked strangely goofy, as if they concealed the punch line to some outrageous joke. Suddenly, without offering any explanations, they all bolted from the tree and disappeared, leaving me to stand there completely bewildered.

Two years earlier, in the spring of 1988, I had the good fortune to move into an old cottage on San Francisco's Telegraph Hill. The most appealing aspect of my new home was not the house itself, but its location on the hill's some-what isolated eastern slope. Most of the area is too steep for roads, so the only way to pass through is on a network of staircases and paths. As a consequence, the noise and chaos of city traffic are blessedly remote. The housing is a friend-ly mix of small apartment buildings and old cottages, many of which have views of long stretches of San Francisco Bay. But the neighborhood's most attractive feature is its large gardens. Lush and, in places, wildly overgrown, they stretch up the entire 300-foot height of the hill in a two-block-wide corridor. The gardens are a real paradise for urban birds. They attract all sorts: scrub jays, humming-birds, kestrels, mourning doves, house finches, hooded ori-oles, sparrows, and more. There is a wide variety of trees to forage from, and the parrots began showing up as regularly as any of the native birds. I watched them for several years, still as fascinated and confused as I'd been at that first sight-ing. The most puzzling thing to me was that the flock was increasing in size. How could that be? They couldn't be breeding, not in San Francisco.

In early 1993, I moved up in the world. I became the care-taker of the top two floors of a three-story house that stood right behind my cottage. Compared to what I'd been living in, it was absolute luxury. The house had some of the best views on the hill, and it provided me with a lofty, unob-structed perch from which to observe the parrots. Every day I saw them fly in from the distance in their typically ragged formations. I spent hours watching from the win-dows as they ate from the trees and fought and played on

the power lines. There were more than twenty now. Their
mystery still gnawed at me. Nobody I talked to knew a thing
about them. At the very least, it seemed that I should be able
to figure out what species they were. One evening I went
down to a bookstore and sat on the floor comparing photographs of different parrot species. They were somewhat
small for parrots, about a foot in length, but with fairly long
tails. The plumage of the feathers on their torso was green,
and they had bright red caps and a red stripe on the bend of
each wing. After an hour of comparing photographs, I nar-
rowed it down to one species, the cherry-headed conure
(*Aratinga erythrogenys*). At last, I knew one true thing about
them.

One day in October, on nothing more than a whim, I
bought a bag of wild birdseed. The seeds weren't for the
parrots — I had never seen any of them come near the houses
and I wasn't particularly interested in birds. I was bored. It
just seemed like something to do. Maybe I'd enjoy bird-
watching. I poured the seeds into a bowl and placed it out
on the fire escape. Occasionally, I'd watch the native birds
eat, but I didn't get any real pleasure from it. I wasn't sure
what I was supposed to be looking for. Then one afternoon,
while gazing absent-mindedly at the bowl, I saw a parrot fly
over to see what the scrub jays were eating. The first parrot
was quickly joined by two others. They ate for a few minutes and then flew away. I felt like a little kid. I was *thrilled*.
It had never occurred to me that this might happen. I was
eager to see if they'd come again the next day. I stuck
around the house the entire morning waiting for them. This
time, they *all* came. I could not believe my good luck.

The door to the fire escape was a Dutch door with a large glass window in each half. We had a clear view of one another. Not wanting to scare them off, I stayed back about ten feet. They continued to come every day, and at each feeding I moved a little closer. Within a week, I was right up against the door. I slowly lowered myself to the floor and sat down to watch. It was chaos, a wild jumble of birds screaming and squabbling, biting each other's legs and wings, fighting to get to the bowl. A bird would jump up onto the lip and bump off the bird next to him with his chest. It was like watching the Three Stooges, only much funnier. I loved their bright colors and those eyes. Many birds have an iris that is nearly as dark as the pupil, and it's difficult to distinguish the two. The cherry heads have a light brown iris and the pupil stands out distinctly. Through their eyes, I could read their moods. They were feisty, diligently so, but also playful and curious. I got such a kick out of them that I returned day after day to watch "just one more time." In the beginning, they were skittish, bolting whenever I made the slightest move. But gradually they got used to me sitting there and became less fearful.

In time, the chaos lessened. I began to recognize individual birds and give them names. The first was Connor. He was easy to pick out. He was a blue-crowned conure (*Aratinga acuticaudata*), one of only two blue crowns in the flock. I chose the name because it sounded like the word "conure." Then there was Marlon. He got his name because he was so cool, like Marlon Brando. No matter how intense the fighting at the bowl, he seemed oblivious to it, working calmly on one seed after another. Eric got his name because he had a more extensive red cap than the others—Eric the Red. Another bird was thug-like, a bully. He frequently assaulted the weaker flock members. He reminded me of a mafioso, so I named him Sonny after Sonny Corleone from *The Godfather.*

Since I couldn't afford to feed both the parrots and the native birds, I put out the bowl only upon the flock's arrival. After a few weeks, they came to associate me with the bowl and the sunflower seeds it contained. Occasionally, some event would show me that their trust had grown. I sat and watched them every day, three or four times a day, for six months. It was great fun, but as spring arrived I began to lose my enthusiasm. It seemed time to hang the whole thing up. Before I was able to get serious about stopping, I got into a huge argument with the neighbor below me. The fight turned out to be a great blessing.

My neighbor, Harvey, liked to open a louvered window that was directly below the feeding area. The angled panes were catching feathers, shells, and bird droppings. He'd been stewing about it for months, but had never told me. One day, Harvey decided to launch guerrilla warfare against the parrots. He started slamming the window shut to scare them away. I couldn't hear the slamming at first, so I couldn't understand what was going on. The flock kept bolting away from the fire escape and then returning, only to bolt again. When I finally figured it out, I became livid. I'd worked hard to earn their trust, and now I was losing them to their fear of this damn slamming window. A few days later, Harvey and I had a public showdown on the street. Obscenities were exchanged in loud, heated voices.

Eventually, we both cooled off and worked out an agreement. It was a simple and fair one: I was not to feed the parrots on days that he had the window open. I really couldn't complain.

One day in April, I saw that the window was open. For the first time ever, I had to refuse them. It was not an easy thing to do. For two hours they called to me, pecking away at my sympathy. But I couldn't break the agreement with my neighbor. Eventually, they all left except for Connor. At the time, he was my favorite bird in the flock. He has a particular way of opening sunflower seeds. He leans over the bowl as he cracks each seed and then drops the empty hull back into it. No mess. I loved Connor, so I took what I thought to be the slim risk of putting out the bowl just for him. Two minutes later, a contingent of ten cherry heads came swooping around the corner of the building and landed on the fire escape railing. I was in a terrible bind. I couldn't let them eat, but I did not want to lose their trust. I loathed the idea of deliberately scaring them away. The only thing I could think to do was to step out onto the fire escape in an aloof, relaxed manner. I knew it would force them to flee, but I hoped that my casualness might mitigate the severity of my trespass. But they didn't leave! I was so shocked that I had difficulty breathing and my legs were trembling. They stared at me softly with cautious, puzzled eyes. "What's the matter? Why won't you feed us?" I still had to keep them from going to the bowl. I dropped to my knees and sat next to it. It was a standoff. After a few minutes, they gave up and left. I was ecstatic. I had to tell *somebody*. The only person at home was Harvey. It's an odd thing. I never would have stepped out among them if we hadn't argued. I ran to his door and knocked. The instant that he opened the door, I began to hose him down with my excitement. Considering that we were not on good terms, he was remarkably cordial. I was rushing so hard that I pretty much had him pinned anyway. He seemed to agree with me that this was an extraordinary development. For whatever reason, he relented and gave me complete freedom with the flock.

The next day, I chose a spot three feet from the bowl and sat down. I was delighted to be sitting so close, to hear the rustling of their feathers and the immediacy of their screaming and squawking. They accepted the new situation with one condition: I was not to move a muscle. The instant that I scratched an itch or stretched a cramped leg muscle, they all bolted in unison. They usually came back after a minute or two. As pleasant as this was, after a couple of weeks I became restless. I was in a cramped space and my back was getting stiff. I stood up and walked to the other end of the fire escape. I wanted to think things over. I wanted even closer contact, but I wasn't sure how to go about it. Occasionally, one bird would pass by me on the railing and I would offer him, jokingly, a sunflower seed. Each time he gave me a startled look and flew away in alarm, which is exactly what I expected. One day I saw the bird hesitate for a moment and then decline the invitation. I hadn't seriously considered trying to feed them by hand, but this made me think. Maybe it was possible.

The next day, the same bird came my way again. As he drew near, I slowly extended the seed toward him. He kept his torso as far back from me as possible while cautiously stretching his neck toward my fingertips. Suddenly, he snatched the seed and took off down the railing. I always had to act cool around the parrots or I alarmed them. Maybe it was this restraint, or maybe I saw it coming, but I didn't feel excitement this time; I felt satisfaction. I made a careful note of the bird's markings and named him Noah.

I think that, at times, all of us sense an eerie poetry to the Universe, strange coincidences that speak to us in a strong way. This was the case for me when Noah took that seed. In my personal life at the time, I'd been having to deal with the issue of trust. Someone wanted my trust and there was someone whose trust I wanted. Both were fairly heavy situations. In a very precise manner, the issue was being mirrored back to me in my experience with the flock. How do you win trust? The answer seems ridiculously simple, but I had never given it serious thought. You win trust by being trustworthy, not just most of the time, but constantly. The first time that you cut even the smallest corner, where is the trust then? Doubt must enter the game. I played with the parrots by a very strict set of rules. I never did anything whatsoever that might damage their trust, and their trust grew. Like many virtues, it's easy to understand but difficult to put into practice. Whenever trust is an issue, it's usually due to the presence of some temptation. The parrots were obviously tempting; it was the reason that they were here in the first place. They had been taken out of their natural home and put in cages to be sold to people who desired their beauty and personality. I had no intention of ever trapping them, but I can't say the desire never entered my mind.

As Noah got more comfortable taking seeds, others came to join him. Competition for seeds at the bowl was intense, sometimes violent. That I was handing out free seeds, and that there seemed to be no danger involved, was a boon to the weaker birds. Over the next months, more of them came to me until I had nearly the entire flock eating from my hand. As I became more familiar with them, I began to understand many of the behaviors and vocalizations that had puzzled me for so long. I began taking notes, and, over time, I began to unravel some of their mysteries. One thing I learned was that they actually were breeding.

In 1994, three couples bred successfully, and I saw nine babies. Of those nine, only two survived an entire year. In 1995, another three couples were successful, and I saw eight babies, only two of which, again, ultimately survived. For those two years, through births and deaths, the flock population remained fairly constant, running down to the mid-twenties and then back up again to the low-thirties. These seemed like precarious numbers to me. One bad year could have gone a long way toward completely wiping out the flock. I fretted over the loss of each bird. I'd come to see them as my friends, and I wanted to see my friends flourish. As the summer of 1996 approached, I found myself pulling for the breeders, hoping that they might fatten the flock's ranks a bit.

Every February, the flock begins to break down into smaller groups, although the females don't begin laying their eggs until around the first day of summer. In June, while the males and immature females fly their territory in several small groups, the breeding females disappear entirely to sit in their nests. The nests are not what one usually thinks of as a bird nest; they're cavities high up the trunks of trees. In San Francisco, the most commonly used tree for nesting is the Canary Island date palm. Holes are often created where the old frond ends break off. Parrots will not start a hole from scratch, but they will enlarge a preexisting cavity. The old frond material is soft and brittle and easy work for their strong jaws and sharp beaks.

For approximately four weeks, while the female sits on her eggs, the male cruises the flock's territory looking for food, returning at intervals throughout the day to feed her. In late July, looking greasy, matted, and skinny, the females emerge from the nests to feed themselves as well as to help gather food for the newly-hatched chicks. As the flock prepares for the fledging of the young, it also slowly begins to reestablish its cohesiveness. That summer I was seeing twenty-four birds, typical for the time of year. They were growing especially noisy and quarrelsome. The usual squabbling for position at feedings seemed more intense than in previous years.

In the early morning of September the 4th, while talking to a neighbor, I saw a group of nine parrots come into the gardens. They scream as they fly, and I could hear that Olive was in this group. Olive is the flock's sole mitred conure. She had shown up one day in the summer of 1995, undoubtedly an escaped pet as were all the other founding members of the flock. Her voice is distinct from that of a cherry head. It's louder and more metallic, sounding much like a gull's. My eye was now well-trained to the flock's most subtle nuances. I recognized immediately that something was out of the ordinary. I had been awaiting the arrival of the first babies, and here they were, two of them. As they drew near, I saw something that astounded me. One of the chicks had a red patch on its forehead. This had never occurred in a cherry head baby. I knew instantly to whom they belonged. Earlier in the year, Olive had paired off with Gibson, one of the cherry heads. They were hers. *Hybrids.* Except for a larger body and beak, the other hybrid chick looked very much like a typical cherry head fledgling.

Two days later, the flock came up with another surprise: two more babies, this time the offspring of Bo and Sticky Chest. The reason for my surprise was twofold. First of all, Bo is one of the weaker males in the flock. In the previous two years, only couples that contained a dominant male had bred successfully. It's difficult for a parrot to find a nest hole of just the right size, shape, and location. I had assumed that only the stronger males were able to secure them. The second reason for my surprise was that only three months earlier Bo had lost his first mate, Mandela, to another male in a fight. I was impressed that he'd been able to find a new mate and to start a family within such a short window of opportunity. Maybe Bo's success was a good omen for the flock as a whole.

Two days after Bo and Sticky Chest's fledglings appeared, I saw two more babies. These belonged to Sam and Kristine. This was nothing extraordinary. Although the flock does not have a strict pecking order, Sam is one of the more consistently dominant males. I'd now seen six babies in five days. It seemed like a decent beginning. In the previous two years, at least one set of parents had brought out four babies. All the flock needed was one such set and I would have felt content enough with the situation.

The babies are sweet balls of fluff and, like all babies, a joy to watch. For their first few days out in the world, they are delightfully clumsy. As they gain coordination, they begin to spend a considerable amount of time hanging upside down from the power lines, swaying back and forth while trying to bite each other. Sometimes they dangle by just one leg, and, on occasion, they even hang by their beaks. For me, the most enjoyable part of the breeding season is watching the parents feed the young. When the babies beg for food, they make a sound that I love. It's something of a cross between a chuckle and a lamb's bleat. The mother (or father—both parents share the duty) energetically bounces her head up and down to bring food up from her crop. She then takes the baby's beak into her own and, while rapidly shaking the baby's head up and down, regurgitates. The baby squats with his wings held away from his sides, his head lifted straight up to receive the food. After each serving, he looks as if he's entered a state of utter bliss. His wings remain limply extended, his body and head feathers puff up, and with eyes wide open, he trembles and bleats ecstatically.

For several days after the last two fledglings appeared, I never saw more than six babies. More often, I saw fewer. The parents often stash their children in a tree and fly off to forage. In previous years, one or two chicks had died shortly after fledging. Because of their restlessness, I couldn't always be certain which babies were with which adults.

I had no way of knowing if I was always seeing the same six or not. After a week had gone by without any change, I began to get frustrated. It looked like the year was going to be a bust, their poorest yet.

Nine days after the last two fledged, and just as I had come to accept the situation, the floodgates began to open. I came out one morning to find ten babies playing on the power lines, their parents eagerly calling to me to bring out the sunflower seeds. I was *elated*. This surpassed their best effort of two years before. Five days later, four more appeared. And a week after that, three more showed up. Seventeen babies! This went far beyond my most optimistic hopes for them. The flock now stood at forty-one members, the strongest it had ever been. Seven different couples— Olive and Gibson, Bo and Sticky Chest, Sam and Kristine, Sonny and Lucia, Guy and Doll, Erica and Russell, Noah and Grace—had successfully brought out offspring. The only individuals more exhilarated about this than I were the parrots themselves. They were growing noisier day by day as if celebrating the flock's new strength.

I encountered them one afternoon as I was bicycling past Washington Square. They were perched in the pine trees that line the park's eastern perimeter and screaming like lunatics. They often start up a flock scream as they prepare to take flight, but this one was especially loud. Their excitement was reaching such a noisy level of pandemo-nium that no one in the park could have been aware of anything else. At the instant that the volume hit its peak, they all bolted from the trees, spiraled upward like smoke, and disappeared in the direction of Telegraph Hill. The people sitting in the park applauded. I laughed, got back on my bike, and rode up the hill. When I got home, the flock was waiting for me.

After years of trying almost everything else, Mark Bittner has returned to his first love: writing. It was the parrots that carried him back. He is now working on his first book, *Tales from an Urban Jungle: The Wild Parrots of Telegraph Hill*. He has lived his entire life on the West Coast, and finds that he much prefers nature to his computer.

Honey Guide

H. V. MORTON

A small bird leads the way.

I T IS NOT EASY TO SURPRISE DURBAN IN THAT slipshod, half-awake condition so familiar to the early riser in London and Paris. When seven o'clock strikes in the morning the place is fairly humming with activity: by eight o'clock not only can you buy almost anything, but you can also ring a man up at his office. By nine o'clock you begin to seek the shady side of the street and to understand why Durban begins its day so early.

An institution which gave me a great deal of pleasure is Durban's large and beautifully run museum. What the Stone Age, the Bronze Age, Celtic, Roman, Anglo-Saxon, and so on, are to us, animal life is to the museums in South Africa. The bewildering variety of life on wings, crawling on its stomach, and walking on all fours, fills one with astonishment.

The South African birds which you begin to know very quickly are the egret, or tick-bird, the secretary bird, the big eagle, the lammervanger, who is sometimes seen sitting on a rock brooding, or more often gliding about the sky on unmoving wings, the cranes, and wild duck; but the great number of smaller birds remain unidentified until you go to a museum of this kind. One of the strangest birds I have ever heard of is the honey guide. It is not much larger than a sparrow and is greyish-brown in colour, with a spot of yellow on each shoulder. Its habits were described by Andrew Sparrmann in 1772, but no one believed him.

This bird, which is found in many parts of Africa, guides men and animals to bees' nests, and, when they have taken the honey, the bird expects to be left a portion of the comb as a reward, preferably a piece containing larvae.

"When I was trekking in South Rhodesia [now Zimbabwe] some years ago on a collecting expedition," the director told me, "I noticed a small bird following me and obviously calling to attract my attention. One of my guides told me it was a bird that led people to honey. I decided to follow it. It would wait until I came close, then it would fly on and wait for me, calling to me all the time. This continued for an hour or so, and I began to think of giving up!

"Soon, however, instead of continuing its flight, the bird began to fly 'round in a most excited way giving an entirely different cry, and I noticed that bees were leaving and entering a hole in the ground. I had the nest dug out and left the comb containing the brood, which the bird immediately claimed. The natives say that should you leave nothing behind for the honey guide, the next time it will lead you to a cobra, a puff adder, or a mamba!"

The director told me the story of a friend who was led by a honey guide on a long chase which, to his irritation, ended near the starting place, but on the other side of a ravine. When he had taken the honey, he decided to go the short way back, but found it impossible. After several attempts, he realised that the honey guide had taken him along the only possible route for a human being.

H. V. Morton was born in 1892 and died in 1979 in Capetown, South Africa. He was the author of many wonderful travel books, including *In Search of South Africa*, from which this piece was excerpted.

Wild Owls

BERND HEINRICH

*An unruly roommate creates changes
in the schedule.*

B Y MID-MARCH IN VERMONT, THE SNOW
from the winter storms has already become crusty
as the first midday thaws refreeze during the cold
nights. A solid white cap compacts the snow, and you can
walk on it without breaking through to your waist. The
maple sap is starting to run on warm days, and one's blood
quickens.

Spring is just around the corner, and the birds act as if
they know. The hairy and downy woodpeckers drum on
dry branches and on the loose flakes of maple bark, and
purple finches sing merrily from the spruces. This year the
reedy voices of the pine siskins can be heard everywhere on
the ridge where the hemlocks grow, as can the chickadees'
two-note, plaintive song. Down in the bog, the first red-
winged blackbirds have just returned, and they can be

heard yodeling from the tops of dry cattails. Flocks of rusty blackbirds fly over in long skeins, heading north.

From where I stand at the edge of the woods overlooking Shelburne Bog, I feel a slight breeze and hear a moaning gust sweeping through the forest behind me. It is getting dark. There are eerie creaking and scraping noises. Inside the pine forest it is becoming black, pitch black. The songbirds are silent. Only the sound of the wind can be heard above the distant honks of Canada geese flying below the now starry skies. Suddenly I hear a booming, hollow "hoo-hoo-*hoo*-hoo—." The deep, resonating hoot can send a chill down any spine, as indeed it has done to peoples of many cultures. But I know what the sound is, and it gives me great pleasure.…

From my vantage point [in a pine tree] I could see that the old crow's nest which the owls had taken over was now in a shambles. It had already been a year old and hit hard by winter storms when the owls had selected it as their home, and they had not improved it. The nest's rim was completely battered down, and three fuzzy owlets standing on the shaky platform were fully exposed. Two of them were probably all of twelve inches tall, the third smaller. Although all three were still covered with fluff, their bills and talons looked like they could do some damage. I doubted that these chicks were in any danger of crows.

I saw no fresh food in the nest, only the remnants of past meals—crow wings and bare bones. To me it looked as if the hunting of these owlets' parents had not been very good. In comparison, Arthur Bent reported that an occupied great horned owl nest he had seen was stocked with a mouse, a young muskrat, two eels, four catfish, a woodcock, four ruffed grouse, one rabbit, and eleven rats, the whole provender totaling eighteen pounds.

When food is available only in limited amounts, as is commonly the case in nature, the practice among some owls is that the largest—that is the oldest—owlet gets fed first. If the last owlet to hatch from a clutch of eggs is able to feed regardless of the competition from its stronger nestmates, it will survive; otherwise it is neglected and dies or is eaten. The opportunity for siblicide exists if the mother needs to leave the nest to hunt. Eggs in a clutch are laid on successive days or every other day, and the female starts to incubate as soon as she begins laying so that the young are hatched on different days. If push comes to shove during food competition at the nest, the first bird to hatch is soon larger than the rest and has the edge. This practice ensures that at least some of the offspring survive when food is scarce. In most other birds not subjected to extreme variations in food supply, incubation is delayed until the last egg is laid. In this way the parents prevent one offspring from getting a head start and dominating the others.

There are other means of matching the number of mouths to feed to the available food supply. For example, when food is scarce at the beginning of the breeding cycle, great horned owls do not breed at all, or, like snowy owls, they may adjust their clutch size to fit the food supply. For example, snowy owls in Barrow, Alaska, do not breed when lemmings are scarce, but will lay up to two dozen eggs per clutch in peak lemming years, and as few as two in moderate to poor conditions.

As I lingered in observing the nest, the mother owl continued to snap her bill, to call out in a hoarse gurgle, and occasionally she hooted while staring at me with her huge yellow eyes. She made no attempt to attack, and her mate did not appear at all. Apparently he had left as soon as I had come into sight, and he stayed away while the female alone kept a continuous watch. But crows kept me informed of his whereabouts.

Events showed again how much of what really makes a difference in individual lives is often a matter of random chance, in this case at least for one of the three young owls.

Two days later the skies turned dark as storm clouds drifted in from the north. The wind stopped, and in the hushed silence sticky, wet snow began to fall. It clung to the pine needles, the twigs, and the branches. And it continued to fall. Slowly the weight of the gathering whiteness depressed the branches. Lower and lower they sagged, until the stillness was shattered as brittle pine limbs, loaded with heavy snow, came crashing down. I anxiously returned to the site of the nest. It was not left unscathed. The nest tree was damaged, and tangles of branches lay beneath it in piles of snow. Miraculously, two young owls were perched on some fallen branches, and the third was mired in the snow. I was immediately compelled to save the soggy, sorry-looking bundle of misery, haplessly lying there amid the snowstorm's debris. It would be a chance once again to feel close to nature by raising the wild creature, as I had often done in my childhood. In addition, I quickly reasoned, I could per-haps study the development of its hunting behavior and determine how or whether an owl's hunting techniques had anything to do with the way crows and other birds so often mob and attack these birds of prey.

There was a problem, however. Taking an owl—or for that matter a robin, a blackbird, or a crow—from the wild is against the law, and there are many bureaucratic impedi-ments to thwart a legal adoption. Taking an animal from the wild is something one does not do casually. It requires much time and commitment to care for another creature, and one must be prepared to provide not only for its physi-cal needs but also for its psychological ones. With a fellow human, we can take intelligence and understanding for granted; we can verbalize our feelings or make symbolic gestures to help define our relationships. Animals, however, especially wild ones, don't always have the sense or ability to tell us what they require or want, so we have to study them closely for signs of their needs; then we must make ourselves available to minister to those needs. To keep an animal is a constant commitment. And such commitment brings obligations and responsibilities for which many of us are not suited.

I chose to make such a commitment with this owl. I cleared the appropriate paperwork through the state and federal bureaucracies and made my acquisition legal....

June 3
It already seems late in the day. The robin started to sing about two hours ago, while it was still dark, and it has long

since stopped. The robin's song was followed by that of the Swainson's and hermit thrushes, and they, too, have already stopped singing. The white-throated sparrows also started early, but they still continue their serenade. The ovenbirds occasionally interrupt the melodious singing of the other birds with their loud, raucous stanzas. Blue jays on their morning errands scream to each other at odd intervals in the forest, and the Nashville warbler near the blueberry patch by the cabin repeats his monotonous cascading call over and over again. The late riser, the rose-breasted grosbeaks and the scarlet tanagers, are only now starting to sing. It is 5:50 a.m.

Before Bubo came into my life I usually started my day a little later. Thanks to his rearrangement of my schedule, however, I have already had breakfast, and I am enjoying my second cup of coffee in front of a warm fire in the wood stove. Up here on the hill in Maine, the mornings are still cold.

All was quiet in Bubo's cage during the night. But at the first flush of dawn he taps on the windowpane next to my head. He is persistent, and when I open the window he hops onto the sill. He studiously surveys the room for a few minutes: the coast is clear. Bunny, the cat, is fast asleep on the bed, having retired from his nocturnal hunt. Bubo launches himself across the cabin and lands on one of the beams.

Many large birds have difficulty lifting off in flight. Not Bubo. He has long, strong legs hidden under his flowing garb, and he can leap-fly straight up from the floor and land on the beam seven feet above his head. It looks effortless. It also looks incongruous in one who waddles like a goose and who reminds you of a very short, stubby, and overweight man.

7 a.m. Bubo continues to be active, even though the sun is now shining brightly. He finds a roll of fish line and works it into a frazzle. He hops from floor to beams and back down. He preens and shakes, explores some more, then relaxes by peering out the window.

And then again, as if on second thought, he puts his head down, spreads his wings, and hisses at Bunny who is still resting on the bed. He does not clack his bill, but advances toward the cat, head close to the floor and body rocking from side to side. Bunny calls his bluff and does not budge, whereupon Bubo proceeds to waddle about elsewhere on the floor in a slow trot, each footstep making clicking noises as his talons hit the pine boards like the studs on hobnailed boots.

Yesterday his main focus had been the inside of the cabin. Today he is almost finished with cabin inspection and spends much more time looking out the windows. Perhaps I need to arrange some entertainment for him inside. I have two live crayfish that might be of interest.

Crayfish number 1 is lying on its back on the floor, moving its legs slowly and flexing its abdomen. Bubo stares at it from the beam above, with an occasional violent shake of his head, in apparent disgust at what he is seeing. Soon enough, curiosity gets the best of him, and he hops down for a closer look. He continues to give his head an occasional quick shake (as he did after he tasted toads, bullfrogs, and clams) as he walks closer. By the time he has made a close inspection, the crayfish has stopped moving its spindly legs, and Bubo loses interest.

I now put the crayfish into several inches of water in the dishpan. The water revives it and Bubo's interest is renewed. He walks around and around the dishpan, ambivalently reaching in for the crayfish but his bill missing the mark and coming up with water instead. He likes the water, takes a drink and hops in, making the high-pitched squealing noises he used to make last year whenever he took a bath.

The dishpan is too small to splash in, and he rediscovers the crayfish at his feet. He grabs it with his bill, crunches it, hops out, and crunches some more. Mmm—not bad. He swallows it.

Half an hour later I present crayfish number 2. This time he goes through the same maneuvers, only this crustacean is committed to the stomach much, much faster.

When I return to the cabin later in the morning after a four-hour absence, Bubo is fluffed out and asleep on the rafters, and Bunny is asleep on the bed as usual. They have the utmost respect for each other, and like the two top carnivores they are, they have made their peace out of mutual fear.

Bubo has not been altogether unoccupied while I was out. My second green washcloth is on my desk, torn into long shreds. I look up: "Bubo, did you do this?" Bubo looks down at me, and as if on cue stretches his neck, opens his mouth wide, and out pops a large green pellet composed of a twelve-inch crumbled strip of green cotton terrycloth, enclosing the exoskeleton fragments of the crayfish. I know he could not possibly have understood my question, but I am reminded of how easy it is sometimes to overrate the intelligence of one's pets. Also, sometimes to underrate it....

June 10

I'm ready for bed early because I get up before 5 a.m. every morning, adhering to Bubo's strict schedule. But Bubo's schedule sometimes demands even greater altruism. Not long after dark, as I am trying to sleep, Bubo taps on the window. I try to ignore him, but the tapping continues at intervals of two or three minutes, and I become irritated. The tapping becomes louder, but I think I can sleep through it, until a new concern keeps me awake: the ancient windowpanes are thin. Should I let him stay outside and risk his cracking the window, or let him in and risk a good night's sleep? I opt for the latter choice, thinking that he will settle on a rafter and sleep, since he sleeps most of the night when in his cage anyway.

Bubo, who had been flying about in the cage for the last half hour, now settles peacefully on the back of the chair next to my bed. Relief! Except that it is another hot night— nearly 90 degrees Fahrenheit. I lie on top of the covers, listening to the evening chorus of mosquitoes. They can be heard from afar as they search around methodically in the dark cabin. When one of them starts to home in on its target (me) and pays particularly close tribute, I wait patiently for it to land and terminate its mission.

Bubo, meanwhile, is also hot. Through the drone of the mosquitoes, his gular flutter sounds like a butterfly beating its papery wings on the windowpane. His thick coat of feathers protects him from mosquitoes better than any screen. But blackflies, when they hover about him during the day, will occasionally bite him on the eyelids. And now he also has Achilles' heels—the jesses that had restrained him at the Raptor Center have worn off the feathers on the back of his legs. Mosquitoes and blackflies gather there to gorge themselves into rotund purple blobs, and fly off replete and unscathed.

Biting flies are most prevalent in the north, and some northern owls can become quite anemic from the bites. Could the furry legs and feet of northern owls have a function besides insulation? It is hard to know how these northern owls would fare if they did not have feathered legs, but the small bare patches on Bubo's legs give a good hint. Feathers are a remarkable evolutionary invention that has been put to a variety of uses. What other adaptation could simultaneously serve as a sun shield, insulation, armor, raincoat, a device to make flight possible, decoration for sexual signaling, camouflage, and a guard against bloodsucking insects and the deadly parasites they sometimes transmit? Sand grouse in Africa even use their belly feathers as a sponge to carry water to their young.

Biology teaches one broadmindedness, because often a number of entirely different hypotheses are simultaneously true, to varying degrees, in different species. Each species is different, because each is better at occupying one specific niche than another one. And it is precisely because each is a unique adaptation that makes it possible for us to see patterns and to understand in what ways and why we are all alike.

But now my thoughts of a peaceful night are terminated with the sound of a "splat." I hear the flutter of wing beats in the dark. A mysterious clang. A little swish. Rattling silverware. Nothing serious. I try to block out the sounds, but I seem to be listening, nevertheless. A long silence. "Click, clack, click"—he is walking across the floor. Splat. Another flutter. "Rip." Silence. "Rip." Silence. Now I'm on full alert. Bubo is on my table and the beam of my flashlight catches him holding my favorite shirt—what is left of it. I jump up and yank it out from under him. He chitters indignantly.

All is quiet for a few minutes after I crash back into bed. As I slowly drowse off, the tap of his toes marching on the floor does not sound reassuring. A flutter. He makes a soft landing at the end of the bed, close to my toes—too close. Visions of his massaging my naked legs keep me awake. Enough! I jerk out of bed. End of experiment. I won't spend the night in the same room with a great horned owl. Period.

I open the window and reach for The Glove. I can't waste time. The mosquitoes, as always, do not. I hold the glove near Bubo's toes so he can hop on and I can maneuver him out the window, but I get no cooperation at all. He chitters, and the chittering picks up volume like an engine revving up. He is angry and snaps at the glove, no doubt remembering that I once used it to hold him forcibly on my fist. Like a fox who condemns the trap instead of the trapper, Bubo blames the glove, not me. As I shove the glove under him he applies his death grip, bites down hard, screams, and then hops off. This won't do. I grab a chair and hold him at bay, maneuvering him toward the window. He first holds his ground and attacks the chair, then flies over it to the opposite end of the room. It is a contest now, and I am determined to win. I am well motivated to get him out, knowing quite well that he'll wake me up at 4:30 a.m., not a very long time from now. Finally he is out, and I slam the

window down behind a hissing, bill-snapping, biting, claw-
ing fiend in the dark.

June 11

Like an alarm clock, Bubo wakes me at 4:30 a.m. by drumming on the window beside my ear. He joins me for breakfast, sharing some of my pancakes; I make them by mixing
whole wheat flour with lots of eggs, some canned milk, and
a little water and salt. He likes my pancakes either with or
without Maine maple syrup. He swallows a mouse for
dessert, and I opt for some toast instead. Then it's onto the
back of my chair, where he makes his friendly grunts while
I caress his head and he nibbles on my fingers. After I've
had enough of our morning session of touch-and-feel, I try
to write, but Bubo keeps inserting himself between me and
my pencil. He wants fingers to nibble on, and fingers he
gets. I do not disagree with a great horned owl unless it is
absolutely necessary.

I can understand Bubo so thoroughly now that I know
why he is the way he is, and I *expect* him to be the way he is,
even though I sometimes don't like his ways and will defend
myself against him if I have to. My understanding tran-
scends any feeling of blame or forgiveness. I can only accept
facts about him and work within them to achieve our mutual well-being....

June 23

Bubo has been spending much of his time at the skeleton of
the new log cabin. Every day he perches up on the collar ties
under the roof where it is dark and dry; from here he can

survey the clearing and see the woods. The gable ends of
the cabin are still not closed—a project for rainy days.

Margaret is now anxious to admire our handiwork from
last year and to add more to it. But Bubo begins to hoot
ominously as we start walking toward it across the field. He
is sporting his "mean" look, eyeing Margaret, who is carrying Stuart in a backpack. As we get closer, he flies down
and stands guard directly in the door opening, hooting ever
louder. He intends to defend that doorstep, and Margaret
gets the message. We decide to continue on to the swimming
hole instead, and even then he chases us, flying from tree to
tree close over our heads. Margaret remains close to me,
clutching a pine branch all the way.

In the afternoon I go to the cabin alone to visit Bubo.
This time he hoots from the collar ties without coming down
to stand guard at the door. He inserts coughing sounds
before each series of hoots. In addition, he makes an entirely different sound—one I have never heard before—a series
of high-pitched clucks, emitted after each series of hoots. It
sounds as if two different birds are in the cabin, one
answering the other. I have no idea what the sounds mean.
[And since I never heard them again I have no clue as to
their context.] They simply remind me that much information has been collected over millions of years and packed
into his 41 pairs of chromosomes, and I don't have access to
most of it. I suspect the variety of strange sounds reflects
the variety of confusing emotions he is experiencing. He
might still be angry at me, jealous, glad to see me, frightened, or all or some of these at the same time. I know how
to ease his mind from all that confusion. I pull a dead robin

out of my pocket. His hoots and clucks change into friendly chuckles. He flies down to me and I sit beside him as he plucks and eats. After he finishes eating he stares at me for a full minute, then he comes closer. I hold out my hand in apprehension, wondering if I should risk the gesture.

It was worth it. His nibbles on my hand and fingers are rough at first, but they get gentler and eventually become caresses. His eyes close, he continues to hoot all the while, even as I'm trying to soothe him by stroking his head feathers. He is still disturbed. We continue to play for 50 minutes, and in time his hoots become softer, until they are almost whispers. This is the first time ever he has hooted while being stroked.

I am glad we have made peace, and I do not break off our play, waiting for Bubo to do so. He eventually does—by pouncing on a roll of twine. He grabs the roll in one foot, and hops all over the piled lumber with the other foot, with some wing assistance here and there. But not enough. He loses his balance and flops on his side. No matter. He is up again quickly, grabbing and releasing the roll. I have not seen him play so exuberantly since last year, when he was young.

Having patched things up between us, I am about to leave and step out the doorstep. But he comes, too, and he perches, all fluffed out, in the bright sunshine on the front steps. I decide to stay a while longer and recline in the grass. He hops down next to me and sprawls out, with his feathers fluffed and his wings spread. His head looks huge.

He stares ahead and remains motionless, as if in a dream or trance. After four minutes without moving, his eyes gradually close into slits, and then they close entirely. After

another eight minutes, a fly lands first on my ever-present
note pad and then on Bubo's bill. He shakes his head, opens
his eyes again, and scratches his head with a talon on his left
foot. Looking up, he stares at a high-flying jet. Then he
hops back onto the doorstep, looks over his shoulder once
more at the jet, and flies up onto a collar tie in the shade
under the roof. When he begins to preen I go back up the
trail to Kaflunk, secure in the knowledge that we still have
a meaningful relationship.

Bubo is a one-man owl, or perhaps I am one owl's man,
and Margaret, who was once fond of him, now prefers the
crows. The crows hang out around Kaflunk, and they caw
loudly whenever Bubo comes by for a visit. Margaret is
glad to have them near, because they are her watchbirds.

The crows follow me into the woods, and we come near
a family of blue jays—two adults and some recently fledged
young that can barely fly. The adult jays mob the crows in
exactly the same way they mobbed the owl—by divebomb-
ing from above and behind when their target's head is
averted. As soon as a crow begins to preen or peck at a
branch, a jay is certain to attack immediately. But as soon
as the crow looks up, the jays stop their attacks, sidetrack-
ing those in progress by veering off in flight. I watch a total
of 30 attacks before I, and the crows, leave.

In the evening I go back to the log cabin for a third time,
this time with Stuart in my backpack. Bubo is "home"
inside the log cabin. I make my introductions, but Bubo is
not impressed. I am glad he ignores Stuart, though I'm puzzled as to why it is so.

Evening. My other nephew, Chris, and his friend Jeff

come up to Kaflunk for a visit. They bring blankets and sleeping bags, planning to spend the night. They know *of* Bubo, but they do not yet know much *about* him.

Bubo makes his usual evening appearance at Kaflunk shortly after everyone is settled in and chatting around the table. Unlike other evenings, we hear loud hoots from the tall spruce: apparently Bubo knows we have company. He comes down and perches low in the birch for a closer look through the front windows, his head bobbing excitedly. Now he flies to the rear window and presses his head to the windowpane. Jeff approaches Bubo, who is still looking in the window, and he feigns an aggressive gesture. This was a mistake. Bubo, reading Jeff's obscene gesture perfectly, throws himself against the window with a crash, and Jeff jerks back in surprise. Bubo is not deterred by a mere closed window and he now looks for another way to get in. Round and round the cabin he flies, checking all the windows and the doors for a place to enter. The hooting rises to a crescendo pitch.

Neither Jeff nor Chris is eager to be the first one out to set up the tent while Bubo stands guard. Can I lure him away with a piece of meat? Nothing doing. He looks right past me into the cabin, as if I, and even the piece of meat, do not exist. It is *Jeff* he wants. Jeff opens the door, and Bubo instantly lunges from the birch. Jeff trips backward, and in his shock neglects to close the door. Bubo barges in, but Jeff quickly grabs the broom next to the door. Bubo attacks the broom before he is beaten back out the door with it.

Both boys laugh, but I detect tension in their laughter. Jeff, who weighs 190 pounds, jokes about being "intimidated by a fifteen-pound owl." (I leave well enough alone and do not tell him that Bubo doesn't weigh a lick over three and a half pounds.) Nice bluff, Bubo! The boys' outward show of humor increases as they realize they may well be defeated by this owl. They will not be able to camp near the cabin, nor will any of us be able to sleep inside with the infernal hooting, and the banging on the windows. It is becoming clear to all that Chris and Jeff must leave, and the sooner they get out, the better: it will soon be dark, and Bubo will enjoy an even greater advantage.

For some not-so-strange reason Bunny has already disappeared, so we cannot use him as a hostage again. I suggest that the boys use their blankets as shields or as diversionary targets, like a matador's red cape. Perhaps they can make it down the trail to the field near the road, well out of his territory, and put up their tent down there. They are ready for a charge, bravely facing an unknown fate. But they lack resolve and hesitate a few seconds too long in front of the screen door. Bubo advances on foot, swaggering up closer to show his annoyance with the situation, and the idea of going out becomes less and less appealing to Jeff and Chris. Finally it becomes downright unpalatable. More nervous laughter. What next?

Bubo is positioned at the door, knowing quite well by now that the enemy must exit that way sooner or later. It appears that it will be later—the enemy's courage has waned and the standoff continues. Bubo's mood is not improving at all.

Necessity is the mother of invention; we must try new tactics. I would not dare to grab him, even with leather gloves. But there might be one way to foil him: drop the blanket *on* him. I go out with a blanket, and he pays no heed to me at all: he wants one of those enemies inside, not me. Because his focus is elsewhere, I'm able to drop the blanket on him, and I carefully roll up a very surprised Bubo. In a blanket he sounds more muffled than before, but is no less animated, possibly even more so. Bulges pop out in all directions.

The boys seize the moment by grabbing their things and running out the door and down the trail. Ten minutes later, after they have had enough time to reach the field, I release my grip on the blanket. Bubo unravels himself, pokes his head out without missing a hoot, looks wildly in all directions, and fixes a long stare down the trail they have just descended. I am surprised he knows they are no longer in the cabin, and where they have gone. The look on his face tells me he knows more than I'm willing to concede, so I try to hold him at Kaflunk with a bribe. Luckily, he has worked up an appetite and eagerly accepts a large chunk of woodchuck meat. I expect that it will take him at least twenty minutes to tear it apart and eat it, so I jog down the trail to console our company.

The boys are relaxing in the field and about ready to set up their tent, relieved that they made a bloodless escape. But the joy is premature. We hear some hooting. We look up and see Bubo flying down the trail directly toward us. He lands on a large maple, eyeing Jeff without making one blink. It is getting dark, and Bubo's presence is even less reassuring now than it was before, especially after he lands on the ground and starts going after Jeff. Jeff, who is still Bubo's primary target (because of his aggressive gesture?), gathers his wits and wraps himself in a blanket. Right idea, wrong object — Bubo is no friend of blankets. Bubo continues to stalk closer. In the last second, Jeff throws the blanket off himself and onto Bubo. An excellent maneuver. The muffled hoots sound increasingly strident, and the dancing dervish under the blanket threatens to escape rather sooner than was intended. Jeff tries to hold him down, but Bubo manages to bite through and inflicts a nasty finger pinch. Enough. The boys bolt down the road for a final escape — and with a host of tales to tell. I am again left holding the blanket. I resolve to leave a sign on the path: "Beware of Owl."

Until this evening I had thought Bubo's behavior toward Margaret was aggressive. But now I think he had treated her relatively well.

After this episode, Bubo no longer bothered Margaret at all, maybe because he did not realize who his friends were until he met his enemies.

Bernd Heinrich, Professor of Zoology at the University of Vermont, has written several books including *Ravens in Winter* and *Bumblebee Economics*. *One Man's Owl*, from which this story was excerpted, has also been adapted into an award-winning children's story called, *An Owl in the House*.

III

Odd Ducks

The Legend of Jesse Mew

PETE DUNNE

*It was written: There shall be
no birder before him.*

"THERE HE IS," A NAMELESS FOLLOWER whispered hoarsely. A voice at the other end of the platform croaked, "It's him." All eyes turned to watch the dramatic entrance of the 1966 Dodge sedan, the car known as "White Trash." Fred Hamer, Official Hawk Counter at the Cape May hawk watch, brought up his binoculars like a salute to offer official confirmation.

"Yup, it's him all right." (There was no mistaking the awe in his voice.)

Trash moved stately as a queen in her court through the peak-season crush in the parking lot and turned lightly into a vacant spot that opened right in front of the hawk-watch platform, just as if she knew it would be there.

Several of the hawk-watch faithful nodded knowingly to each other. It was written: A WAY WOULD BE MADE FOR HIM

IN CROWDED LOTS AND FAST FOOD DRIVE-IN WINDOWS.

The engine dieseled heavily for thirty seconds. Thin blue smoke hung like incense over the gutsy old heap and billowed uncaringly over the crowd standing open-mouthed and shoulder-to-shoulder on the platform. One or two asthmatics coughed irreverently.

Trash gave one final, thunderous belch of smoke, then shut down, making a noise like a Bessemer furnace giving breech birth to a Boeing 747. The hawk-watch platform was enveloped in thick, oily fumes. The faithful, to a man, woman, and child, were brought to their knees by wracking coughs.

And when the smoke cleared, there he stood, the legendary Jesse Mew — Professional Peregrine Watcher. Several of the faithful, their eyes streaming tears that ran rivulets down smog-blackened faces, nodded knowingly to each other. It was written: HIS MOVEMENTS ARE AS A CIVET CAT UNDER A NEW MOON — which was no small feat when you consider that removed of his Acme high-rise prairie stompers, Jesse stood six foot, seven and three-quarter inches.

Few, upon seeing the man for the first time, could describe him accurately — probably because to take in the whole unit at once would overload anything that approximated a normal functioning mind. And no individual seemed able to see Jesse the same way twice. This is particularly hard to understand, since Jesse never wore anything but the same crusty pair of Levi bellbottoms, a checkered shirt that looked as if it seconded as a dipstick rag, and a sun-bleached denim jacket that gave every appearance of having spent over half its life at the bottom of a bird cage.

His neck was long and sported a convulsively animated Adam's apple the size of a cue ball. His features were coyote sharp—the nose prominent, regal; the chin deeply notched. His hair was long, bleached white, and the consistency of spaghetti about thirty minutes overdone.

It went with the jacket.

Including guano, the whole unit weighed in at just over 109 pounds. Jesse Mew had the physique of a man just cut down from the cross.

But the color of his eyes was a matter of deep mystery and a subject of controversy. Jesse was never seen in public without his aviator sunglasses. Most believed that his eyes were deformed—the result of incalculable hours spent looking into the sun for towering peregrines. One school said his eyes looked like twin hamburger patties, well larded; another said that they were a matched set of charcoal briquettes. But whatever their color, it was no secret that as organs of sight, they were remarkable. Jesse could read the Manhattan Telephone Directory White Pages at 70 paces.

His feats were clouded in myth and it might be that only half of what was attributed to him was true. It was believed that his father was a plastic injection mold technician specializing in geodesic dome interiors. His mother is nameless. Rumor has it that Jesse was born in the underground parking garage of an L.A. hospital. Admission was delayed because Mrs. Mew's Blue Cross/Blue Shield cards were not in hand for a polite but inflexible admissions nurse.

Little about Jesse's boyhood is known, but his grammar, spelling, and inability to figure outside of the base three certified that he was the product of a public school education. Not until he reached the age of nineteen did there emerge a story whose roots are verifiable. It seems that while the family was visiting relatives in Ithaca, New York, Jesse and his parents became separated. After a long search, his father is said to have found him instructing a graduate seminar at the Laboratory of Ornithology on camber, aspect ratios, and wing-loading of North American falcons.

During his undergraduate years, Jesse bounced widely and often between universities—taking courses that he rarely completed, arguing with professors of ornithology, and having the unforgivable temerity to be right.

It was almost certain that during these early peregrinations he formulated his now-famous creed of "Natural Noninterference":

"THAT ENVIRONMENT IS MAINTAINED BEST WHICH IS JUGGLED LEAST."

"If civilization," he would explain, "does some stupid and unwitting thing that blows a hole in the whole natural structure, anything done to try to right the situation will probably only make it worse."

Jesse particularly denounced that arcane backwash of the natural sciences known as: The School of Wildlife Management. "Why 'management'?" he would ask his followers. "Why not 'maintenance' or 'preservation' or 'wildlife, leave-it-the-hell-alone'? Who says that after two and a half billion years of working things out, a three-million-year-old hominid has the wherewithal to elbow his way onto the scene and do a better job?"

His teachings grew popular with the poor, the downtrodden—the undergraduates. The high nooky-nooks of Academe grew jealous of his popularity and watched nervously as their course enrollment declined. Jesse was brought before a joint faculty/student board (packed with political science and home economics majors), denounced publicly on the trumped-up charge that his library card was overdrawn—and expelled.

Following this public humiliation, Jesse withdrew into the desert of the Southwest, where he apprenticed himself to some half-cracked, Navajo medicine man turned falconer-and-bunco-artist who spent half his time bootlegging funny mushrooms and the other half trying to cross peregrine falcons with caracaras in the hope that he might interest the Arizona Highway Department in ordering wholesale lots of highly efficient roadkill remover that could be flown from the fist. It is whispered among raptor cultists at their gatherings in the back rooms of sandal shops and coffeehouses that the Indian could leave his mortal being and his spirit could fly free with peregrines. Maybe it was true. Jesse believed it anyway.

Forty days later, Jesse was found face down in the Rio Grande by a seasonal park ranger leading a morning herp walk. He was naked, delirious, and barely alive when admitted to the hospital emergency room. The official park report reads "mugged and robbed." The doctor's diagnosis: "severe malnutrition, dehydration, and acute wind burn. Patient admitted in semi-conscious state, suffering delirium and under the apparent illusion that he could fly."

Recovery was slow. After a week, Jesse stopped trying to leap from eighth floor windows but continued to sleep perched on the headboard and bated frantically whenever meals were served.

Following a two-year recovery in a nice quiet place out in the country, Jesse rocked the ornithological community by conducting a milestone study on autumn peregrine migration by strapping himself to a jettisoned bale of hemp and dog-paddling around the Baltimore Canyon, 100 miles east of Ocean City, Maryland, during September and October. The following year he covered himself with plaster of Paris. Thus disguised as a 300-year-old accumulation of whitewash, he staked out a nest ledge on the Coleville River of Alaska and observed the nesting strategy of tundra peregrines from courtship to departure.

He returned next spring, but midway through the incubation, the tiercel disappeared. After a brief but decent interval, Jesse made known his intentions to the young widow, was accepted, and proved to be a good provider and capable father. At season's end, he and his new bride got off four strapping young pup peregrines.

That was nine seasons ago. Each fall, filling in as a relief hawk counter at various hawk watches during peak-peregrine period, Jesse made his way down the coast. During the winter he disappeared into the neotropics, but each spring he returned to his ledge overlooking the Coleville and to his lady. And now he was standing in the parking lot of Cape May Point State Park.

Jesse moved unhurriedly toward the trunk, rooted around through the mound of empties, and emerged with five cans of Skunkhead 10/40 motor oil. He unlatched the hood, inserted a magnum-sized funnel, and dumped all five cans into the crankcase simultaneously. Trash gurgled happily like a suckling child.

Having seen to the needs of his mount, Jesse made his way toward the platform. He took the steps two at a time and reached for Fred's extended hand.

"How you doing, Jesse?"

"Tolerable, Fred, tolerable. How 'bout yerself?"

"Just fine. How's the wife and kids? Everyone get off all right this year?"

"Got off without a hitch," Jesse answered proudly. "How's the flight been?"

"Oh, pretty fair," Fred pronounced. "How'd you like to count some peregrines while I concentrate on other stuff?"

Jesse grinned widely, "Well, Ah guess Ah can do that. Ah guess Ah'd like that jes' fine."

Smiling shyly, Jesse moved through the press toward the other end of the platform. He stopped abruptly, brought his hand up to block the morning sun, and announced casually, "Peregrine coming in."

A blue-backed bird arched over the trees, threw on the after-burners, and burned a hole through the early morning haze hanging over the marsh. A paunchy, balding man wearing Italian climbing boots, a string tie, and an Abercrombie and Fitch safari jacket bedecked with no fewer than 60 bird club patches elbowed his way to Jesse's side. In a voice heard from one end of the platform to the other he announced, "Peregrine, all right. Second after hatching year immature female I make it: subspecies *borealis*." He turned with staged familiarity, gazed (one expert to another) at the figure towering three heads above him, and dug himself in just a little bit deeper. "Not much question about that one."

Jesse gazed mildly at the upturned face for a pensive few seconds and replied, "Her name's Albert." Jesse whistled shrilly and hailed, "Yo, Albert, you old plover-eater, you."

Albert altered his course 40 degrees to pass directly over the platform, executed a neat little wing dip, and climbed steadily as he moved out over Delaware Bay.

The "expert" pulled his head down between his shoulders and moved, quickly, toward the exit ramp. Several of the faithful nodded knowingly to each other. It was written: THE CHARLATANS SHALL TRIP OVER THEIR OWN WORDS. AND ALL MUMMERY BE LAID BARE IN HIS PRESENCE.

"That a friend of yours, Jesse?" Fred inquired.

"Neighbor," said Jesse. "Two bluffs up."

Jesse, completing his shift to the south side of the platform, was heedless of the friends, followers, and admirers who stared in unabashed veneration; the few bolder ones reached out to touch the hem of his bellbottoms. From his daypack, Jesse pulled a pair of beat-up Hensolt binoculars (which he was never seen to use), a rebuilt stainless-steel hand counter, and two six-packs of Dr. Pepper. Jesse was a Pepper addict.

Life on the platform returned to a semblance of normalcy. Fred clicked off sharpies and kestrels on the north side; Jesse pulled peregrines out of the ozone on the right. He averaged fifteen to twenty an hour.

Occasionally, Jesse turned his head sideways, Adam's apple abob, peered upward into what looked for all the world like empty sky, and made a notation on his data form.

Seeing the puzzled looks around him, Jesse smiled and explained.

"Stealth peregrines—flying beyond the limit of conjecture. That'd be a code-eight bird on the data sheets (if they went up that high.) It is kinda tough picking 'em up on a day like this," he added generously. "Lots of heat inversions—blocks reception."

As he was taking the three o'clock weather reading, Jesse's face turned pale and he grasped the rail as if for support. Almost immediately, a young hawk-watcher called out, "Peregrine! Peregrine coming in three fields over Cape May." The masses gasped, thunderstruck, the foundation of their faith rocked. Jesse Mew beat to a call by a total unknown! Such a thing had never happened in memory.

Fred, his face the picture of concern, looked down the length of the platform and inquired anxiously, "Jesse, you O.K.?"

Jesse smiled weakly and shook his head in affirmation. With an effort he said, "Yeah, no problem, jes' a little dizzy is all." And then turning to the young hawk-watcher, he said apologetically, "It's not a wild peregrine, I'm afraid. It's a Pseudogrine, *Falko pseudogrinus*. It's one of them test-tube birds with the garbled bloodlines; the ones they used to grow indoors back in the DDT-panic when the sensible thing would have been jes' to let the birds go an re-establish themselves naturally. Folks jes' don't seem to have no faith in nature workin' things out herself—and less patience. It do beat all."

"Oh," the youngster said (more relieved than hurt). "But how could you tell it wasn't a real bird?"

"Ah felt a weakening in the force," Jesse allowed.

Several of the faithful nodded knowingly to each other. It was written: THOU SHALT HAVE NO ERSATZ PEREGRINES BEFORE THEE.

The flight dwindled as the afternoon wore on. The shadow of the lighthouse reached slowly but inexorably for the hawk-watch platform. The faithful, singly or in small groups, departed. Most would be late for wherever it was they were going.

On the empty platform, Fred closed the space separating himself and Jesse. They both stood for a time saying nothing, savoring the deepening evening. Words weren't necessary. Indeed, sometimes words impede communication.

Fred finally broke the silence.

"So how long you planning on staying, Jesse?"

"Contract with the pirate at the Observatory runs to the fifteenth but Ah may stay on a few more days if the flight looks good—and he knows it, too. But Ah got to git goin' by the twentieth at the latest. Ah got a ways to go, yet."

"I guess so," Fred said. "Well, I'm calling it a day; flight seems to have died. You going to watch for a bit?"

"Yea, Ah guess Ah'll hang on 'n keep an eye on things for a bit. Ah got me some friends that like to travel at night. Less traffic, they insist, and it's easier on the eyes."

With this, Jesse reached up and casually removed his shades. Fred was one of the handful of people on earth who *knew* what color Jesse's eyes were. And although Fred noted that the effect wasn't as startling as the first time, it was still hard to feel comfortable looking into eyes that drew all the shapes and colors of the world into themselves and reflected nothing but mystery in return. It was a gaze that was both benign and piercing, and he could never decide, somehow, whether the eyes seemed shallow, like standing water on an asphalt highway, or like two holes cut through the dark universe where depth has no meaning.

They might have been blue once. But maybe the medicine man wasn't so cracked after all.

Pete Dunne also contributed "Gift of Seed" in Part One. This story was excerpted from his book, *Tales of a Low-Rent Birder*.

How the Pimpernel Saved His Pigeons

PIPPA STUART

He acted in the spirit of history's great heroes.

THE FIRST TIME I NOTICED THIS SMALL, gray-haired man, I was seated on the train, looking out my window. He was hurrying along the platform, carefully carrying a large cardboard box. When he appeared a second time, a third, and then a fourth, always with the same scurrying haste and the same box, my curiosity was aroused. Once he had boarded the train he invariably made his way to the empty front carriage where he sat, aloof from his fellow passengers, the box held firmly on his knees.

Sherlock Holmes would have solved the mystery of what was in it at once, but I only found out the day the little traveler nearly missed the train.

The green flag had been waved, the whistle blown, and the door was about to close when along he rushed. The ticket collector grabbed him; he dropped the box; I caught it; and he was heaved aboard.

"Never jump on a moving train," the ticket collector said sternly. "Never!"

The man was too breathless to reply, but meekly followed me as I carried the box for him to his customary seat. "Some run!" he wrought out at last.

"A close shave," I agreed. He had begun to eye me closely, as if weighing me in the balance: Could he trust me with a secret?

"Perhaps," he began tentatively as the train rattled out of the Central, heading for the country. "Perhaps," he said, tapping the lid of the box, "you'd like to know what's inside."

"I certainly would!"

"I don't think that I could be arrested for what I'm doing."

"What on earth are you doing?" I asked, more curious than ever.

He half-opened the box. What did I expect to see? Certainly not what I did: two bedraggled, grimy-winged pigeons huddling together, peering out at us. He replaced the lid, watching my reaction.

"Do you breed pigeons?"

"Well, not exactly, though it might come to that." He paused, obviously eager to confide.

"Do tell me how," I begged.

"It all began with books," he said.

"But where do the pigeons come in?"

"They come in later. I had such a dreary job, you see, standing behind a counter all day, selling things like clothespegs, dusters, boot laces, and mothballs—not very inspiring. When my boss left me in charge and no customers came, I'd sit reading all the adventure stories I could lay my hands on—escapes from the Gulag or Colditz, rescues from Devil's Island, but especially from the Bastille. My favorite was a book called *The Scarlet Pimpernel*. This Pimpernel saved prisoners during the French Revolution. He'd turn up just as the tumbrels came rolling along to the foot of the guillotine, somehow managing to snatch victims from the jaws of death."

"But where's the link with those pigeons?" I insisted. "Oh, here's my station."

"Mine's the last one on the line," he said. "I'll tell you next week." He waved to me and held up his box as a pledge of the next installment.

A week later there he was, eager for more talk. "Last year was a milestone; I became an old-age pensioner," he continued. "No more mothballs or shoelaces! I started to come to the Central to look up at the departures board and dream of the places I might travel to. It was then that I noticed the pigeons, not lined up for the guillotine, perhaps, but doomed to a lingering death from starvation. Some had trailing wings, others broken beaks, withered claws, depending on travelers for crumbs. Remember the lame man at the Pool of Bethesda, always waiting for his turn in the healing water—someone always got in before him? The pushing pigeons were just like that, always nipping in first for food."

"I've never thought of the Central as Revolutionary Paris or the Pool of Bethesda, but it's an interesting analogy."

He chuckled at that. "I thought that if I smuggled

pigeons out of town and freed them in the country, it might not be heroic but at least it was a beginning."

"You're a benefactor of the railways," I told him. "Plenty of people object to pigeons flying in their faces and skimming over their heads. You should be rewarded for smuggling services!" The idea delighted him.

"Perhaps you've noticed how worried most of those travelers look, mainly about money and the fear of losing it or not having enough," he began. "All I need is my old-age-pensioner ticket—fifty pence return—and there's happiness!" he exclaimed.

"They should all take to pigeon smuggling," I said.

"There's quite a skill in it," the little traveler said. "First you pick out your pigeon—the most starved and persecuted. At first I would get flustered, and the pigeon panicked and pecked. I soon learned, however, you scoop it up, fold the wings closely together, gentle but firm, then pop it into the box."

"Doesn't anybody ever catch you at work?" I asked.

"Never. There's the advantage of being small. I've become part of the Central landscape. Who would take me for the Scarlet Pimpernel! To make it more like those exciting rescue stories, I'd pretend that the station police were after me and run for the train as if my life depended on it—you've seen me."

The spring weeks of travel to the country were filled with his happy chucklings and tales of adventure on the rails. "One day I opened the box a chink to see if my two birds had enough air, and out they flew, perching on a very neat businessman, sound asleep over some computer thing.

He woke to find a pigeon roosting on his shoulder, another on his knees. They took some catching, feathers flying. He forgot all his stock-exchange calculations in the chase!"

"When you get out into the country, what do you do then?" I asked.

"Ah then!" His face lit up with a blissful smile. "I walk over the fields and into the woods. Then I sprinkle some grain and lift out my bird. I open my hands, and up he soars into the clear air, a country bird not a city one. There's nothing to beat that moment." A kind of cheerful comradeship had grown between us, so that I almost expected our talks, as we traveled countryward, to continue indefinitely. I might even learn the gentle art of pigeon smuggling. Then, all at once, he was no longer there. For a long time I kept expecting to see him come fluttering and flapping along, bird-like, clutching his precious box, but he never came.

Now when I stroll through the beechwoods around our village and a silvery-gray cloud of pigeons rises up from feasting on beechnuts, I think: The Scarlet Pimpernel of the Central rescued them! I was not likely to forget him.

Pippa Stuart has an obsession for European languages and birds, which she attributes to her good fortune to be born to a father with a passion for birds and poetry and a mother whose special passion was for those human birds known as "lame ducks." She has traveled extensively throughout Europe and Russia and now makes her home in a village in Scotland where she devotes her time to birdsong and poetry.

Nothing Tastes Like Roadkill

ROBERT H. BOYLE

And on the menu today we have rotten squirrel.

JUST WHAT I NEEDED FOR MY BIRD FEEDER: A road-killed woodchuck. I slammed on the brake, pulled the car to the side of the road, dashed out, shooed away the flies, grabbed the bloated corpse by the tail and popped open the trunk. As I was about to drop the body in—my wife will never notice the bloodstains, I thought—a passing driver slowed down and gave me the once-over. Better a suspicious stranger eyeing me than the couple who surprised me the other day as I pawed through a supermarket dumpster in quest of a spoiled chicken.

Let others feed robins, cardinals, or purple martins; the birds for me are turkey vultures. My vulture feeder is in a brushy field a hundred feet downhill from my house, and the three-by-three-foot feeding platform, set six feet above the ground, is high enough and large enough to assure the vultures that they won't be ambushed by a predator. Despite their fearsome appearance—bald red head, big beak, and a wingspread of about six feet—vultures are very wary birds, and why another creature would even dream of attacking one is beyond my comprehension. The stinking breath of a turkey vulture, so the saying goes, "would cloud a photographer's lens." And, to top it off, vultures vomit on strangers. Like all birds of prey the turkey vulture has superb eyesight, but it may also have the keenest sense of smell of any soaring bird in the world.

As a rule I set out the day's fare around 10 a.m., because the vultures are late risers that like to stretch their wings and sun themselves before taking to the air. (If I set the table the night before, crows are likely to have had at the food by the first light of dawn.) On heavy-rain days I don't put out food, because without the sun the birds tend to stay put, rather than fly.

Vultures quickly become accustomed to a free lunch, and on a sunny day they show up promptly to check out the menu, which might be dead mice, chipmunks, and squirrels; chicken, meat, and cold cuts; extraordinarily ripe Brie, Roquefort, and mozzarella cheese; and the vultures' favorites: filleted carcasses of largemouth bass, sunnies and crappies, and the heads of brown trout.

Vultures are masters of soaring and gliding flight. With their wings set in a dihedral position, a slight V, they seem to stay aloft for hours without a single beat of their wings. They do this by getting lifts from thermals (rising currents of hot air) and updrafts (caused when the wind is deflected upward off a hill or a mountainside). Inasmuch as vultures feed on animals only if they are already dead and dead animals are not as numerous as live animals, vultures have to be capable of sustained flight, with no unnecessary expenditure of energy.

All this helps to attract turkey vultures to a well-placed feeder; the birds don't have to work very hard. After they've been south for the winter, they check out my feeder upon returning north. They won't land and eat if people are around, so when I see them coming I hide behind a window to watch. Ever on the alert, they glide downward from a thousand feet above me, slowly circling down and around and down again. As they fly by me at eye level, their beguiling aerial ballet, performed by from one to a half-dozen vultures, is four-star theater that can last as long as twenty minutes. Turkey vultures are like giant feathered versions of the paper airplanes I made as a boy, except that my planes always crashed, while the vultures keep on gliding by.

Eventually one will put on the wing brakes, land gently on the platform and look around, then look around again and yet again before holding down the day's special with a foot and tearing into it with its beak. Should another vulture venture to land on the platform, the original occupant is likely to reach over and expel the interloper by biting it on the neck.

For all their love of the dead, vultures won't dine on just any stiff. The major dictum of la *cuisine de vautours* is, "The more rotten the better." This is an important consideration for anyone who wants to feed turkey vultures. Along with other New World vultures, turkey vultures lack the razor-sharp bills of their Old World counterparts. The griffon vultures of Africa, for example, can strip off a rhino's hide with the ease of a chef peeling a ripe avocado. Turkey vultures apparently depend on other creatures, such as maggots and flies, to soften the flesh of a fresh cadaver. In fact, several days passed before the vultures finished the road-killed woodchuck mentioned above, and even then they began by probing the soft spots—the eyes and the anus.

Both New World and Old World vultures evolved some 50 million years ago—but strange as it may seem, they are not related. They look alike because of what scientists call convergence. This occurs when unrelated species in distant regions occupy similar niches. And it explains why the Tasmanian wolf resembles the North American wolf and why the South American fish known as the dorado looks like a salmon.

Old World vultures belong to the same order as eagles, hawks, and falcons (*Falconiformes*), while New World vultures belong to the order that includes storks (*Ciconiiformes*). One behavioral trait that vultures and storks share is that they excrete waste on their legs to cool themselves.

There are seven species of New World vultures, and two besides the turkey vulture are native to the U.S. These are the California condor, an endangered species, and the black vulture, mostly found in southern states but moving north these days. The turkey vulture, in contrast, is the most successful and widespread of all New World vultures, ranging seasonally from southern Canada and the continental U.S. down through South America to Patagonia. In the early 19th century the species rarely ventured north of New Jersey on the East Coast. Its movement north since then has been attributed to warmer temperatures and to highway construction that has resulted in more roadkills.

When winter comes to the northern states, turkey vultures migrate south. The folks in Hinckley, Ohio, celebrate their return with a one-day festival. Hinckley residents claim that, like the swallows that return to San Juan Capistrano, California, the "buzzards" show up in Hinckley every March 15, regardless of the weather.

Turkey vultures nest as far as possible from people. Actually, there is no nest, because the female simply lays two eggs on a bare rock cliff, in a hollow log, in a cave, or even on the floor of an abandoned house. Vulture parents feed their young by regurgitating food into their mouths. One theory is that regurgitation transfers antibodies, in the form of immunoglobulins, that make the young immune to botulism, anthrax, and other lethal bacteria or viruses in carrion.

The idea that the digestive system of the turkey vulture could be of significance in human medical research helped lead to the founding in 1994 of The Turkey Vulture Society, based in Reno. The society's aim, according to Bill Kohlmoos, a former rancher and the society's CEO, is "to study the turkey vulture and to give it the proper understanding and respect to allow it to continue its vital role in the natural environment of living things on earth."

One study cited by Kohlmoos will be on the vulture's ability "to disinfect rodent carcasses carrying the deadly hantavirus." Another study, conducted by the General Accounting Office, measured the threat of birds to military aircraft safety. Ingestion of birds into jet engines caused 16,198 accidents over a five-year period, with nine fatalities, according to the study. The U.S. Air Force warns its pilots to avoid flying through areas known to have dense vulture populations.

I have always been doubly taken with the scientific name of the turkey vulture: *Cathartes aura*, from the Greek *kathartes*, "cleanser," because the vulture cleans carrion, and *aura*, meaning invisible breath of radiation, because of the bird's bald red head. Then again, to my mind, *Cathartes aura* rhymes with the lyrics from the song "The Party's Over." This holds true for the dead upon which the vultures feast, but for me, when I see the birds glide toward my feeder, the party is just beginning.

Robert H. Boyle has been writing for *Sports Illustrated* since it started 45 years ago. He is the president of the Hudson River Keeper, a conservation organization, which looks after the integrity of the Hudson watershed.

Close to the End

KENN KAUFMAN

A record-setting birder questions the meaning of his accomplishments and hits the road for redemption.

"**N**OW YOU CAN DIE HAPPY," JANET WITZE-man told me.

I couldn't resist teasing. "Thanks a lot," I said. "Trying to get rid of me, now that your Christmas Count is over?"

"You know what I mean. You've done something now, something to be proud of. Your Big Year—and finding a first for California. It's an accomplishment."

But was it? Had I accomplished anything? I wondered about that during the next two days, as I took to the road one more time, heading for the upper Texas coast.

I must have been a disappointing rider for the drivers who picked me up in those last days, near the end of the year: lost in thought, I probably failed to make much conversation. But I was tired of hitchhiking—tired of the small talk that was repeated, with minor variation, on virtually every ride. By my rough calculations I had thumbed my way some 69,000 miles that year, on top of many thousands over the preceding three years, riding with many hundreds of drivers. I was grateful to them all. But I was tired of being grateful. Now I never wanted to get a free ride, or a free anything else, ever again. I wanted to work for every inch, pay for every mile.

Had I accomplished anything? That was a good question. Maybe I had set a record—if it meant anything to set a record in a sport that had few fans, no professionals, and no referees.

Or maybe I was an also-ran. There was no way to know. Somewhere out there, Floyd Murdoch was still seeking a Bohemian waxwing, which I had seen in Alaska in July; he might also get word of some fantastic rarity someplace, and jump a plane to go see it. Floyd still had potential new birds to list. I did not. Black rail had been my last serious possibility for the year in North America.

Now Mexico beckoned, with the promise of dazzling tropical birdlife, a world of birds that I could enjoy without having to focus on list-keeping. I would heed the call before December ended and start the new year in the teeming birdland of southern Veracruz. But first I had an appointment with birding tradition.

A few years earlier, as an energetic teenager, Victor Emanuel had started a Christmas Bird Count at Freeport, Texas. With his organizing, planning, and recruiting, he had made it one of the top counts in the nation. In 1971, close to the end of his Big Year, Ted Parker had taken part in the count; that year, naturally, Freeport had set an all-time national high, with 226 species. Although I could not expect any additions to my year list there, I would go to Freeport for tradition, and for fun.

So it was back across Interstate 10 one more time, and then angling down a series of state highways toward the coast, to avoid the Houston-to-Galveston traffic. As we approached Freeport and the coast, the horizon was filled with tall oil tanks, chemical tanks, steel towers for power-lines, factory buildings, dozens of smokestacks, and der-ricks and cranes for ongoing construction. It looked like some bad dream of a science-fiction future. I was just as amazed as when I had passed this way the preceding April: amazed that Victor Emanuel had been able to see past this surface ugliness, to see that the surrounding habitats would add up to the most diverse Christmas Bird Count circle in North America.

Past this technoscape, over the high bridge across the Intracoastal Waterway, the highway came down to the beach at Surfside. Victor had reserved an A-frame house on the beach as a rendezvous point and accommodations for the counters. When I arrived, late in the afternoon, hardly anyone was there: the earlier arrivals were out scouting the count circle. As daylight faded they drifted in, dozens of birders, from all over Texas and from farther afield.

Victor Emanuel was radiating energy as he orbited around the room, welcoming all the counters, discussing the prospects for the morrow, planning where to position the available observers. Jim Tucker arrived, and we talked about our Big Day exploits from the preceeding April, the

Kenmare convention in June, and things that had happened since. Rose Ann and Pelican came in, all smiles and good cheer as usual, brightening the A-frame with their presence. They had failed to drag the hard-working Edgar Kincaid away from his desk to take part in the count, but to demonstrate his support he had sent along his best wishes and his good telescope.

We ate that night in a seafood diner just down the beach from the A-frame, a place called the Shrimp Hut, where the waitresses wore little mock sailor suits. Dozens of birders were there. An air of cheerful confusion reigned. In the midst of it all, Victor was still debating, planning, organizing, trying to find the perfect allotment of birders to birding areas. This count circle contained so many patches of different habitats, each with a different potential. Counters had to be assigned to the old groves of live oak, to the willow–saltcedar thickets, to the marshes, to the open fields, to the suburbs with their feeders, and so on. I could hear Victor giving out final assignments, mentioning some of the key birds to watch for, telling each person how important his or her particular area was. When Victor got to me, he had an inspired look in his eye.

"Western Kingbird!" he said, greeting me by my Texas bird name. "We have an excellent assignment for you, if you're willing. This is a Noble Task. There are certain seabirds that are probably present offshore every year; but we rarely record them. We need someone with stamina and skill to stand out at the end of the Freeport jetty all day, watching for pelagics."

Sure, I thought, kids from Kansas are always good at

seabirds. But I was complimented. "Yeah, I'll do it."

"You'll need a telescope," Peli told me, "Why don't you take Edgar Kincaid's 'scope? Rosie and I will be in the woods, so we won't need it."

"Just make sure you don't drop it in the water," Rose Ann added. We all laughed.

Morning came to the A-frame as a chorus of rustlings and shufflings, as people crawled out of their sleeping bags in the dark and started off to reach their birding areas by first light. I lingered in the warm blankets awhile—there was no point in looking for seabirds in the dark—but as soon as gray dawn lit the windows, I shoved my backpack into a corner and started off alone down the beach.

A gusty cold wind was blowing under a dark and restless sky. The pale sand beach was deserted except for a few sanderlings, nervously skittering ahead of me. Behind the dunes the tawny beach grass whipped in the wind, and the wooden houses on stilts look shuttered up and empty.

In the mile between the A-frame and the base of the jetty, as I was waking up more thoroughly, I began to notice just how loud the ocean was. The jumbled gray peaks of the waves turned to brown as they roiled up silt in the shallows, and then to white as they smashed on the beach. Big waves were visible as far out as I could see, all the way to where the gray ocean blended into gray sky; the lack of any stable horizon gave an unsettled feeling to the scene.

The Freeport jetty was a massive pile of stone blocks, incredibly long, extending perhaps half a mile out to sea. A similar jetty paralleled it a few hundred yards away;

between the two ran the ship channel that led to the inner harbor. No boats seemed to be traversing the channel today.

Looking out along the jetty, I could see waves breaking violently out near the end. *Hot rats*, I thought; *it's no wonder they can't usually get anyone to go out there.* I was too unfamiliar with the area to realize just how much the weather had worsened since the afternoon before. *Well, this is the West*, I said to myself; *I'm not going to chicken out on my assignment.* There was no point in hesitating. The big gray slabs of stone that formed the center of the jetty were almost level, and I started out toward the end, leaping from rock to rock, in a hurry now to get out there and man my post.

Out at the very tip of the jetty, I found a solid place to station myself, a huge level block of stone. Planting the tripod firmly on the rock, I aimed Edgar Kincaid's telescope out to sea. I was determined that no seabird would slip past me unnoticed. Alternating between scanning with binoculars and sweeping the distant waves with the telescope, I began my day's vigil.

It was good to be just birding, just looking to see what was there, not trying to build any personal list. At the precount gathering the night before, so many people had been asking, "Could you get any new year birds tomorrow?" "Do you think you'll win the Big Year competition?" It was impossible to explain to them that I really did not care anymore.

The Big Year had been a great excuse to go birding. To both Floyd Murdoch and me, that had mattered more than the numerical outcome. All along, Floyd had been more interested in the protection of birds and their habitats than in the accumulation of check marks. As for me, my own passion for list-chasing was dwindling fast, while my interest in the birds themselves was becoming stronger than ever. So the contest was coming to matter least of all to the contestants.

The whistling wind that flapped my poncho around also drove each breaker against the base of the jetty at my feet. The waves seemed to be getting bigger. I was being misted with spray from every wave now, and some of them broke high enough that water washed around the soles of my beat-up hiking boots. As a whimsical precaution, I tied the drawstring of my poncho to the tripod that held the borrowed telescope.

Gulls were tacking into the wind, hanging on updrafts where the gusts were deflected by the jetty, streaking downwind on backswept wings like errant boomerangs. They were wonderful to watch, but did I really know them? All the North American species of gulls were on my list, so I should have recognized each one here with confidence. But I didn't. Not really. In the past I had always checked them off by finding the adults in their distinctive plumages, ignoring most of the motley younger birds. So, what were all these young gulls flying past now? I thought they were probably all ring-bills and herring gulls; but if something rare had been among them, I would not have recognized it. I still had a lot to learn.

One thing was becoming obvious to me now: list-chasing was not the best way to learn birds. It had been a good way to start, an incentive for getting to a lot of places and seeing a lot of species. But the lure of running up a big list made it

all too tempting to simply check off a bird and run on to the
next, without taking time to really get to know them. And
there was so much that I did not know.

So much left to learn…. And one other lesson was sinking in, near the end of 1973, as I ran into the expectations of
other birders. Just because I had broken listing records,
they expected me to be a top-notch birder—and I was not.
They were comparing me to Ted Parker, who had set the
record just two years before—but there was really no comparison. None of us realized then just how fast the world of
bird listing had been changing. Indeed, the entire approach
to doing a Big Year had been undergoing a radical change.

Ted Parker had set his record in 1971 on the strength of
sheer skill and knowledge and energy. For me, as for Floyd
Murdoch, the mix had involved less skill and a lot more
information: just two years had made that much difference,
as the fledgling American Birding Association had broad-
cast the directions to dozens of good sites for scarce birds.
The totals amassed by Murdoch and me would be edged
out in 1976, as a young ornithology student named Scott
Robinson made a low-budget, high-knowledge run around
the continent. But that would be the last time that any
record could be set by a birder who focused on the normally
occurring birds.

The information explosion, in birding as in everything
else, was bringing us more and more data, faster and faster.
The new bird-finding booklets let us know about good birding spots that had been productive within the last year or so,
even within the last few months. But before long, the bur-
geoning communication among birders would bring news of

rarities that were really current: found today, even found within the last few hours.

A couple of times in 1973 I had heard about rare visitors in time to go and look for them, like the loggerhead king-bird that had spent the whole winter in Florida. But before the end of the 1970s, the growth of birding "hotlines" would make it possible for birders to find out about such strays almost instantly. A birder with money could then jump on the next flight, rent a car, and check off a bird that he had never even heard of just a few hours earlier. It was inevitable that Big Year listing would come to focus more and more on such rarities. Listing would shift away from knowl-edge and planning and experience, toward contacts and hotlines and money.

And no doubt, it would continue to be a tremendous amount of fun for those who could afford it, the greatest of games. But list-chasing had lost most of its appeal for me. What I needed to do now was to go back and look at all those birds again, taking more time.

By now the sea was in a frenzy all around my perch near the end of the jetty. The waves were still coming from ahead and to my right. I could not see them approaching as indi-vidual waves, only as a dance of whitecaps, but I could tell each time one arrived, running *wham*! into the massive rocks and sending up a curtain of spray. If I looked quick-ly back along the jetty I could see how the angle of the breaker would run itself out against the line of rocks, and at the same time I would feel the water from the spent wave washing over my feet. Gradually it was coming to me that this must be unusual weather, and that perhaps I should move back a little from the end of the jetty. But I would take one more scan out over the ocean first.

Gulls had been flying past the jetty and out over the whitecaps, but scanning farther out I suddenly picked up one that looked different. With a start, I realized it was a species I could recognize with certainty, one I'd seen by the thousands in Alaska, a black-legged kittiwake, a rare bird in Texas, the kind of prize that Victor had hoped would come out of my vigil on the jetty. I strained to follow it in the telescope as the wind rocked me and spray stung my eyes.

Seeing the kittiwake brought back sudden images of Gambell, Alaska, the magical place that I had visited half a year and most of a continent earlier. Perhaps my Big Year attempt had no value in itself, but it had led me to incredible places, a whole series of extraordinary destinations. It had taken me through life-changing experiences. Regardless of final list totals, it had been worthwhile.

Listing, at its best, could be a wonderful quest, I reflected. We list-chasing birders, at our best, could be like knights seeking the Holy Grail—except that the birds were real, and we birders were rewarded at every turn. If we made an honest effort, the birds would come. This kittiwake, appearing out of the storm like a winged messenger, seemed to confirm that. Inspired, I began another scan of the ocean.

Just then I felt another wave washing over my feet, tugging at my ankles. The breakers were obviously getting high. Despite all my macho intentions, common sense was insisting that I really should move back a little. But at that moment, I picked up something flying far out over the horizon. A dark gull, flapping hard—No! it was a jaeger, another bird that would be a great addition to the count. But which kind? With difficulty I found it in the telescope and struggled to see field marks. White flashes at the bend of the wing, dark chest band; could be either pomarine or parasitic. Salt stung my eyes and I lost the bird, still undecided about which it was. But maybe I could find it again. I would take one more scan—

The next wave rumbled up onto the jetty, and I could feel that this would be a big one. Instinctively I flexed my knees to brace against the current, but it was futile. With a sense of unreality I felt my feet slipping, and then I was sliding sideways, flailing for the telescope, tumbling off the top of the jetty. My shoulder hit a rock with a tooth-rattling crunch, and then I was gulping saltwater and thrashing in the cold green darkness.

When I came to the surface I was looking up at the jetty, now seeming to tower above me, several yards away. My tattered jeans and boots were heavy as lead, and my poncho wrapped around my arms like a shroud, but when I reached for the poncho drawstring that had been tied to the tripod and 'scope I felt nothing—the cord had pulled free, and the telescope was gone.

Another wave crashed over the top of the jetty, and I was underwater again. Floundering toward the boulders at the jetty's base, I grabbed them and pulled myself up. The rocks were covered with barnacles, and their razor edges sliced my palms. Surprised, I loosened my grip, and another wave knocked me off again.

Treading water heavily, I tried to think rationally about what to do. The sharp little cones of barnacles appeared to cover every inch of the jetty rocks near water level. For a moment I considered trying to swim to shore, but the beach was so far away; I doubted I could swim that far in my sodden clothes. I had to go up the rocks to survive.

Twice more I tried to climb the rough boulders. Twice more, waves coming over the top of the jetty knocked me loose, sending me sliding down, barnacles ripping my palms and the knees of my jeans. But finally I was able to clamber up to the top of the jetty, above the level of the barnacles. Slowly, half crouching and half crawling, clinging to the rough rocks when each wave broke, I made my way back toward shore. It seemed like an eternity before I was finally standing on the beach again.

My hands were bleeding and stinging so badly that I could not even hold my binoculars. There was no point in looking for assistance at the deserted houses behind the line of dunes. Then I remembered the Shrimp Hut, up the beach near the A-frame, where the group had had dinner the night before. Maybe it was open today. Shivering now in the cold wind, I walked back in that direction.

The waitresses in the Shrimp Hut were shocked by my appearance—and no wonder. As unkempt as I usually looked, I was now also sopping wet, bleeding, and probably wild-eyed. But when they saw my hands, their expressions changed. Although the waitresses were no older than I, their maternal instincts seemed to take over. They sat me down, washed and soaked and bandaged my hands, and even spoon-fed me some warm soup. Silently I rebuked myself for having laughed at their mock sailor uniforms the night before; regardless of their uniforms, they looked like angels to me now.

I tried to pay for the bandages and the soup, but they refused the wet dollar bills I fished out of my wallet. So I thanked them again and turned to leave.

"You're not going back out on the jetty, are you?"

"I have to," I said. "This is our big bird count."

Trudging back up the beach, I hardly noticed that the waves still pounded the sand, the wind still gusted and cried; I was inured to the weather. Once again I picked my way out onto the jetty, jumping from rock to rock, gauging how far I could go in safety. A little more that halfway out, just before the first stretch where the waves began to get bad, I took my stand.

You're not going back out there, are you? But of course I was. It was the only thing to do. The certainty of that decision gave me a sense of calm. In the midst of the turbulent sea and sky, I was overcome by a great feeling of peace: I was doing exactly what I was meant to do today. *Any day could be a special day, and you just had to get outside, and see what the birds were doing….* Birding is what I came here for; this is how I spend this day and my days and my life.

The borrowed telescope was gone, my hands were bandaged, and my cheap binoculars were clouded with salt water, but I was keeping my vigil. I could still see rare seabirds if they came in close. As the afternoon waned, the sun might find a break in the clouds, and then it would be low in the western sky behind me—flooding everything in front of me with perfect light.

Somewhere out there, maybe not too far away, jaegers were coursing over the waves. They might come this way again. I was sure they would. Experience had shown me that jaegers and other seabirds might come in closer to shore early in the morning and then again late in the afternoon and evening. Surely in this stormy weather they would come in close. I would be here, ready, when they came.

Now, when I look back many years later, as though from a great distance, I can still see that young man standing out on the jetty. And at least on my better days, I can see myself standing there with him: shaken by experience, perhaps, but still confident that the light will be better, that the birds will come in closer, that we will see everything more clearly at last, before the day is over.

Kenn Kaufman is the author of *Lives of North American Birds*, *Peterson Field Guide to Advanced Birding*, and *Kingbird Highway: The Story of a Natural Obsession That Got a Little Out of Hand*, from which this story was excerpted. He lives in Tucson with his wife, Lynn.

After the Fires

PETER DAVIS

Would the neighborhood's most enchanting character be a casualty?

NO ONE TOLD US TO GET OUT. INDEED many people in our street chose to stay. But we knew that our cedar home wouldn't stand a chance against the ferocity of the fire that was consuming the national park less than 300 metres away. We packed the cars (with computer discs, photographs, personal letters, and the big Oxford dictionary from the study) and we cruised down to the village.

From there we monitored the wind, listened to the radio, and watched the big planes water-bomb our precious hill in a desperate attempt to contain the fire. For years the national park has provided us with exercise, recreation, and reflection. Often we would hike the steep slopes from our front door, up the dry western side where the scent of eucalypti lingers on a hot day, to the top of the hill. We would then continue down the eastern slope where the vegetation is moist, the ferns are large, and water flows gently under giant mossy tree roots into gullies.

And that's where we first met Henry, early one morning just near the big mossy tree. We actually heard him before we saw him. He was singing in the way that lyre birds do, switching abruptly from one tune to another, from one key to the next.

We made pathetic attempts to emulate his tones. Suddenly he appeared from the lush undergrowth. He hopped onto a tree and, less than three metres from where we stood, he demonstrated an impressive repertoire. One minute he would sound like a chorus of kookaburras, then came the rosellas, a screeching cockatoo, a dog, a magpie, and some indistinct human voices.

After twenty minutes it seemed like Henry had no intention of stopping. But we had other commitments so we applauded and then made our way down the hill. Henry ceased his singing and followed. He emitted a sorrowful whimper as he trailed behind us almost to the bottom. Then he disappeared.

From that day on we saw Henry (that's the name the rangers give him) on a regular basis, usually early in the morning. Other walkers smiled as they passed. They too had experienced Henry's song, dance, and general hospitality.

Just before the fires we carried cameras and a professional tape recorder. Henry didn't let us down; his repertoire was even more extensive. In mid-song he jumped off his perch, onto the ground, and danced rhythmically as if performing a corroboree. With his lyre bent over his head he made what can only be described as the sound of a space invaders' machine interspersed with drumming. For 30 minutes we recorded his extraordinary music and photographed his dance.

Again we had to leave. And again Henry followed us almost to the bottom. The next morning an eagle perched low on a branch as Henry pranced beneath. That was the morning the fires came.

As the planes continued their sorties and the people in yellow sped past in red trucks, we thought of all our friends who had chosen to live in the peaceful surrounds of the hills. We thought of how we might begin again if the house went. We joked with other residents about what we packed and what we left behind. We expressed despair at the rumour (later confirmed) that the fires were deliberately lit. And we expressed outrage at the ghoulish goons who invaded the neighbourhood for a better view. And of course we thought of Henry.

The homes in our street survived. Two days later we walked through the smouldering remains of the western slope. Fallen trees littered the landscape. Not a speck of green was visible. The eerie silence was punctuated by the cacophony of cockatoos. They looked even more brilliant in their whiteness as they flew from one blackened tree to the next, screeching with every take-off and landing. Kookaburras hovered above the scorched earth maintaining a keen eye for fried worms and lizards. We were looking for Henry so we walked to the other side.

Here things seemed untouched. The green was as it had been. And the water continued its summer trickle. We yelled a *cooee*, we walked a little farther, and then we stopped.

Our efforts were met with silence. Could the damage on the other side cause such a stillness? Were we bearing witness to the post-traumatic shock of the forest? Again we yelled, self-consciously this time because we felt we were disturbing the forest that was trying to heal itself. We stood motionless. The only sound we heard was the comforting gurgle of the underground stream. Then we heard it. Far in the distance was the familiar sound of the space invaders' machine. Henry was performing somewhere. The east/west divide had assured his safety. We walked on to our usual rendezvous point, and waited. Within moments Henry emerged. He hopped onto a tree and, just as he had done before the fires, he played his repertoire.

His imitation of kookaburras, cockatoos, magpies, and machines was more than just entertaining. It was reassuring. Our laughter and applause seemed to encourage him. With each sound he revealed something of his unique world, something of what he had heard and what he had seen. This performance poet of the forest was nothing if not a diligent chronicler of his times. We wondered whether he sensed our concern about his fate in the fires because his performance on this day was especially earnest. It was as if he were trying to show us that all is well and he had survived.

As we continued to be an attentive audience, we detected something different, the faint strains of a sound we had not previously heard. It was strangely akin to the noise of a low flying airplane, perhaps the one that water-bombed our hill and helped save our homes.

What else had Henry seen and heard? Next time he performs we'll pay even closer attention. Maybe he'll mimic some deranged person striking a match and then beating a hasty retreat on a trail bike. Henry is a key witness and we should all take note.

Peter Davis lives in the hills outside Melbourne, Australia. After graduating in economics (for reasons he still can't understand), he landed a job selling fire extinguishers. He regards this as the beginning of his extinguished career. From there he drifted into freelance writing and photography. He contributes to a wide range of publications, lectures part-time in non-fiction writing at Deakin University and in photojournalism at Photography Studies College, and is a contributing author to the Lonely Planet books on India. He is also the co-author/photographer of the book *Aliya: Stories of the Elephants of Sri Lanka*.

The Ramble of Central Park

MARIE WINN

*Hours pass like minutes in the
dark mysterious wood.*

I F IT IS POSSIBLE TO FALL IN LOVE WITH A
thing, I believe I fell in love with the Bird Register the
day I first opened it. The emotions were familiar: the
same feeling of excitement, of undeserved luck, the mildly
deluded sensation that a new kind of happiness was just
around the corner, the certainty that life was about to divide
forever into a before and after.

The Loeb Boathouse, a nondescript building located at
the east end of Central Park's rowboat lake, is where the
Register resides, though not always in the same place.
During the years I've known it, the Bird Book, as it is often
called, has lived on the frozen-yogurt bar, on a shelf behind
it, and on the cafeteria counter where the little packets of
sugar, mayonnaise, mustard, and grape jelly are kept.
Currently it may be found behind the podium where reser-

vations are taken for the Boathouse Café, a private restaurant. It may have moved again by the time you read this, but keep looking. It's sure to be there, somewhere, sitting right out in the open as if it were an inconsequential thing instead of a local tribe's central treasure.

I remember casually picking up the plain, blue canvas loose-leaf notebook with its sloppily hand-lettered legend on the front cover: CENTRAL PARK BIRD REGISTER AND NATURE NOTES: ENJOY BUT PLEASE DO NOT REMOVE. I opened it for a quick glance at its contents. Then, with that greedy feeling one gets after cautiously tasting some unpromising new dish and discovering it to be delicious, I stood there devouring page after page.

I had known there were robins and sparrows and blue jays in Central Park. I had even seen a warbler or two on occasion. Now I read of owls and snipes, goshawks and scarlet tanagers, flycatchers, vireos, kinglets, and twenty, thirty species of warbler—all, it appeared, more accessible than in any wild forest or meadow.

Squirrels, rats, and dogs were the only mammals I had encountered in my past visits to the park. Here were raccoons and woodchucks and bats. And snapping turtles laying eggs. And bullfrogs croaking at dawn. And butterflies and dragonflies. And so much more, all to be found at such intriguing locations as the Humming Tombstone, Willow Rock, the Oven, Muggers Woods, the Point, the Azalea Pond. Where were these places? I wanted to find them. They weren't on any Central Park map.

The detailed observations, notations, exhortations, invitations, descriptions, maps, diagrams, even poems in the

Bird Register gave me a tantalizing glimpse not only of the
unexpected wildlife treasures of Central Park but of a community as well. Who were these people? I longed to know
them, to learn their secrets. And there was the Bird Register
right out in the open. "Don't be an eavesdropper," its voices
seemed to be saying. "Come and join us, come and learn."

Everyone in the bird-watching tribe knows Sarah Elliott. A
trim, redheaded, trenchant woman in her sixties, Sarah once
roamed the park with a different band of Regulars from
those active today. She remains a vital link with the past, for
it was she who started the Bird Register in the first place.

A native of Chicago, Sarah was not solidly hooked on
birds until she moved to New York in the early 1960s. There
she began birdwatching in earnest, learning to identify birds
in the company of some of the city's top birders of the time:
Richard Harrison, Dick Plunkett, Bert Hale. Central Park
was where most of her bird studies took place. There, in
1972, she met Lambert Pohner and began her journey from
bird-watcher to naturalist—a person who studies nature in
all its forms.

Lambert Pohner's obituary in *The New York Times* on July
13, 1986, described him as "an elf of a man, with a white
beard and a bush hat…who watched over the birds and butterflies of Central Park for more than forty years." Sarah
had often wandered through the park with Lambert, picking up an approach to learning that appealed to her, one that
took in the whole picture—the trees, flowers, frogs, turtles,
butterflies of the park, as well as the birds.

Sarah soon revealed an organizing skill all her own. As

she rambled through the woodlands, she kept two lists: one, of the birds she had seen that day; the other, of the bird-watchers she ran into. Until then, Central Park's birders knew each other slightly, or not at all. Sarah became a common link. Around 1975 Sarah took the crucial step that marked the bird-watching community's true beginning: she started the Bird Register. Now Central Park's bird-watchers had a place to meet, if only on paper.

In 1980, the Central Park Conservancy, then a newly formed organization seeking to rehabilitate a down-at-the-heels park, asked Lambert to lead bird walks in the Ramble, a 37-acre wilderness in the heart of the park. He accepted the invitation, and invited Sarah to share the job.

There had been regular bird-watching walks in the park before Lambert and Sarah's. There was the legendary Farida A. Wiley, who began leading walks in 1938 under the aegis of the American Museum of Natural History and continued for almost 50 years. Lambert and Sarah's walks were different, slower, as likely to focus on a plant or grasshopper or bat or raccoon as on a bird.

After Lambert's death, Sarah kept his memory alive by continuing the Wednesday and Saturday morning walks during the spring and fall migrations, on her own now, but still in Lambert's uncompetitive, reflective style. Many of the park's most ardent bird-watchers and nature lovers first caught the Central Park bug, as it were, in one of Sarah Elliott's bird classes.

Though Sarah was to be my entry into the vibrant world of Central Park's bird-watchers, it was dead birds that first brought us together. That was in late May of 1991. I had come upon an article she'd written in the New York City Audubon Society newsletter in which she'd declared that the city's brightly illuminated skyscrapers were deathtraps for passing migratory birds. To save birds' lives, she proposed a letter writing campaign: Write to the owners of well-lit skyscrapers to tell them to turn off their bright lights during the migration seasons, at least on foggy and rainy nights, she instructed.

I had begun writing an occasional column about birds for *The Wall Street Journal.* I called her for an interview about her crusade and she chuckled at the opportunity to reach a nice pack of fat-cat skyscraper owners.

We arranged to go on a fact-finding expedition the next foggy or rainy day. Our mission: to look for dead birds near the Empire State Building, the Met Life Building, the World Trade Center, and other illuminated towers.

On a highly propitious (i.e., dismal) morning a few days later our inspection tour turned up no dead birds at all, merely one dazed warbler that zipped off the moment we tried to pick it up. Perhaps Sarah thought she owed me more birds, for as we parted that morning she offered to take me on a bird walk in Central Park some day. I called her that very afternoon to set a definite date. Open Sesame.

We met at the Boathouse. There's an expensive restaurant at one end where tourists and swanky New Yorkers congregate. The Regulars, a little band of the park's most devoted birdwatchers and nature lovers, prefer the plain cafeteria next door. That's where they warm up on cold days, they shelter from rain, and find out where the action is. The vegetable soup isn't bad, the blueberry muffins are homemade, and the Bird Register is kept there—the major attraction.

From the moment we set off, I began scribbling notes and drawing maps filled with kindergarten-style representations of rocks, fences, and lampposts where a path to somewhere or other is to be found. It was my first walk in the Ramble and I wanted to remember what I was learning—the names of trees, flowers, birds, streams, bridges, people, everything!

Most of all I wanted to be sure I wouldn't get lost when I came the next time. This was Central Park, after all, and everyone knows it's not the safest place in the world. I'd been to the park many times before, to be sure, for I grew up nearby, but I had never been in the Ramble. That dense woodland had always been out-of-bounds—a scary place. The feeling still lingered on that day in mid-June.

As Sarah Elliott led me up the steep footpath that begins behind the Boathouse at lamppost 7401 and leads into the Ramble, I learned the first of many park secrets: the last two digits on each lamppost tell its location relative to the nearest city street. (North of 99th Street the numbers begin with 00, indicating 100th Street.) In this case it revealed that we were somewhere near 74th Street. For the park's bird-watchers the numbers serve to pinpoint important spots where birds have been sighted so others can easily find them.

We were hardly halfway to the top when the show began. Suddenly a pair of tufted titmice appeared on a branch just ahead and seemed to be keeping up with us as we walked. They were pronouncing their raucous version of the black-capped chickadee call as they flew from branch to branch. Dee-dee-dee!

As Sarah stopped and fumbled with something in her bag, the titmice hopped to a branch so near I could no longer focus my binoculars on them. The birds continued yelling, making little forays out towards us and then back onto the branch.

Sarah unscrewed a small black plastic film canister, removed a peanut fragment, and held it out on her hand. One of the titmice promptly landed and snatched the peanut away. She provided another peanut tidbit for me to do the same. I'm embarrassed to find in my notes that a bird's feet on the palm of the hand feel "like fairy wings." In years to come I was to see this little drama many times, for most of the Regulars hand-feed the resident birds on occasion. Chickadees, blue jays, and cardinals are others that yammer to be fed when the Regulars walk by, though they only come close; titmice and chickadees alone actually come to the outstretched hand, with a downy woodpecker taking the plunge once in a blue moon.

The Ramble proper starts at the top of the hill and an unmistakable landmark — the Balancing Boulder — marks its beginning. One of the park's many naturalistic artifices, it is a huge upended rock that from a certain angle appears to be balancing so precariously on top of another, horizontal boulder that a good, firm push should send it toppling. Children seem compelled to give it a try.

Just past the boulder, at a crossroads of sorts where three paths diverge, we bore left. "You'll see a few warblers in a moment," Sarah promised. And so we did, soon after we arrived at the Point, a wooded promontory jutting out into the rowboat lake. This little spit of land is a famous bird-watching spot during the spring and fall migration.

Standing at an elevation high above a heavily wooded depression just to its west, known as the Oven, observers at the Point can look down into the crowns of the Oven's oaks and willows and get an exceptionally good look at such elusive warblers as the Cape May and cerulean, treetop feeders. Thus bird-watchers can avoid the occupational hazard know as warbler neck, a painful condition brought on by long-term upward gazing.

Bird-watchers have long joked about warbler neck, but the ailment may be more serious than people believe. Neurologists have discovered that when people assume extreme neck positions for extended periods of time, blood flow through the vertebral arteries is reduced, leading to an increased vulnerability to strokes. Researchers singled out the tilted-back head position of women having a shampoo at the beauty salon. But it happens to be the very posture of bird-watchers craning to see a warbler at the top of a tree.

At the Point, according to my notes: "2 magnolia warblers, female redstart, blackpoll warbler; warblers eat berries in fall, otherwise bugs; big uproar about Point and Ramble in '81 when Conservancy chopped down trees to restore historic views—bird-watchers still mad."

Birders sometimes see more than twenty species of warblers at the Point, Sarah told me. But by the beginning of June the spring migration is winding down. The birds we saw that day were the stragglers—mostly first-year birds (last summer's fledglings) and females. The bright-colored

males in breeding plumage had raced ahead to their breeding grounds farther north to get the choicest nesting spots,
Sarah said. The females would join them a week or so later,
after the males had worked out their territorial disputes

From the Point, we walked a short distance to Willow
Rock, a flat outcrop high above a peaceful lobe of the Lake.
It was named for the two thick black willows growing nearby, Sarah explained. (One of them fell in a storm in 1994.)
There was a small tree, almost a sapling, growing out of a
crevice in the rock, near the edge. "Look at this," said Sarah.
"It's a real peach tree. Maybe somebody planted a pit here."
I could see dozens of unmistakable mini-peaches growing all
over the little tree. They were still green—though already
covered with the characteristic fuzzy down botanists call
pubescence.

Willow Rock offered easy views of the *same* treetop
activity we had seen from the Point but from a different
angle, as Willow Rock is directly across from it. What a
splendid opportunity this affords bird-watchers: with the
sun behind them they can spend their morning hours gazing
at warblers from the Point, and then do the same at Willow
Rock in the afternoons.

Like many impassioned novices, I wanted to know
everything all at once—the names of every plant, every bird,
every *part* of a bird. Sarah, it was clear, did not suffer such
acquisitive fools gladly. "What's that tree with the bunches
of red berries?" I asked—it was probably my hundredth
question. "Oh, that's the bunches-of-red-berries tree," she
answered with a smile. A few moments later, as we saw a
black-crowned night heron land on a willow overhanging

the Lake, I wondered out loud about one of the bird's most conspicuous features: "Is that called a bill or a beak?" I asked Sarah. "Yes," she answered firmly, and that was that.

Her message sank in. Don't worry about nomenclature when a bird is sitting in front of your nose. Look at it. Notice everything you can about it—its yellow-green legs, its blackish back and cap. Look at that orange eye. Later I checked out the bills vs. beak question in *The Birdwatcher's Companion*, a reliable reference book by Christopher Leahy. His entry for *beak* says: "Essentially synonymous with *bill*. In more restrictive usage, refers particularly to larger bills, especially the hooked beaks (or bills) of birds of prey. In general 'bill' is the preferred term in ornithological/bird-watching contexts." Yes.

Next we walked up a small incline, passing another large boulder—Warbler Rock, Sarah called it. I was growing more and more uncertain of our orientation as we veered away from the Lake and open sky and entered the deeper woods. Soon the leafy canopy was closed all around us. Even the air felt different—more carbon dioxide, I imagined.

Once in the woods, I gave up mapmaking entirely. I had completely lost my sense of direction and was too embarrassed to keep asking Sarah which way was which. In other parts of Central Park one can orient oneself by the surrounding tall buildings—the Fifth Avenue skyline is east, the twin towers of the El Dorado and the San Remo are west. But in the heart of the Ramble the city has vanished; all reminders of civilization are obscured by trees.

An illusion begins to take over: you are in an enchanted woodland. Even the park furniture seems to belong. "Sit on us," the dark green benches command. "Look at the birds, look at that flower. Stay awhile. Don't hurry or you'll miss something." The black wrought-iron lampposts no longer foreshadow the feared nightmares of Central Park in the dark. At nightfall their soft light will show owls and bats and gaudy moths attracted as if by moonlight.

We had entered a virtual maze of little paths, all unmarked, winding, twisting, taking us past ravines, waterfalls, rustic benches, scenic vistas. By then my notes had become as confusing as the Ramble itself, a jumble of bird names, people names, plant names, and samples of Sarah's botany and ornithology sound bites: "parula, magnolia, Wilson's — warblers, Ruth, George, Ira, Dave — Regulars, double-file viburnum has 2 rows of white flowers in May, Swainson's thrush has buffy eye-ring, gray-cheeked thrush doesn't, spice bush — smells good, sassafras has 3 kinds of leaves, grackles walk, crows hop."

We reached the area birdwatchers call the Swampy Pin Oak (sticklers prefer to call it the Pin Oak swamp, for there is no such tree as a swampy pin oak). Within a little grove of trees growing in a moist sumpy spot, there is one significantly larger tree right in the center, *the* "swampy" pin oak. That day it was hopping with a variety of small birds while the wet ground below revealed others busily poking around in the mud. Watching the action from two ringside benches were a variety of bird-watchers as well: Alice and Ira, Max and Nellie, David Monk, Sheila and Lou, Mary Birchard, Chris and Marianne, Judy — some of them, I soon learned, were Regulars, others Seasonal Migrants, bird-watchers who show up regularly only during the migration seasons.

There I learned yet another secret from Sarah. The eggs of minute aphids hatch on the leaves of pin oaks in May and June, attracting a great variety of migrating songbirds. So head for the pin oaks if you want to score heavily during spring migration.

On our way to the Azalea Pond—our last destination, said Sarah—we came to a couple of thick holly trees just to the right of the path. M. M. Graff, author of *Tree Trails in Central Park*, disapproved of these particular trees, accusing them of being "a gloomy black-green at best and made even more funereal by a coating of city soot." They looked shiny and handsome to me. I was even more taken with them when Sarah told me these were a favorite roosting place for owls. I kept returning to the spot over the next few weeks, hoping to find a roosting owl, until a kindly birdwatcher informed me that owls show up in Central Park only in the late fall and winter.

After turning right at the second holly tree, we found ourselves out of the deepest woods. Now the skyline of Central Park West was visible once again. Walking north-ward along the same path, we soon came to a grassy knoll where a small group of bird-watchers were standing in a classic pose looking upward, watching something invisible to the naked eye. Their binoculars all pointed to the same spot in the same tangle of wisteria vines. Sarah did not ask, "What are you looking at?" as I might have done, but main-tained birders' etiquette, merely raising her own binoculars in the same direction. It took her hardly a minute to locate the bird—a "good bird," she told me with some excitement. "A hooded warbler." A good bird? All the other birds we had seen on our walk had been just as good, as far as I was concerned.

At the edge of that little clearing was a large, rectangular granite block. "Do you hear anything coming from that block?" Sarah asked me. At first I heard nothing but the sounds of birds all around and dogs barking in the distance. Then I did hear it—a faint buzzing sound. "We call that the Humming Tombstone," Sarah said, and I immediately realized that the block did resemble a large cemetery monument. "Some birders use the sound as a hearing test. Every year they see how near they have to get before they hear the buzz."

I stepped away until I couldn't hear it, and noted the place. I still check every year to see if I hear the buzz at the same spot. So far so good.

It took me years to discover what makes the Humming Tombstone hum: a mechanism within that controls all the lights in the vicinity, turning them off in the morning and on at night. One year in the early spring I found myself at the Tombstone at sunrise. I thought I had gone deaf, for it was silent. A few moments later, at 6 a.m. sharp, it started to buzz.

After another few twists and turns of the path where we encountered, according to my notes, "common yellowthroat, ovenbird, three raccoon babies up a tree, Mo & Sylvia," we crossed a small rustic bridge known as (surprise) the Rustic Bridge and I began to hear a crescendo of bird sounds. We were approaching the Azalea Pond feeding station.

The Azalea Pond is a small body of water fed by the Gill, one of the Ramble's most picturesque features. This replica of a meandering stream is turned on and off by a hidden faucet. Though winter was long over, and official bird-feeding would not resume until cold weather set in, the place was still well stocked: birdseed was scattered all around, bits of bread, and some brownish lumps that looked like dry dog food. (They were.) Chunks of suet had been attached to nearby tree trunks. And birds were everywhere.

Sparrows, pigeons, cowbirds, and mourning doves were eating seed on the bare ground in front of six scraggly bushes. These were the azaleas for which the place was named, a rather garish carmine variety called "*hinode-giri*," which M. M. Graff called "an offense to the eye in almost any garden setting and a shrieking dissonance in this quiet spot."

As I took in the scene, entranced, other birds flew in and out, mainly titmice and cardinals, grabbing bits of peanuts from a sardine tin attached to the trunk of an oak. Several woodpeckers were working the suet, squirrels were racing up and down the tree trunks, trying to get at the peanuts, while a man with a shock of white hair threw sticks at them and shouted, "Go away!" After the bucolic serenity of Willow Rock and the Swampy Pin Oak, the place seemed a madhouse of activity.

Bird-watchers were everywhere too. The Azalea Pond is one of their major gathering spots, and some we had met earlier were now sitting on the benches facing the feeders. "George, Joe Richner (keeps list of bird-watchers, not birds)—white-breasted nuthatch, red-bellied woodpecker goes Chork!" read my notes.

Sarah was on her way home, but I decided to stay just a

few more minutes. "I'll find my way out," I assured her, knowing it wouldn't be easy. Bill, the white-haired man who had been throwing sticks at the squirrels, was now throwing peanuts to a pair of cardinals. "Get this!" he was saying with each throw. The male was bolder and got more than the female. Joe Richner put my name on his People list. "I have four Marys and you're the second Marie," he informed me. A red-bellied woodpecker arrived and grabbed one of the cardinal's peanuts. George and Ira were talking about vitamins. Before I knew it, an hour had gone by and I was still at the Azalea Pond. Hours pass like minutes there.

A spell must have come over me in that dark, mysterious wood, for I came back the next day and the next, and never stopped coming. I still get lost in the Ramble at times, and most of the Regulars admit that they do too.

Anne Shanahan's fascination with hawks began a few months after the Fifth Avenue nest was discovered. She remembers the moment well. On Friday, May 21st, at 1:15 p.m. to be exact, she was walking up 82nd Street between Madison and Fifth with her little dog Bijou, a bichon frisé. Just as she approached the Metropolitan Museum of Art, she saw a hawk swoop down to the sidewalk a mere ten or twenty feet in front of her. "It gave an incredible scream as it dove down," she recalls. "What's that?" she asked a workman outside the museum, and he answered, "It's the red-tailed hawk hunting." He said it matter-of-factly, as if a hawk hunting in the heart of Manhattan were a commonplace event for him—that impressed her particularly.

She watched the bird on the sidewalk and quickly

snapped a few shots of it with a point-and-shoot camera she happened to have with her. Then she saw the hawk fly to the balcony of a small building on Fifth Avenue. It perched there for a few minutes before flying directly into the park. She knew she wanted to follow it. She entered the park too. And that was the beginning of a new life.

A slender, soft-spoken woman, neither young nor old, who listens far more than she speaks, Anne has been following the hawks in the park for more than five years now, photographing them with ever better equipment and greater artistry. She takes a great interest in the other wildlife of the park too, and her photographs are beginning to show up at exhibitions, including a recent one at the American Museum of Natural History. One of her butterfly photos appeared on the cover of *Mulberry Wing*, the magazine of the New York Butterfly Club. But hawks are her passion.

Anne knows the Fifth Avenue hawks. She knows their favorite roosting places, their most successful hunting perches. She can detect their presence long before anyone else does. Anne rarely carries binoculars, occasionally using the long lens of her camera for a closer look at something that has caught her eye or, more often, her ear. Using a keen sense of hearing more than her eyes, she listens for sounds from other birds and especially other animals indicating the presence of a predator. Squirrels, for example, flatten themselves on tree trunks and branches and emit a low steady whine when a hawk is in the immediate vicinity. Using such clues, Anne regularly locates one or both of the red-tail pair where others have gone right by them.

Though Anne sets forth alone in the park, most of the

Regulars unobtrusively attach themselves to her whenever they can. For she always seems to arrive at the place just as the hawk action is about to begin. "There's a hawk somewhere over there," she'll say as she runs into a little group of bird-watchers. Only then will the others hear what Anne's ear alone had detected: regular, sharp little chips coming out of a nearby tree—alarm notes of robins announcing a hawk in the vicinity. She can tell one boisterous blue jay cry that means "Here I come! Stay out of my territory" from a similar cry that means "Hawk nearby! Come on, birds, let's mob 'em."

Anne is modest and self-effacing, rare and devalued traits in an era when self-esteem is the *summum bonum*. Yet her intimate knowledge of the hawks has gained her the admiration and respect of all—the Regulars, the Hawkwatchers, even the Big Guns. When there is a question about the hawks that requires resolution, Anne Shanahan is the first to be consulted.

Her enthusiasm is infectious, and somewhat surprising for a woman of gentle sensibilities, since most of the hawk action she follows would not receive a PG rating: Pale Male plucking a recently caught pigeon on the Killing Tree; the pair soaring together in a courtship flight, talons locked, tumbling down in the air; the couple mating on the railing of the Octagonal building—each time she witnesses such a hawk event she grows excited, as if it were the first time she was seeing it and not the hundredth. "Isn't this wonderful?" she'll exclaim, always a little breathless. "Aren't we lucky to see this?"

One day early in the hawks' nest-building phase, I arrived at the hawk bench and found myself the only one there. When I raised my binoculars to the nest, my feeling of isolation grew: nobody at home up there. Standing at the edge of the model-boat pond, I scanned the sky in all directions. I needed my red-tail fix.

As I stood there staring upward, an unkempt young man came up to me in a state of excitement. His somewhat sinister aspect—the impression was partly based on grooming, or lack of it, partly on some indefinable "attire"—made me glad I hadn't run into him in a less populated part of the park. "You looking at birds? There's a humongous bird on a tree over there. It's eating a pigeon!"

He half-walked, half-ran in the direction of Pilgrim Hill. I followed him, and a few minutes later I was not surprised to see that the humongous bird was Pale Male. Perched on a low branch of an evergreen halfway up the hill, he was busily eviscerating a plump dark-gray pigeon. Feathers were flying. The hawk's talons and beak were visibly bloody, and something about the perspective of our vantage point made him look particularly huge.

The comradeship of hawk-watching swiftly dispelled my previous caution. In the way of the hawk-watchers, I introduced myself by first name to the young man. He did the same: Johnny. Together we stood there for a good ten minutes, transfixed.

Suddenly, as if from nowhere, another hawk materialized on the branch beside the dining male. It was the female, the one we had started calling Chocolate.

"Holy shit!" said Johnny. For the next ten minutes he

and I and the lady hawk watched Pale Male scarf down the pigeon. All three of us gazed with unwavering attention.

When the pigeon was almost consumed, the young man and I heard the female give a little snort that I translated to mean: "Some gentleman you are!" A moment later she reached over with a talon and grabbed the remains of the pigeon. Pale Male tugged for a few seconds, but without much enthusiasm. Then he emitted a snort of his own that I understood as: "Hey, I was just about to pass it over." With that the pale hawk flew off the branch and headed for Fifth Avenue, while his lady finished the pigeon.

I lent Johnny my binoculars and pointed out the nest. I knew exactly the moment he found the nest because he uttered the same comment as before. He was genuinely flabbergasted to learn that hawks had taken up residence in such an unlikely spot.

The next day Johnny reappeared at the hawk bench. He had brought a friend — José — to see the hawks. This time, as luck would have it, both hawks were sitting on the nest. I passed Johnny my binoculars and he was just as enthusiastic as on the previous visit — a potential bird-watcher, I thought. José, it must be said, seemed to be in a different space entirely.

Part of hawk-watcher etiquette is not to ask the usual cocktail-party questions, "What do you do?" and the like. But curiosity is always there, so I was glad when Johnny's next remark answered some of my unspoken question about his life history.

"I told my caseworker at drug rehab that I saw a pair of hawks making a nest on a building on Fifth Avenue,"

Johnny told me. "She looked at me funny and asked, 'What have you been smoking?'"

Marie Winn is a contributor on nature and bird-watching to *The Wall Street Journal*. Among her books are *The Plug-In Drug: Television, Children & the Family*, *Children Without Childhood*, and *Red-Tails in Love: A Wildlife Drama in Central Park*, from which this story was excerpted. Married to the filmmaker and palindromist Allan Miller, she spends part of every day in Central Park.

IV

Brushes with
Divinity

Actual Field Conditions

JAMES KILGO

*A birder breaks away from the pack
and wades into creation.*

"WHEN I WAS A BOY THERE WERE MEN IN my hometown who were respected for their knowledge of birds. They were not bird lovers in the usual sense of that term but farmers and foresters who spoke without self-consciousness about such things as declines in the red-headed woodpecker population or the rare occurrence in our area of a painted bunting.

Once, when we were fishing on the creek below our house, my father suddenly gripped me by the shoulder and whispered, "Look!" He put his hand on the back of my head and aimed my gaze toward a ferny spot on the far bank. There, flitting about among the sun-splotched leaves, was a small yellow bird I had never seen before. "That's a prothonotary warbler," he said. The conjunction of that improbable name with the brilliant flame color of its breast seemed marvelous to me.

The first bird I identified on my own was a black and white warbler. I was ten or eleven years old, sitting one morning on a log near the creek, when I spied it in the low canopy overhead. Although I was familiar with the species from an illustration by Louis Agassiz Fuertes in a set of cards I had ordered from Arm & Hammer Soda, I was not prepared for the precision of zebra striping on a bird so tiny. I ran all the way home, excited by a wild conviction that something had been settled.

What had been settled, I understood much later, was my experience of that particular species. The sight of the bird required a response—I had to do something about it. A camera would have worked—even a gun, I'm afraid, because I wanted to have the bird—but the name alone was enough. Armed only with that I applied it, ratified the act of seeing, and appropriated the black and white warbler.

Perhaps the obvious way of seizing and holding such moments of delight, especially for one who is able to draw, is by painting the bird. For some reason, that possibility did not occur to me until I was grown. By the time it did, I had devoted several years to avid birding, naming every new species I could find until my fascination with birds was reduced to a mere game of listing, in which the checking off of a species amounts almost to a cancellation of it. As if that weren't enough, the game became for me a competition with other such binocular-visioned people.

Then one day on the beach of Sapelo, a barrier island off the coast of Georgia, something happened that changed my way of looking at birds. I was participating in a Christmas bird count with a small group of experienced birders and ornithologists. On Saturday night one of them reported having seen what he thought was a stilt sandpiper on the south end of the beach. Because that species occurs rarely on the South Atlantic coast, most of us needed it for our lists, so early the next morning the whole crowd piled into a couple of vehicles and headed down the strand.

We must have presented quite a spectacle as we climbed from the jeeps—a brigade of birders, wrapped in heavy coats and armed with binoculars, some even with a 'scope and tripod, tramping down an empty winter beach to "get" a sandpiper. According to Roger Tory Peterson's description, the bird is almost indistinguishable at that time of year from dowitchers and lesser yellowlegs. Even the man who had reported seeing it had had trouble confirming identification because it was part of a mixed flock of small shorebirds.

The sun stood before us upon the water, its reflection blazing on the wet sand where the waves reached and retreated, and a cold salt wind was blowing off the ocean. I began to doubt that I would have the patience to sort out a stilt sandpiper from a large flock of sand-colored shorebirds, and I was bothered as well by the legitimacy of my recording it if someone else identified it first.

On the point at the end of the beach hundreds of birds were racing along the edge of the surf; hundreds more lay dozing in the dry sand, their feathers ruffled by the steady wind; and a few big, solitary willets stood here and there like unhappy schoolteachers watching children at recess. I took one look through my binoculars into the glare and realized that I didn't care enough about a stilt sandpiper to bother.

Looking for something to pick up—driftwood, bottle, or shell—I left the crowd and climbed the high dunes. On the other side, between me and the marsh, lay a long, shallow lagoon. It appeared to be connected to the sound at high tide, but now with the ebb it was an isolated pool. A flock of large birds, all of a kind, was wading in it, stretching, preening, and feeding. They were marbled godwits—a species I had seen before—but I grabbed my binoculars anyway and focused on one bird. From that angle the light upon its mottled brown plumage was ideal; I could even detect the flesh-colored base of its recurved bill. Then I lowered the glasses in favor of the whole choreography. There must be 50 of them, I thought, and I marveled at their obedience to the common will that moved them all in one direction, comprehending a dozen little sideshows of casual interaction. I delighted in the repetition of muted color and graceful form, reflected 50 times in blue water.

Suddenly, by a shared impulse the godwits rose crying from the pool and wheeled in an arc above me, their cinnamon wings flashing in the sun. I watched them fly south toward St. Simons, hearing their cries after I could no longer distinguish the flock in the shimmering air.

With the dying away of their cries I sat down on the dune. The other bird-watchers were scattered on the beach below me, still focused on the flock of sandpipers, but I was not ready yet to rejoin them. For I had seen godwits rising in the sun—a glory of godwits crying down upon the marshes—and I felt strangely abandoned. I wanted to grab hold of that moment with both hands, before it faded away with the birds, and keep it; and I wanted to tell my friends on the beach about it so they could see it too. If only I could paint it in watercolor, bathed in that light, those who saw it would feel something of the loneliness I had felt.

Not long after the Christmas count on Sapelo I saw the illustrations by Robert Verity Clem for *The Shorebirds of North America*. They represented exactly the kind of thing I wanted to do. For the next year I studied them as well as the work of Fuertes and George Miksch Sutton, sketched hundreds of birds in the field, and often picked up road-kills to learn anatomy and plumage patterns. It was not mere illustration I sought but a representation of the experience of seeing a particular bird in its habitat, as I had seen the black and white warbler that day on the creek or those godwits rising above me in the sun.

The ornithologist who introduced me to the behavior of birds under actual field conditions was a south Georgia farmer named Calvin Hardy, one of the group on the Christmas count. When I met him on the dock, waiting for the boat to Sapelo, I could see right away that he was different from the rest of us. Big and sturdy, as though cut to a larger pattern than most men, he gave the impression that if something broke he could fix it.

I was not surprised to hear that Calvin was a farmer and a forester. In fact, he reminded me of those men whose interest in birds I had noticed when growing up. Before the weekend was over I learned, partly by talking to him but mostly from a mutual friend, that he was also an airplane pilot and a carpenter of better-than-average skill; that he had published papers on herpetology, mammalogy, and

ornithology; that he photographed wildflowers and collected
stamps and coins, antique turpentining equipment, and local
folklore; and that he lived in an old railroad depot that he
had moved two miles from its original site after cutting it in
half with a chain saw.

Somehow Calvin and I discovered quickly that each of
us had stories the other wanted to hear, so we spent the late
night hours of that weekend drinking coffee and talking. By
the time we left the island Sunday afternoon, I knew that he,
like me, was one of those people who has to do something
about birds. Painting, I had just realized, was the thing I
would do; Calvin's was science. At that time he was working
on the nesting habits of herons and egrets. "Come on down to
south Georgia in June," he said, "and we'll go into a rookery."

Most wading birds are colonial nesters. The colony is
called a rookery, or by some a heronry. In south Georgia the
birds often select lime-sink ponds as nesting sites. As long as
a colony site remains undisturbed the birds will return to it
year after year until they eventually fill the capacity of the
place; an established rookery may contain six different species
of wading birds and as many as two thousand nests. Calvin
had been going into rookeries in his part of the state for several years, mainly for the purpose of determining and mon-
itoring fluctuations in the populations of the predominant
species—the little blue heron and the cattle egret, the latter
an exotic that made its way across the Atlantic from Africa
at the end of the nineteenth century and has since worked
its way north to our continent. Though the intruder does not
compete for food with native species, Calvin suspected that
it was taking over sites formerly held by the little blues.

In May he called to remind me of the invitation. The nesting season would be at its peak in a few weeks, he said; we might find as many as five or six species. I needed no encouragement. The rookery would afford a rare opportunity to photograph and sketch the wading birds in their own bedroom. I could hardly wait.

The morning was already hot when we climbed from the truck and started across a brush field. Ahead of us stood the woods, quietly shimmering through the heat waves as though nothing remarkable were happening within its shadow. But presently we began to detect a commotion, a murmur of flaps and squawks. As we drew nearer, the trees before us seemed to bloom with white birds. Herons were ascending, reluctantly it appeared, to hover above the canopy, legs a-dangle, and complain at our intrusion. Still nearer, we caught a vague whiff of organic effluvium that grew stronger as we approached the trees.

Beneath the canopy we paused at the edge of what appeared to be not water but a pale green floor; through it rose a thin forest of tupelo gum, red maple, pond cypress, and pine. The flapping activity of the adult birds receded before us to the far reaches of the rookery, and for a moment I could neither see nor hear young birds. After the clamor that had greeted us, the silence seemed unnatural. I thought of alligators, prehistoric submarines cruising noiselessly beneath the green floor, and I felt some reluctance to enter the rookery. Calvin had not mentioned gators to me, but since we were entering their habitat I thought I might ask.

"I wouldn't worry about them," he said. Then he smiled,

"But if you do get tangled up with one, remember now that his belly is the soft part."

His smile was no sure sign that he was kidding because he smiled most of the time—so I checked a bit furtively to see that my Randall skinning knife was still securely fastened on my hip. Then I followed him in.

A thick mat of vegetation, streaked and splashed with chalky excrement, lay upon the surface of the pond. Beneath this, the water was a warm chowder. Ten yards out we were waist-deep in it, pushing the surface before us like a buckling rug and releasing smells that engulfed us as we moved.

Calvin was already busy recording data with a pad and a mechanical counter as he moved confidently through the trees. I was dropping behind, still a little conscious of my legs but mainly marveling at the nests—frail platforms, four or five to a tree sometimes, lying in the forks of branches six to eight feet above the water. Looking up from underneath I could see the sky through them, and many of them held clutches of three eggs. By climbing onto the roots of a tree and holding on to the trunk I was able to look into several nests. The eggs were of the palest blue-green, as large as golf balls and oval in form. What astonished me most was the capacity of such slight nests to support their weight.

Many of the nests contained newly-hatched chicks, nestled in damp clumps (sometimes around an addled egg), and looking back at me with yellow reptilian eyes. From the number of fledglings standing about on the edges of nests and neighboring branches, I figured that these birds, in their ravenous determination to receive food before their siblings, quickly developed the strong legs that enabled them to climb out of their flimsy quarters. Once out, however, they remained in the immediate vicinity, jostling each other in clumsy sidestep as they awaited the return of their parents with food. Most of the birds we saw were in this stage of development, ineffectual sentinels protesting our presence by gaping and squawking and, in their excitement, sometimes regurgitating or defecating as we passed by or paused to take pictures of them.

Most birds in the fledgling stage are ungainly—hence the tale of the ugly duckling—but few species present a greater contrast between the immature stages and the adult than wading birds. Crowned with ludicrous patches of hairy down, these tailless white creatures seemed badly put together—too much neck, too much leg, and none of it under control. They looked to be in constant danger of toppling from the branches, and occasionally a chick would lose its balance. We saw one hanging upside down, wings fallen open so that the light shone through the membranes, and clutching its perch with the toes of one desperate foot.

I wondered how long the bird could last in that position and how long a gator would take to find it once it had let go. Calvin said he doubted that alligator predation was a significant factor in the mortality of immature birds, though he was sure that the reptiles took an occasional victim as they scavenged the rookery. Just then he pointed out a young bird crawling from the thick gravy at the base of a tree and clambering laboriously up its trunk, using beak, claws, and even wings like some prehistoric creature moving from the amphibian stage through the reptilian to the avian in one heroic action. But I was not moved to admiration. In its mindless determination to survive, the creature seemed hideous to me—but I was hot and filthy, and I had already seen too many birds, too many eggs.

On our way out of the rookery Calvin spied a pair of anhinga chicks perched in their nest about ten feet up and had me stand on his shoulders to photograph them. Their buff down looked as thick as the nap on a baby harp seal, and I had to restrain an impulse to stroke them. After snapping several pictures I lowered the camera to Calvin and embraced the tree to shinny down the trunk. As I glanced over my shoulder at the green surface beneath me, I felt suddenly that I was suspended above the primal generative slime itself, composite of earth, air, fire, and water, secreted from the earth by what Annie Dillard had called "the pressure of fecundity." I clung to the tree, appalled by the terrific energy that digested sticks, eggs, leaves, excrement, even baby birds, and bubbled up a scum of duckweed, releasing in the process a blast of heat and odor.

"You need some help?" Calvin asked. The question restored my equilibrium. This was after all only a rookery. So I climbed down and followed in his wake toward dry land As we approached the edge, adult herons and egrets with a clapping and beating of wings began to reclaim the area we had deserted, young birds commenced to clamor again for food, and the rookery resumed its normal business. Give them a wooded lime-sink pond, I thought, and they would do the rest—these ethereal white creatures— by dropping sticks and laying eggs and regurgitating a mash of protein and defecating thousands of times a day.

And the result? New egrets, hundreds of them, emerging from the rank miasma to glide like angels upon fields of summer hay or to float upon their individual images in quiet ponds.

Near the edge of the rookery a white egret rose up from a low nest ahead of us and flapped off through the trees. Calvin sensed it was something different, but he resisted a conclusion. In the nest we found a wet, new chick and two eggs, one cracking even as we looked into it. "Snowy egret," he guessed, but the scientist in him required confirmation so we hid and waited for the parent to return.

The most elegant of American wading birds, the snowy is a predominantly coastal species, and we were over a hundred miles inland. Calvin suspected that this might be a nesting record for the interior of the state—he had never found snowies in a rookery before. I shared a little of his excitement, but my thoughts were of a different nature. As wading birds go, the stumpy little cattle egrets we had been observing occupy the lower end of the aesthethic yardstick. Somehow, it seemed to me, that fact had something to do with the evidence we had just seen of the birds' appetite for breeding. I had no trouble envisioning a field of cattle egrets shamelessly engaged in the business of reproduction, but the image of snowy egrets copulating had never before occurred to me.

When the adult returned to the nest we spotted instantly the bright yellow toes on black feet that confirmed Calvin's impression. Grasping a thin branch, the egret seemed to reverse the direction of its wing beats in a frantic effort to balance itself. I couldn't tell which parent this was, but the bird's white flurry in that shadowed place startled me into a vision of a gorgeous male, nuptial plumes aquiver as he climbed the back of a crouching female and held her neck in his beak.

I didn't give much thought to painting that night. As we sat in front of his house, watching purple martins in the heavy twilight, Calvin interpreted the statistics we had gathered, and his eyes sparkled as he recalled various details of our trip. But my skull was filled with a green stew that sloshed when I lay down to sleep, and my imagination struggled with wet wings to climb out of it. If I was praying to the same God who charged egrets with the procreative urge, I didn't see how I could expect much of an audience.

The next morning Calvin took me up in his Taylorcraft, a flying machine of uncertain vintage that reminded me more of a kite than an airplane. He thought he had discovered the general location of a new rookery in the next county and wanted to see if he could verify it from the air. About 10 miles west of town, at 1,500 feet, he pointed out a cool green spot on the ground that looked exactly like a mint, dropped down onto the patchwork of fields and woods. "Recognize that?" he asked. White specks, brilliant particles against the dark ground were converging upon the spot and radiating from it in slow, deliberate flight. I felt as though I were looking down through clear water at something going on in another world. The effects of the day before were already beginning to diminish; nothing about the mint-green spot prompted memory of the rookery's reek and clamor. I began to understand the lofty point of view. It was easy up here to ignore rookeries, even to deny the fall of baby birds, and I saw that there might be some chance for the imagination in the clean, cold, blue air.

Then came the hawks. They appeared at first as a dark shape out in front of us. We didn't recognize it immediately, the thing not in flight but falling, and hurtling not away but toward us. Then, for a single instant, we saw clearly *two* birds in clasped union; for that frozen moment they seemed suspended in the force of their own energy. Almost into the prop, they split apart, one blown past the windshield, the other peeling away below. If I had been standing up, my knees would have buckled.

"What was that?" I shouted above the engine.

"Red-tails, weren't they?"

"I mean, what were they doing?"

"What did it look like?"

"You mean they really do it in the air like that?"

"What do you think?" he asked.

But I couldn't answer. I was so exhilarated by that incredible intersection, thinking was out of the question.

On the ground again, I remembered Walt Whitman's poem about the free fall of copulating eagles: "A swirling mass tight grappling,/In tumbling turning clustering loops, straight downward falling." A single, graphic image of what he calls their dalliance, it risks no statement of meaning, evidently because Whitman thought the image was message enough. I agree with his judgment, but I had made closer contact with the birds I saw. Their attractive force clapped me to them. And though the roar of the plane had interrupted their long tumble and blasted them apart, I continue to fall with them, convinced that the whole green earth below was one damned rookery, its power as strong as gravity.

James Kilgo recently retired from the University of Georgia, where he had taught since 1971. During his tenure as professor, he helped develop a graduate program in creative writing and served as Director of Creative Writing. He began his second career as a writer at the age of 40 and has authored numerous books including *Inheritance of Horses*, *Daughter of My People*, and *Deep Enough for Ivorybills*, from which this story was excerpted. He lives in Atherns, Georgia.

The Setting of Wings

BUDDY LEVY

*A rite of passage takes an
unexpected turn.*

ANYONE WHO HAS EVER SAT IN A DUCK blind and watched birds fly knows the thrill of the setting of wings. Once it might be a steady, sure braking when the bird pulls up with full flaps and is on the ground or water so fast you want to see it again to try to understand how it happened. Often, as with mallards, the wing set has an air of style to it. They set their wings quite early, the slope of their trajectory decided far away from the intended landing pad. As they descend, the wingtips vacillate, like the waving of a crop duster or a bush plane, and then there is the exhalation sound of wind cupped in wings as the mallards land with a shudder on the water.

One winter afternoon, before just such a moment, I was sitting on the deck of my cabin near Silver Creek in south-central Idaho, simply waiting. The air was so cold I could nearly hear my breath crystallizing, and the feet of my deck chair squeaked in the dry snow. As I watched the sky, the outline of a single Canada goose appeared on the horizon to the west, flapping in from some great distance beyond my ability to imagine. The goose flew too low for such a clear day, and I wondered about his instincts. Hunting season was on, and at sunset the valley would be littered with the cough-reports of shotguns booming from river bend and slough. By late season the birds were usually quite wary, having been conditioned to come in higher on clear nights, but this bird seemed less concerned with the consequences of his flight than with the freedom and perfection of it. The goose drew closer until it was upon me, flying right over my head, as it made one huge parabola and turned back across the barley stubble. Setting its wings with panache, it landed on Loving Creek at the big bend below the headgate.

The eldest of three sons, I was the most accomplished hunter, but I was the only one of us who had never shot a goose. Having no goose notched into my mythical belt was no great assault on my machismo, but my brothers wouldn't let me forget it. In some families, and in some places, shooting a goose is a rite of passage that catapults you from stripling to seasoned in the time it takes to pull a trigger. You must be strong to end the life of a wounded goose. You must be strong to sling the goose over your shoulder and carry the great bird home by the neck, its heavy body slapping against your hip as you stomp across the snowfield.

I'm not certain whether sibling rivalry influenced my decision to go inside that day and grab the Browning 12-gauge shotgun, but something moved me. Something about the solitary quality of this bird, its aura of nonchalance. I wouldn't be lying in wait in the frozen palm of a grain field for some anonymous bird, one of many in a group, setting to land. I would be stalking this particular goose, just the two of us crystallized in time.

Before I knew it the shells were in my parka pocket, and I was skiing along the irrigation ditch that ran parallel to Loving Creek. I had marked the bird's descent precisely, and as I moved across the landscape, I was transformed from birder to hunter.

A few hundred yards from the creek I paused to load the Browning. The barrels of the gun were clean and blue-black and shiny against the skyline. When I got to the willow belt I snapped the gun shut and moved in behind a dense bunch of thicket and paused again, feeling the pulse of blood in my chest and my head. Then ever so slowly I leaned out and peeked at the bank of the creek, the rolling snowdrifts unfurling themselves to the smooth water of the bend.

The goose paddled calmly in the slack water of the curve, its gallant head bowed slightly. I watched the way it held itself steady, the way its movements sent small ripples along the water, like recurring dimples. I slowly removed the glove from my shooting hand and readied the gun against my chest. Two quick ski steps and I was free of the brush and willows, standing in the open, ready to fire when the goose lifted from the water.

Sensing danger, the bird turned and saw me and flapped all at once, its great wings slapping the water in departure. It rose with surprising quickness for its size, and I pulled up just as fast, swinging my bead past the mottled, gray-white chest and then back along the craning black neck, finally setting my sights on the white feathers slung across its face like a chin strap. It was in perfect range. I clenched my cheek tight against the gun stock and felt the cold trigger on the underside of my index finger—and let the bird go. No resonating click came from the trigger. The sky congealed into a beautiful perfection.

I continued watching the bird's flight through my gun sight. I could see the way the goose gained altitude quickly and honked its frightened distress call, its feet trailing awkwardly behind. It headed straight for Sullivan's Pond on Silver Creek, then banked hard downstream and turned east, staying low, in the direction of Purdy's place. I squinted to watch the flight, seeing the bird diminish in the fading light, its wings set, when one sharp shotgun blast echoed from the vicinity of Kilpatrick Bridge, and the bird was yanked from the sky. I heard a distant whistle and the muffled commands of a man to his dog. Then I, too, crumpled in the snow.

The sky began to fill with birds, and I watched them carefully, studying their dance. I listened to their cries, my head curled in the crook of my arm. Wind blew snowdrifts around me and the sky went dark as I lay there listening to the sounds of evening—the wind shearing across their wings like sirens, the landing slaps as their feet broke the water of the pond.

I remained there until all the birds had stopped talking, until a half moon rose over Timmerman Hill and a coyote yelped from the barren, frozen fields. Then I pulled myself

together and slunk back silently to the cabin, knowing that
now, when someone asked me if I had ever killed a goose, I
could answer, would have to answer, yes.

Buddy Levy is a writer, educator, and life-long sports enthusiast. His first
book, *Echoes on Rimrock: In Pursuit of the Chukar Partridge,* was published in
March 1999.

Whimbrels

TERRY TEMPEST WILLIAMS

*Everyone needs a place
to feel grounded.*

THE BIRD REFUGE HAS REMAINED A CONstant. It is a landscape so familiar to me, there have been times I have felt a species long before I saw it. The long-billed curlews that foraged the grasslands seven miles outside the Refuge were trustworthy. I can count on them year after year. And when six whimbrels joined them—whimbrel entered my mind as an idea. Before I ever saw them mingling with curlews, I recognized them as a new thought in familiar country.

The birds and I share a natural history. It is a matter of rootedness, of living inside a place for so long that the mind and imagination fuse.

Maybe it's the expanse of sky above and water below that soothes my soul. Or maybe it's the anticipation of seeing something new. Whatever the magic of Bear River is—

I appreciate this corner of northern Utah, where the numbers of ducks and geese I find resemble those found by early explorers.

Of the 208 species of birds who use the Refuge, 62 are known to nest here. Such nesting species include eared, western, and pied-billed grebes, great blue herons, snowy egrets, white-faced ibises, American avocets, black-necked stilts, and Wilson's phalaropes. Also nesting at Bear River are Canada geese, mallards, gadwalls, pintails, green-winged, blue-winged, and cinnamon teals, redheads, and ruddy ducks. It is a fertile community where the hope of each day rides on the backs of migrating birds.

These wetlands, emeralds around Great Salt Lake, provide critical habitat for North American waterfowl and shorebirds, supporting hundreds of thousands, even millions of individuals during spring and autumn migrations. The long-legged birds with their eyes focused down transform a seemingly sterile world into a fecund one. It is here in the marshes with the birds that I seal my relationship to Great Salt Lake.

I could never have anticipated its rise.

My mother was aware of a rise on the left side of her abdomen. I was deep in dream. This particular episode found me hiding beneath my grandmother's bed as eight black helicopters flew toward the house. I knew we were in danger.

The phone rang and everything changed.

"Good morning," I answered.

"Good morning, dear," my mother replied.

This is how my days always began. Mother and I checking in—a long extension cord on the telephone lets me talk and eat breakfast at the same time.

"You're back. So how was the river trip?" I asked, pouring myself a glass of orange juice.

"It was wonderful," she answered. "I loved the river and I loved the people. The Grand Canyon is a…"

There was a break in her voice. I set my glass on the counter.

She paused. "I didn't want to do this, Terry."

I think I knew what she was going to say before she said it. The same way, twelve years before, I knew something was wrong when I walked into our house after school and Mother was gone. In 1971, it had been breast cancer.

With my back against the kitchen wall, I slowly sank to the floor and stared at the yellow flowered wallpaper I had always intended to change.

"What I was going to say is that the Grand Canyon is a perfect place to heal—I've found a tumor, a fairly large mass in my lower abdomen. I was wondering if you could go with me to the hospital. John has to work. I'm scheduled for an ultrasound this afternoon."

I closed my eyes. "Of course."

Another pause.

"How long have you known about this?"

"I discovered it about a month ago."

I found myself getting angry until she answered the next obvious question.

"I needed time to live with it, to think about it—and more than anything else, I wanted to float down the Colorado River. This was the trip John and I had been dreaming about for years. I knew the days in the Canyon would give me peace. And Terry, they did."

I sat on the white linoleum floor in my nightgown with my knees pulled in toward my chest, my head bowed.

"Maybe it's nothing, Mother. Maybe it's only a cyst. It could be benign, you know."

She did not answer.

"How do you feel?" I asked.

"I feel fine," she said. "But I would like to go shopping for a robe before my appointment at one."

We agreed to meet at eleven.

"I'm glad you're home." I said.

"So am I."

She hung up. The dial tone returned. I listened to the line until it became clear I had heard what I heard.

It's strange to feel change coming. It's easy to ignore. An underlying restlessness seems to accompany it like birds flocking before a storm. We go about our business with the usual alacrity, while in the pit of our stomach there is a sense of something tenuous.

These moments of peripheral perceptions are short, sharp flashes of insight we tend to discount like seeing the movement of an animal from the corner of our eye. We turn and there is nothing there. They are the strong and subtle impressions we allow to slip away.

I had been feeling fey for months.

Mother and I drove downtown, parked the car, and walked into Nordstrom's. I recalled the last department store we were in when the only agenda was which lipstick to choose.

We rode the escalator up two floors to sleepwear. Mother appeared to have nothing else on her mind but a beautiful piece of lingerie.

"What do you think about this one?" she asked as she held a navy blue satin robe up to her in the mirror.

"It's stunning," I answered. "I love the tiny white stars."

"So do I. It's quite dramatic." She turned to the clerk. "I'll take this, please," and handed her the robe.

"Would you like this gift wrapped?" asked the saleswoman.

I started to say no. Mother said yes. "Thank you, that would be very nice."

My mother's flair for drama always caught me off guard. Her love of spontaneity made the most mundane enterprise an occasion. She entered a room, mystery followed her. She left and her presence lingered.

I thought of the last time we were in New York together. We slept late, rising midmorning to partake of steaming hot blueberry muffins downtown in a sidewalk café. It was my mother's sacrament. We shopped in the finest stores and twirled in front of mirrors. We lived in the museums. Having overspent our allotment of time at the Met in the Caravaggio exhibit, we opted for a quick make-over at Bloomingdale's to revive us for the theatre. The brass and glass of the department store's first floor was blinding until we finally bumped into the Lancôme counter.

"It's wonderful to be in a place where no one knows you," Mother said as she sat in the chair reserved for customers. "I would never do this at home."

The salesclerk acquainted her with options. She looked

at my mother's hazel eyes, the structure of her face, her dark hair cut short.

"Great bones," the makeup artist said. "For you, less is more."

I watched the woman sweep blush across my mother's cheekbones. A hint of brown eyeshadow deepened her eyes as framboise was painted across her lips.

"How do I look?" she said.

"Dazzling," I answered.

Mother gave me her chair. The Lancôme woman looked at my face and shook her head.

"Do you spend a lot of time in the wind?"

The hospital doors seemed heavy as I pushed them open against the air trapped inside the vestibule. Once inside, it reeked of disease whitewashed with antiseptics. A trip to the hospital is always a descent into the macabre. I have never trusted a place with shiny floors.

We found our way to the lab through the maze of hallways by following the color-coded tape on the floors. Mother was given instructions to change into the hospital's blue and white seersucker robe. They say the gowns are for convenience, so they can do what they have to do fast. But their robes seem more like socialistic wraps that let you know that you belong to the fraternity of the ill waiting patiently in rooms all across America.

"Diane Tempest."

She looked too beautiful to be sick. Wearing their white foam slippers, she disappeared down the hall into a room with closed doors.

I waited.

My eyes studied each person in the room. Why were they there and what were they facing? They all seemed to share an unnatural color. I checked my hands against theirs. I tried to pick up snippets of conversation that pieced together their stories. But voices were soft and words were few.

I could not read the expression on Mother's face when she came out of X-ray. She changed into her clothes and we walked out of the hospital to the car.

"It doesn't look good," she said. "It's about the size of a grapefruit, filled with fluid. They are calling in the results to the doctor. We need to go to his office to find out what to do next."

There was little emotion in her face. This was a time for details. Pragmatism replaced sentiment.

At Krehl Smith's office, the future was drawn on an 8½ by 11-inch pad of yellow paper. The doctor (her obstetrician who had delivered two of her four babies) proceeded to draw the tumor in relationship to her ovaries. He stumbled over his own words, not having the adequate vocabulary to tell a patient who was also a friend that she most likely had ovarian cancer.

We got the picture. There was an awkward silence.

"So what are my options?" Mother asked.

"A hysterectomy as soon as you are ready. If it is ovarian cancer then we'll follow it up with chemotherapy and go from there…"

"I'll make that decision," she said.

The tears I had wanted to remain hidden splashed down on the notes I was taking, blurring the ink.

Arrangements were made for surgery on Monday morn-ing. Mother wanted to prepare the family over the week-end. Dr. Smith suggested that two oncologists be called in on the case; Gary Smith and Gary Johnson. Mother agreed, requesting that she be able to meet with them before the operation for questions.

There was another awkward silence. Details done. Mother stood up from the straight back chair.

"Thank you, Krehl."

Their eyes met. She turned to walk out the door, when Krehl Smith put his arm through hers. "I'm so sorry, Diane. I know what you went through before. I wish I had more encouraging news."

"So do I," she said. "So do I."

Mother and I got into the car. It started to rain. In a peculiar sort of way, the weather gave us permission to cry.

Driving home, Mother stared out her window. "You know, I hear the words on the outside, that I might have ovarian cancer, but they don't register on the inside. I keep saying to myself, this isn't happening to me, but then why shouldn't it? I am facing my own mortality—again—some-thing I thought I had already done twelve years ago. Do you know how strange it is to know your days are limited? To have no future?"

Home. The family gathered in the living room. Mother had her legs on Dad's lap. Dad had his left arm around her, his right hand rubbing her knees and thighs. My brothers, Steve, Dan, and Hank were seated across the room. I sat on the hearth. A fire was burning, so were candles. Twelve years ago, we had been too young to see beyond our own pain; children of four, eight, twelve, and fifteen. Dad was thirty-seven, in shock from the thought of losing his wife. We did not do well. She did. Things were different now. We would do it together. We made promises that we would be here for her this time, that she would not have to carry us.

The conversation shifted to mountain climbing, the men's desire to climb the Grand Teton in the summer, then on to tales of scaling Mount Everest without oxygen—it could be done.

Mother said she would like to work in the garden if the weather cleared. We said we would all help.

"That's funny," she said. "No one has ever offered to help me before."

She then asked that we respect her decisions, that this was her body and her life, not ours, and that if the tumor was malignant, she would choose not to have chemotherapy.

We said nothing.

She went on to explain why she had waited a month before going to the doctor.

"In the long run I didn't think one month would matter. In the short run, it mattered a great deal. The heat of the sandstone penetrated my skin as I lay on the red rocks. Desert light bathed my soul. And traveling through the inner gorge of Vishnu schist, the oldest exposed rock in the West, gave me a perspective that will carry me through whatever I must face. Those days on the river were a meditation, a renewal. I found my strength in its solitude. It is with me now."

She looked at Dad, "Lava Falls, John. We've got some white water ahead."

I know the solitude my mother speaks of. It is what sustains me and protects me from my mind. It renders me fully present. I am desert. I am mountains. I am Great Salt Lake. There are other languages being spoken by wind, water, and wings. There are other lives to consider: avocets, stilts, and stones. Peace is the perspective found in patterns. When I see ring-billed gulls picking on the flesh of decaying carp, I am less afraid of death. We are no more and no less than the life that surrounds us. My fears surface in my isolation. My serenity surfaces in my solitude.

It is raining. And it seems as though it has always been raining. Every day another quilted sky rolls in and covers us with water. Rain. Rain. More rain. The Great Basin is being filled.

It isn't just the clouds' doing. The depth of snowpack in the Wasatch Mountains is the highest on record. It begins to melt, and streams you could jump over become raging rivers with no place to go. Local canyons are splitting at their seams as saturated hillsides slide.

Great Salt Lake is rising.

Brooke and I opt for marriage maintenance and drive out to Black's Rock on the edge of the lake to watch birds. They'll be there in spite of the weather. And they are.

Avocets and black-necked stilts are knee-deep in water alongside Interstate 80. Flocks of California gulls stand on a disappearing beach. We pull over, get out of the car, and begin walking up and over lakeside boulders. I inhale the

salty air. It is like ocean, even the lake is steel-blue with
whitecaps.

Brooke walks ahead while I sit down with my binoculars
and watch grebes. Eared grebes. Their red eyes flash
intensely on the water, and I am amazed by such buoyancy
in small bodies. Scanning the horizon, all I can see is water.
"Lake Bonneville," I think to myself.

It is easy to imagine this lake, born 28,000 years ago, in the
Pleistocene Epoch, just one in the succession of bodies of
water to inhabit the Bonneville Basin over the last fifteen
million years. It inundated nearly 20,000 square miles in
western Utah, spilling into southern Utah and eastern
Nevada—a liquid hand pressing against the landscape that
measured 285 miles long and 140 miles wide, with an estimated depth of 1,000 feet.

Across from where I sit, Stansbury Island looms. Distinct
bench levels tell a story of old shorelines, a record of where
Lake Bonneville paused in its wild fluctuations over the
course of 15,000 years. Its rise was stalled about 23,000
years ago when the lake's elevation was about 4,500 feet
above sea level; over the next 3,000 years, it rose very little.
The relentless erosion of wave against rock during this stable period cut a broad terrace known to geologists as the
Stansbury Shoreline.

The lake began to swell again until it reached the 5,090-
foot level 16,000 years ago. And then for a millennium and
a half, the lake carved the Bonneville Shoreline, the highest
of the three main terraces. Great tongues of ice occupied
canyons in the Wasatch Mountains to the east, while herds

of musk oxen, mammoths, and saber-tooth cats frequented the forested shores of Lake Bonneville. Schools of Bonneville cutthroat trout flashed through these waters (remnants of which still cling to existence in the refuge of small ponds in isolated desert mountains of the Great Basin). Fossil records suggest birds similar to red-tail hawk, sage grouse, mallard, and teal lived here. And packs of dire wolves called up the moon.

About 14,500 years ago, Lake Bonneville spilled over the rim of the Great Basin near Red Rock Pass in southeastern Idaho. Suddenly, the waters broke the Basin breaching the sediments down to bedrock, releasing a flood so spectacular it is estimated the maximum discharge of water was thirty-three million cubic feet per second. This event, known today as the Bonneville Flood, dropped the lake about 350 feet, to 4,740 feet. When the outlet channel was eroded to resistant rock, the lake stabilized once again and the Provo Shoreline was formed.

As the climate warmed drawing moisture from the inland sea, the lake began to shrink, until, eleven thousand years ago, it had fallen to present-day levels of about 4,200 feet. This trend toward warmer and drier conditions signified the end of the Ice Age.

A millennium later, the lake rose slightly to an elevation of about 4,250 feet, forming the Gilbert Shoreline, but soon receded. This marked the end of Lake Bonneville and the birth of its successor, Great Salt Lake.

As children, it was easy to accommodate the idea of Lake Bonneville. The Provo Shoreline looks like a huge bathtub ring around the Salt Lake Valley. It is a bench I know well, because we lived on it. It is the ledge that supported my neighborhood above Salt Lake City. Daily hikes in the foothills of the Wasatch yielded vast harvests of shells.

"Lake Bonneville..." we would say as we pocketed them. Never mind that they were the dried shells of land snails. We would sit on the benches of this ancient lake, stringing white shells into necklaces. We would look west to Great Salt Lake and imagine.

That was in 1963. I was eight years old. Great Salt Lake was a puddle, having retreated to a record low surface elevation of 4,191.35 feet. Local papers ran headlines that read, GREAT SALT LAKE DISAPPEARING? and INLAND SEA SHRINKS.

My mother decided Great Salt Lake was something we should see before it vanished. And so, my brothers and I, with friends from the neighborhood, boarded our red Ford station wagon and headed west. It was a long ride past the airport, industrial complexes, and municipal dumps. It was also hot. The backs of our thighs stuck to the Naugahyde seats. Our towels were wrapped around us. We were ready to swim.

Mother pulled into the Silver Sands Beach. The smell should have been our first clue, noxious hydrogen sulphide gas rising from the brine,

"Phew!" we all complained as we walked toward the beach, brine flies following us. "Smells like rotten eggs."

"You'll get used to it," Mother said. "Now go play. See if you can float."

We were dubious at best. Our second clue should have been the fact that Mother did not bring her bathing suit, but rather chose to sit on the sand in her sunsuit with a thick novel in hand.

The ritual was always the same. Run into the lake, scream, and run back out. The salt seeped into the sores of our scraped knees and lingered. And if the stinging sensation didn't bring you to tears, the brine flies did.

We huddled around Mother, the old Saltair Pavilion was visible behind her, vibrating behind a screen of heatwaves. We begged her to take us home, pleading for dry towels. Total time at the lake: five minutes. She was unsympathetic.

"We're here for the afternoon, kids," she said, and then brought down her sunglasses a bit so we could see her eyes. "I didn't see anyone floating."

She had given us a dare. One by one, we slowly entered Great Salt Lake. Gradually, we would lean backward into the hands of the cool water and find ourselves being held by the very lake that minutes before had betrayed us. For hours we floated on our backs, imprinting on Great Basin skies. It was in these moments of childhood that Great Salt Lake flooded my psyche.

Driving home, Mother asked each of us what we thought of the lake. None of us said much. We were too preoccupied with our discomfort: sunburned and salty, we looked like red gumdrops. Our hair felt like steel wool, and we smelled. With the lake so low and salinity around 26 percent, one pound of salt to every four pounds of water (half a gallon), another hour of floating in Great Salt Lake and we might have risked being pickled and cured.

Brooke brought me back a handful of feathers and sat

behind me. I leaned back into his arms. Three more days until Mother's surgery.

The family spontaneously gathered at Mother's and Dad's; children, spouses, grandparents, and cousins. We sat on the lawn, some talked, others played gin rummy, while Mother planted marigolds in her garden.

Mother and I talked.

"I don't want you to be disappointed, Terry."

"I won't be," I said softly. My hands patted the earth around each flower she planted.

"It's funny how the tears finally leave you," she said, turning her trowel in the soil. "I think I've experienced every possible emotion this week."

"And how do you feel now?" I asked.

She looked out at the lake, wiped her forehead with the back of her gardening glove, and removed more marigolds from the flat.

"I'll be glad to have the operation behind me. I'm ready to get on with my life."

Dad mowed the lawn between clumps of relatives. It felt good to be outside, to feel the heat, and to hear the sounds of neighborhoods on Saturdays in the spring.

The sun set behind Antelope Island. Great Salt Lake was a mirror on the valley floor. One had the sense of water being in this country now, as the quality of light was different lending a high gloss to the foothills.

At dusk, we moved inside to the living room and created a family circle. Mother sat on a chair in the center. As the eldest son, Steve annointed Mother with consecrated olive oil to seal the blessing. The men who held the Melchizedek

Priesthood, the highest order of authority bestowed upon Mormon males, gathered around her, placing their hands on the crown of her head. My father prayed in a low, humble voice, asking that she might be the receptacle of her family's love, that she might know of her influence in our lives and be blessed with strength and courage and peace of mind.

Kneeling next to my grandmother, Mimi, I felt her strength and the generational history of belief Mormon ritual holds. We can heal ourselves, I thought, and we can heal each other.

"These things we pray for in the name of Jesus Christ, amen."

Mother opened her eyes. "Thank you…"

My sister-in-law, Ann, and I slipped into the kitchen to prepare dinner.

Some things don't change. After everyone had eaten, attention shifted to the weather report on the ten o'clock news, a Western ritual, especially when your livelihood depends on it as ours does. A family construction business, now in its fourth generation, has taught me to look up before I look down. You can't lay pipe when the ground is frozen, neither can you have crews digging trenches in mud.

The weatherman not only promised good weather, but announced that most of the planet would be clear tomorrow according to the satellite projection—a powerful omen in itself.

After everyone left, I asked Mother if I could feel the tumor. She lay down on the carpet in the family room and placed my hand on her abdomen. With her help, I found the strange rise on the left side and palpated my fingers around its perimeter.

With my hands on my mother's belly, I prayed.

We wait. Our family is pacing the hall. Other families are pacing other halls. Each tragedy has its own territory. A Tongan family in the room next to Mother's sings mourning songs for the dying. Their melancholy sweeps over us like the shadow of a raven. What songs would we sing, I wonder. Two doors down, a nurse calls for assistance in turning a patient over on a bed of ice. Minutes later, I hear the groaning of the chilled woman.

It has been almost four hours. For most of the time, I have been sitting with my mother's parents. My grandmother, Lettie, is in a wheelchair. She suffers from Parkinson's disease. Her delicate hands tremble as she strokes my hair. I am leaning against the side of her knee. She and my grandfather, Sanky, are heartsick. Mother is their only daughter; one of their two sons is dead. Mother has always cared for her parents. Now that she needs their help, Lettie feels the pain of a mother unable to physically attend to her daughter.

The three doctors appear: Smith, Smith, and Johnson, green-robed and capped. Dad meets them halfway, cowboy boots toe-to-toe with surgical papered shoes. I try to read lips as he receives the bad news followed by the good news.

"Yes, it was malignant. No we didn't get it all, but with the chemotherapy we have to offer, there is reason to be hopeful." The doctors say they will meet with us in a couple of days when they get the pathology report back, then they will go over specific details and options with Mother and the family.

Dad—tall, rugged, and direct—asks one question. "What's the bottom line—how much time do we have?"

The doctors meet his narrow blue eyes. Gary Smith shakes his head. "We can't tell you that. No one can."

The curse and charisma of cancer: the knowledge that from this point forward, all you have is the day at hand.

Dad turned around defeated, frustrated. "I'd like to get some answers." His impatience became his stride as he walked back down the hall.

Bad news is miraculously accommodated. With one hope dashed—the tumor was malignant (an easier word to stomach than cancer)—another hope is adopted: the chemotherapy will cure. Now all we had to do was convince Mother. We made a pact among ourselves that we would not discuss anything with her until the next morning. We wanted her to rest.

Two orderlies wheel Mother back into her room. The tubes, bags, blood, and lines dangling from four directions did not foster the hope we were trying to sustain. Our faith faltered in the presence of her face—white, wan, and weakened. Dad whispered that she looked like a skinned deer.

Mother opened her eyes and faintly chuckled, "That bad, uh?"

No one else laughed. We just looked at one another. We were awkward and ill-prepared.

Dad took Mother's hand and spoke to her reassuringly. He tried stroking her arm but quickly became frustrated and frightened by all the tubing connected to her veins. He sat with her as long as he could maintain his composure and then retreated to the hall where his parents, Mimi and Jack, were standing by.

Steve, Dan, and Hank took over, each one nursing her in his own way.

"Don't worry about fixing dinner for Dad tonight, Mom, we'll take care of him," said Steve.

Dan walked out of the room and came back with a cup of ice chips. "Would you like to suck on these, Mother? Your mouth looks dry."

Hank, sixteen, stood in the corner and watched. Mother looked at him and extended her hand. He walked toward her and took it.

"Love you, Mom."

"I love you, too, dear," she whispered.

My brothers left the room. I stood at the foot of her bed, "How are you feeling, Mother?"

It was a hollow question, I knew, but words don't count when words don't matter. I moved to her side and stroked her forehead. Her eyes pierced mine.

"Did they get it all?"

I blinked and looked away.

"Did they, Terry? Tell me." She grabbed my hand.

I shook my head. "No, Mother."

She closed her eyes and I watched the muscles in her jaw tighten.

"How bad is it?"

Dad walked in and saw the tears streaming down my cheeks. "What happened?"

I shook my head again, left the room and walked down the hall. He followed me and took hold of my shoulder.

"You didn't tell her, did you?"

I turned around, still crying, and faced him. "Yes."

"Why? Why, when we agreed not to say anything until tomorrow? It wasn't your place." His anger flared like the corona of an eclipsed sun.

"I told her because she asked me, and I could not lie."

The pathologist's report defined Mother's tumor as Stage III epithelial ovarian cancer. It had metastasized to the abdominal cavity. Nevertheless, Dr. Gary Smith believes Mother has a very good chance against this type of cancer, given the treatment available. He is recommending one year of chemotherapy using the agents Cytoxan and cisplatin.

Before surgery, Mother said no chemotherapy.

Today, I walked into her room, the blinds were closed.

"Terry," she said through the darkness. "Will you help me? I told myself I would not let them poison me. But now I am afraid not to. I want to live."

I sat down by her bed.

"Perhaps you can help me visualize a river — I can imagine the chemotherapy to be a river running through me, flushing the cancer cells out. Which river, Terry?"

"How about the Colorado?" I said.

It was the first time in weeks I had seen my mother smile.

Ten days have passed and, between all of us, we have kept vigil. Mother's strength is returning and with typical wit, she hinted that a bit of privacy might be nice. I took her cue and drove out to the Bird Refuge.

It looked like any other spring. Western kingbirds lined the fences, their yellow bellies flashing bright above the barbed wire. Avocets and stilts were still occupying the same shallow ponds they had always inhabited, and the white-faced glossy ibises six miles from the Refuge were meticulously separating the grasses with their decurved bills.

Closer in, the alkaline flats, usually dry, stark, and vacant, were wet. A quarter mile out, they were flooded.

The Bear River Migratory Bird Refuge, at an elevation of 4,206 feet, was 2 feet from being inundated. I walked out as far as I could. It had been a long time since I had heard the liquid songs of red-wing blackbirds.

"Konk-la-ree! Konk-la-ree! Konk-la-ree!"

The marsh was flooding. The tips of cattails looked like snorkels jutting a few inches above water. Coots' nests floated. They would fare well. With my binoculars, I could see snowy egrets fishing the small cascades that were breaking over the road's asphalt shoulders.

I could not separate the Bird Refuge from my family. Devastation respects no boundaries. The landscape of my childhood and the landscape of my family, the two things I had always regarded as bedrock, were now subject to change. Quicksand.

Looking out over the water, now an ocean, I felt foolish for standing in the middle of what little road was left. Better to have brought a canoe. But I rolled up my pantlegs over the tops of my rubber boots and continued to walk. I knew my ground.

Up ahead, two dozen white pelicans were creating a spiral staircase as they flew. It looked like a feathered DNA molecule. Their wings reflected the sun. The light shifted, and they disappeared. It shifted again and I found form. Escher's inspiration. The pelicans rose higher and higher on blacktipped wings until they straightened themselves into an arrow pointing west to Gunnison Island.

To my left, long-billed dowitchers, stout and mottled birds, pattered and probed, pattered and probed, perforating the mud in masses. In an instant, they flew, sweeping the sky as one great bird. Flock consciousness.

I turned away from the water and walked east toward the mountains. Foxtails by the roadside gathered light and held it. Dry stalks of rumex, russet from last year's fall, drew hunger pangs—the innocence of those days.

Before leaving, I noticed sago pondweed screening shallow water near the edge of the road. Tiny green circles of chlorophyll were converting sunlight to sugar. I knelt down and scooped up a handful. Microscopic animals and a myriad of larvae drained from my hands. Within seconds, the marsh in microcosm slipped through my fingers.

I was not prepared for the loneliness that followed.

With her first book, *Refuge: An Unnatural History of Family and Place*, Terry Tempest Williams won an immediate reputation as an eloquent and impassioned naturalist-writer in the tradition of John Muir, Rachel Carson, and Wallace Stegner. Her books since then have included *Pieces of White Shell: A Journey to Navajoland, Coyote's Canyon*, and *An Unspoken Hunger: Stories from the Field*, from which this story was excerpted. She lives in Salt Lake City with her husband Brooke.

Redbird

JAKE PAGE

Hope hinges on the color red.

I T IS ONE OF THOSE DAYS WHEN SNOWFALL has settled down to sulk on the landscape and melt. The sky is a uniformly opaque grey, the hedgerow a murky black-brown. The day is short. What light we are permitted is diffuse and without definition: the crisp delights of winter have temporarily turned into old celery. A great dampness. There are people who become frightfully depressed at such times and some of them regain their composure only, medical science seems to think, if they spend part of the day under Gro-lite lamps, the sort used for houseplants. For others, there are less cumbersome solutions.

A cardinal appears, a little packet of tropiclike joy on a wet black twig in a disheveled bush outside, and suddenly there is a small, significant change in the local universe. Color returns for an instant—magical, timeless instant—

focused by the bird's brilliant feathers. For just a moment in the damp, grey emulsion of winter, there is a miniburst of elation, and hope hinges on this bird.

Hope? Hope for what, asks the rationalist?

This is not an easy time for nature writers, the kind of people who have traditionally sought to share the comfort they find in the change of the season, the veins of a leaf, or the apparition of a common bird in the still-life of a winter afternoon. We are told that there is little meaning in such things, never mind one's emotional life—little left that is translatable into a philosophy for making one's way through the days. And nights. This is because they let physicists loose in this realm. Physicists lately presume to be the accounting department of nature, woebegone anchors attached to otherwise free-sailing yachts.

Today, to know nature is to know that it consists mostly of empty spaces inhabited by flashing instants of subatomic energy packets appearing here, then there, evidently without cause. This sounds absurd, of course, but believe me: this is the world according to physics. Nature as you and I perceive it may not even exist in the sense of being real, except that it will respond to a physicist with an answer determined only by the question he asks. Worse, to seek ethical principles from nature is to anthropomorphize it and this is a sin. That there can be sins in a natural world devoid of meaning may seem paradoxical, but not if you are a physicist and have laid claim to the rules of the game. Such is the legacy of the physicists' new world view, quantum mechanics: we populate a dream and no one knows whose dream it is.

Theologians and philosophers, even some physicists, have set out to find god, or at least to redefine god, in this rarefied quantum broth, and what may be emerging is at least a sign of an orderly geometric urge that lies behind the Big Bang origins of our universe. All paradox—and very thin soup indeed. The cardinal outside is at best a temporary fancy in one enormous thought. Same for the rest of us. Under the circumstances, it may make little sense to take up the cause of the cardinal, recently humiliated in print, but one does so anyway, in the hope that a bit of chivalry may lead somewhere useful in the chimerical plane where we obstinately carry on what we are pleased to call our existence.

Some time ago, a writer in *Smithsonian* saw fit to giggle at the expense of six state legislatures which, at various times in the past, unimaginatively chose the cardinal as their state bird. To be sure, the writer doffed his hat at the cardinal's excellent character, noting that the male is an especially adept parent. But he complained that no great raptors, no delightful warblers, not even the burgherlike choice of Ben Franklin's, the wild turkey, had made it onto the roster of state birds.

The male cardinal *is* a good parent, almost exclusively raising the young in spring, an exemplary provider, and ardent and patient teacher of fledglings. And so he must be: his equally exemplary mate is too busy hatching a second clutch of eggs. This activity suggests more virtue, as we see such things, than the sleazy scams of the cowbird, but I am told it can serve us ill in the long run to project our own, often temporary mores upon the actions of creatures we don't really understand all that well.

For example, in a book published in the 20th century, there is the following paean to the virtues of the cardinal: "All through the Southern plantation country, this is the bird that typifies everything that is elegant and chivalric not only to the colored cotton pickers and plantation laborers, but to the country gentlemen."

Well.

Perhaps the scientists of today are right to perceive the cardinal merely as an interesting abstraction called a species, one of the many such abstractions, driven by its own range of hormones and their response to light, all this mediated in the pineal gland, a kind of chemical machine that one could, if one wished, ultimately explain by reference to the nature of electrical potentials and the dance of subatomic energy packets. They, the biochemists, avoid a lot of grief by thinking in such a manner. Individual cardinals are, in such a way of thinking, dispensable: they are all merely role-players following a script written by a particular brand of selfish gene, window dressing for a self-replicating molecule.

What then am I to make of the male cardinal who spent an entire year attacking my kitchen window from a nearby bush? I would wake in the morning, hearing the insistent clatter as it hit the window, over and over, day in and day out, ignoring so far as I could see any parental or other duty, ceasing only when the sun went down.

A research ornithologist—my friend Gene Morton, in fact—suggested that the bird was attacking his own image in the window glass, but I looked at the window from the bird's angle and there was no image. Gene suggested that I place a mirror facing out of the window to see if the bird would attack it. It didn't. Its behavior was pointless and obviously counterproductive—an aberration assuring that whatever motivated this cardinal would not later turn up in the gene pool, evolution taking care of business, ridding the future of an automaton that had somehow become wrongly wired.

Even in the face of science's inability to explain this bird's behavior, it was patently silly for me to think of the aberrant tapping on the window as some sort of a sign, to take it personally as if some pattern in my own behavior was being cosmically frowned upon. Who needs avian reminders of that anyway? No omen here, just a neuronal screw-up, unfortunate for the bird but no reflection on human affairs.

Nevertheless, somewhere between a chemical mix-up leading to maniacal behavior by one cardinal and the magical apparition of another cardinal in a colorless snowscape, with my attendant dose of elation, there was something more than a valueless abstraction. There was something very real. It had to do with the fact that the bird is red.

The tanager is red, too, but it usually skulks in the woods while the cardinal moves in with us all year and stays red all year as well. Nothing about cardinals could be more important than their color, and this is probably why six state legislatures have adopted it. Red sells, say merchandising experts. Everything about the cardinal, it became clear, hinges on its very redness.

In fact, the Latin roots of the word *cardinal* mean hinge, and those exalted members of the early church were named for the crucial role they played in keeping ecclesiastic matters organized and functioning. And in those days when symbolic meanings had a more present reality than nowadays, red meant a host of things but none more present and powerful than the blood of the Savior, which is to say hope against the ineffable odds of the flesh. So, in some such manner, the cardinals of the European church came to wear red and it is no surprise at all how our bird came by its name.

In more recent history, red is also the symbol of anarchy and certain revolutions that did not turn out all that well — by our standards — and it is probably best here to take the line of the scientist and dismiss all those symbolic meanings and religious connotations as alien — certainly alien to the bird. And it is also probably best to stare scientific evidence right smack in the face if one is determined to find virtue or hope in the likes of a common red bird.

The cardinal is red because its feathers contain little packets of pigments — carotenes and others — that reflect the red wavelengths of light and absorb all the other wavelengths. Thus we see it as red. And red, science tells us, is but one component of visible light which itself is seen as white, and light is part of the larger electromagnetic spectrum which includes such esoterica as gamma rays and X-rays, all having different properties in part because they have different wavelengths. The wavelength of red falls at about 620 nanometers on the scale and energy that oscillates at that precise rate produces the sensation of red somewhere in the brain. That is about all that science has to say, in essence, about the red of the cardinal. More thin soup.

Indeed, the physics and chemistry of red are pretty well worked out up to the point of our having, in our brains, the sensation of red. It doesn't make sense to wonder if my wife sees the same red when she looks at the cardinal as I do. My neuronal system is operating on the same wavelength as hers and that is simply all that can be known. In fact, just what the *sensation* of red is lies beyond science, and herein lies hope. The language of science—which is fundamentally numerical—has no color. Numbers are colorless. Wavelengths are themselves colorless. There is no way that science can explain precisely what we know in our minds to be red.

Such anomalies as this have led some philosophers and even some physicists to suppose that there may be more to the mind than a material collection of neural activity, no matter how exquisitely complex it all might be as wiring or biochemical communication. It could be, they suggest, that mind (with its indescribable sense of red) exists beyond or somehow outside matter. Here again we may have what can be thought of as some hope against the ineffable odds of the flesh, a legitimization, at least, of the human sense of elation at the sight of beauty, quantum soup be damned.

The mind-matter question will plague thinkers for a long time. It may never be resolved. But it is enough to think that the answer to this conundrum could hinge on our ability to respond to something as commonplace as the cardinal, the little red burst in January's grey.

Jake Page lives in Corrales, New Mexico with his wife, Susanne, and is the author of numerous books, including *Hopi, Lords of the Air: The Smithsonian Book of Birds, Pastorale: A Natural History of Sorts,* and *Songs to Birds: Essays,* from which this story was excerpted.

The Last Cranes
of Siberia

PETER MATTHIESSEN

*It's a long flight back from the brink for these
legendary birds, but hope remains.*

O N A RARE CLEAR DAY—FIRST DAY OF
summer—as I fly the Bering Strait from the
Yukon Delta toward the Diomede Islands and
the Chukotski Peninsula, it excites me to imagine this gray,
sun-silvered sea from the view on high of the great cranes,
more particularly, the golden eye of the Crane from the
East, as the Canadian, or sandhill, crane of North America
is known in its western breeding territory, in Siberia. Even
the airplane's altitude, of 30,000 feet, might prove no obstacle to the sandhill, which commonly migrates a mile above
the earth, and whose smaller relative, the demoiselle crane,
has been seen in airy passage of the snow peaks of the
Himalayas at 20,000 feet.

That the cranes of the world appear to travel at astonishing altitudes accounts for their ubiquity in the earliest

legends of the world as messengers and harbingers of highest heaven. In Cree legend, Crane carries Rabbit to the moon, and Aesop extolls the crane's singular ability "to rise above the clouds into endless space, and survey the wonders of the heavens, as well as of the earth beneath, with its seas, lakes, and rivers, as far as the eye can reach." In China and Japan, the red-crowned crane—largest and, by all accounts, most beautiful of the world's cranes—has represented longevity and good fortune since ancient times. It is also the most celebrated bird in all world cultures, appearing in all sorts of art forms, designs, and motifs, and on royal robes and kimonos. Being faithful to their mates (it is alleged), the red-crowneds also bedeck wedding cakes and anniversary cards. Indeed, they are granted a spiritual dimension, with heaven-bound sages commonly depicted riding on a crane, or even assuming the crane's beautiful form for their arrival in the clouds of immortality.

The Arctic air numbs the bright-red skin on the sandhill's crown; the long, still wings creak on the wind. As a Family, the first cranes appeared some 50 million years ago, and the sandhill crane, whose bones turn up among Wyoming fossils 10 million years old, is the most ancient bird species on earth. The world's great cranes stir the imagination not only because they are the oldest and the largest of the earth's flying creatures or because the horn notes of their voices summon man's attention to his own swift passage but because they symbolize, like no other living things, the disappearing expanse of clean water, earth, and air upon which their species—and ours, too, though we learn it very late—must ultimately depend for survival.

The brown coast falls away in the bright mists, and there is only the rotted pack ice and gray shallow seas of the vanished land bridge between the continents. "The flight of cranes, the way they form letters" was noted by the poet Hyginus. Ovid attributed the invention of letters to the god Mercury after watching cranes fly. Like wild geese, cranes often fly in V formation, having had long ages and many millions of miles of buffeting by the great winds to absorb the aerodynamic limitation of—let's say—the letter H.

Soon the Diomede Islands—one in the New World, one in the Old—drift off in northern mists and are replaced by Siberian barrens of the Chukotski Peninsula, home of the Chukot or Chukehi aborigines, who share an ancient ancestry with the Inuit. Even in late June, the mountain tundra of Chukotski looks wintry, with hard wind-worn snow in the ravines.

The Arctic distances flown at such altitudes by birds shame the seat-bound airline traveler. Peering out from my plastic aerie over the firmament of wind and light, mightily stirred by the unspoiled world beneath, I strive to experience with Goethe (or with Faust, at least) how "it is inborn in every man that his feeling should press upward and forward...when over precipitous fir-clad heights the eagle floats with wings outspread, or over flatlands, over seas, the crane sweeps onward toward its home"—the German word is *Heimgang* or "home going"—to the virgin earth, the lost paradise at the source of all man's yearnings.

Following old migration instincts, the sandhill will descend each spring to this peninsula, and may continue west along the Arctic coast some 1,500 miles to the Yana

River, where its breeding grounds border upon those of the Siberian crane....

Two years ago, I explored Lake Baikal, in south central Siberia, but this was my first journey to the Russian Far East—more specifically, to the Amur Basin, which also includes large regions of China. The Amur, all but unknown in the West, is the great river of northeast Asia and, at 2,705 miles, drains a watershed of 716,200 square miles on its journey from Mongolia to the Pacific. Despite the enormous floodplains of the lower river, only 5 percent of the Amur Basin is under water, since most of the terrain farther inland rises in small, ancient mountains and upland forest, containing immense resources in timber and minerals. The mighty Amur, unrolling beneath the wings as the airplane starts its long descent to Khabarovsk, is as singular and precious as Baikal itself, the largest free, wild, unbridged, undammed river left on earth.

With its tributary the Ussuri, the Amur defines the Russo-Chinese northeast frontier, all the way from the Mongolian steppes of Central Asia to great Lake Khanka, on the border between northeastern China—formerly Manchuria, now the province of Heilongjiang—and far southeastern Siberia, known as Ussuri Land. For a century, the disputed frontier has prevented extensive settlement along the river, known to the Russians as Dear Father Amur (as in Mother Volga, Mother Lena) and to the Chinese as Heilong Jiang, or Black Dragon River. But in recent years, with the easing of hostilities, the ecology of the entire basin has become threatened by precipitate development, not only by Russians and Chinese but by multinational timber and mining interests seeking to loot eastern Siberia; unfortunately, the verb is not too strong. In these times, Russia is too fragmented and chaotic to protect its resources, not only from ruthless corporations but from its own entrepreneurs. Local officials, politicians, private citizens, and even the military, all seeking shelter from the myriad uncertainties, are selling off every asset that is not nailed down.

Among the rare forms of East Asian wildlife most seriously threatened by the new surge of development are the white-naped and the red-crowned, or Manchurian cranes. To understand better what might be done to help offset the decline, I was on my way to an international environmental conference on the Amur Basin, to be held aboard a ship on a river voyage north and west to the crane-breeding territories in the floodplains of the middle Amur. From the Amur I would return south to Lake Khanka, where, it is hoped, the Russians and Chinese will establish an international refuge for endangered cranes. Since all the migratory cranes breed in more than one Asian country and winter in two or three others, their survival depends on international cooperation of the kind brought by Canada and the United States to the return from near-extinction of the whooping crane, which came back from a mere 15 birds a half century ago to a present population of well over 200, with about 140 living in the wild. After the whooper, the red-crowned is the rarest crane on earth; the species now numbers only 1,400 or 1,500 including a non-migratory population in Japan....

I walked out to the end of a wooded ridge along the lake, and had hardly begun to scan the marsh when a striking red-white-and-black head rose from the reeds perhaps 200 yards away, withdrew mysteriously, and rose again, joined this time by another. Soon two birds stalked out into the open, their black tertials, folded and draped like plumes on the white tail, giving them a striking "black-tailed" look complementing the black on neck and head. In a moment, standing close together, they stretched white necks into the sun to bugle a duet in answer to a cry from the captive male at the research station, which they doubtless perceived as an intruder into their territory. (This "unison call," characteristic of all cranes, is genetically determined, George Archibald says, and offers a strong clue to crane phylogeny.) For a minute they stood, bright heads held high against the far oaks, under a blue sky, then vanished once more into the wind-waved reeds.

Not until the first flush of exultation passed did it occur to me that this pair, wild though they appeared, were too close to the research station not to be associated with it. And, in fact, it turned out that they had been raised by hand from eggs removed from the path of a spring fire, and, having grown accustomed to the station, had not responded to wild cranes that might have led them south in migration. Though these two birds had raised chicks in the wild, they were only "semi-wild," dependent in winter on the help of man. And yet how beautiful was the sight of them—bugling red-crowned cranes in a sunlit marsh!—in those first instants when I saw them, unburdened by the knowledge that their wildness was forever lost.

With George Archibald, Jim Harris, and a few others, I tented for the night at the research station in order to join another helicopter expedition the next day, whose purpose was to capture and fit radio harnesses to those molting white-napeds.

Skidding his big machine around, the copter pilot managed to slow the two big birds, which were flapping and galloping over the wet prairie; then he dropped off Smirenski and Andronov to run them down. Even with more helicopter herding, the run turned out to be an extended effort that exhausted all parties to the chase, and eventually the male escaped entirely. The female was tackled by Smirenski, who was badly cut across the arms by the razor toenails of the big, floundering bird.

An adult crane of a large species is a very strong creature indeed, and the hard, sharp bill at the end of the long neck is a much more dangerous weapon than the claws, all the more so since the crane aims for the eyes. Several pairs of hands were needed to subdue and band this bird without harming it. One person held and taped the hard legs, and another grasped it by the neck as a Japanese ornithologist, Dr. Kiyoaki Ozaki, slipped a bag over its head—a move that usually calms the bird—and wrapped a cloth straight-jacket around it, to pin its wings close to its sides and control its thrashing. The bird was then banded—a red band on the right leg, and a green band on the left, in case anyone wished to look for this bird next winter on the south island of Kyushu, in Japan, or possibly at Poyang Lake, in south-

eastern China. Then it was sexed and weighed and measured, and, finally, Ozaki fitted it with a small radio-teleme-
ter in a back harness, which would permit satellite tracking
during migrations.

When the bag was removed, the enormous bird, its fierce
orange-gold eye blinking at electronic speed in the bare
carmine skin, hissed in threat, like its reptile ancestors, and
also, no doubt, in instinctual distress that in this frayed,
smothered condition it could not properly defend itself, as it
might have in its magnificent full plumage, of royal red,
ivory white, and silver gray.

In the summer silence, on the sunlit Siberian savanna
and wet meadow of iris and lilies, I was struck abruptly by
the spectacle of so much manpower and big machinery—the
noise and time and cost—devoted to the capture and plastic
outfitting of this one dilapidated bird. After this most trau-
matic episode, and as a result of the perils and obstacles it
would meet in the thousands of miles of its migrations (not
excluding those that could be caused by the encumbrance of
a backpack and satellite transmitter), this bird might never
be observed again.

Jim Harris acknowledged that the radio-transmitter
operation might cause the bird to run some risk during its
migration. However, he thought that the risk was worth it,
for the benefit of the species as a whole. There is much
about the white-naped crane, *Grus vipio*, that is still
unknown, including the location of some northern breeding
grounds and certain routes on its migration flyways. The
satellite tracking helps delineate where the birds go when
they cross remote frontiers, and this provides a better

understanding of which staging areas should be monitored to protect the migrants.

I had to agree, but with misgivings, and hoped we would learn next fall that this bird had made it.

A growing sense that I was doomed to miss the wild red-crowned crane was sharply intensified at dawn the next day at the village of Poyarkovo (named, like our ship, for the cossack who led the first exploration down the Amur), where I awoke at six to find the ship docking at a coal depot, with long-necked cranes of the wrong sort elevated all around in the morning mist. Amur falcons, coursing the river like huge swallows in pursuit of insects, were small consolation for the news that the river was too low for the ship to proceed. The captain had counted on monsoon rains, but they were weeks late; now we could not reach our scheduled destination—the old frontier town of Blagoveshchensk, at the confluence of the Amur and Zeya Rivers.

On July 10, 1992, the villagers of Muravyovka, about 50 miles upriver, voted to lease to the Socio-Ecological Union an entirely protected 13,500-acre "nature park" mostly within a partly protected game refuge, for a crane sanctuary; the Wild Bird Society of Japan would donate the payment for this inviolable sanctuary. A historical signing took place in a town-hall ceremony attended by a throng of seventy: it marked the first time since the 1917 revolution that a private organization had acquired Russian land for a nature reserve. This excellent news, brought back by Smirenski, was accompanied by word that twelve cranes had been spotted from a river bluff overlooking the Khinganski Reserve. Although they were seen only from a distance, it was readily perceived that half of them were adult red-crowned cranes.

On the way downriver, the Chinese delegates signed a fervent but nonbinding resolution to work for the preservation of the Amur, and afterward they relaxed somewhat at parties held in the evenings in the dining salon. The monsoon was on the way at last: the Black Dragon skies were low, with rumors of the sullen rain that greeted us on the day of our return to Khabarovsk. George Archibald, Jim Harris, and I, with the Russian wildlife artist Viktor Bakhtim, and Ma-Yiqing and some other Chinese delegates from Heilongjiang, then took the night train south to Spassk, a prosperous town on the Ussuri Plain, east of Lake Khanka, where the I.C.F. hoped to preside over the birth of an international crane reserve, a symbol and a main purpose of our journeys....

The Khanka marshlands represented my last chance on this journey to observe *G. japonensis* in the wild. The aircraft flew over the grain fields west of Spassk, then north across the paddy fields and marshes of the buffer zone between the town and the lake. Xingkai Hu-Lake Khanka, shining silver in the mist, is a shallow basin some fifty miles across; next to Baikal, it is the largest lake east of the Urals, but its average depth is about twelve feet, whereas Baikal, in places, descends more than a mile. This whole flat plain of the upper Ussuri was formerly lake bottom, and in the Pleistocene epoch, when that ancient lake went dry, the northern taiga penetrated this far south; it was cut back by Russian settlers in the last century. Today, the lake is severely polluted by heavy metals from the coal-mining industry, and by herbicides and pesticides from the rice fields.

Spassk was still in sight when, to the northeast of our route, I saw three long white birds in slow, measured flight on a course that would soon intersect our own. I leaned forward and yelled "Red-crowneds!" to Jim Harris, and he waved at me blithely over his shoulder.

The cranes were swinging off toward the north, not in panic, yet increasing speed with a hard wingbeat. Through binoculars I saw that all were adults, with fine white-pennanted black-and-red heads and the striking black pattern on their strong white wings. The birds turned in to the sun, then disappeared.

I sat back in a suffusion of well-being as the helicopter clattered on over the marshes. The wind of its rotors bent fresh reeds and riffled sparkling black sloughs all set about with tall white birds—egrets, swans, and storks—that could not compare in size or majesty with these great cranes.

Perhaps 50 miles north of Spassk, the aircraft approached the frontier, at a small river that divides the two reserves, flowing eastward through wet meadowlands from the misty lake to the Ussuri. Here the helicopter turned back south, following a wooded ridge. Just east of the ridge, stalking the open savanna between ponds, was a red-crowned crane family of four, the adults moving swiftly, without fluttering or flight, to draw two big brown chicks from pale-green meadow into deep-green reeds. The helicopter turned back for a better look, swinging out wide so as not to flare the cranes. In such a setting, the huge birds with their huge chicks evoked those ancestral cranes that walked among the large swamp reptiles in the morning sunlight of the Eocene, fifty million years ago....

In February of the following year,...Harris reported the good news that the white-naped crane whose backpack of radio-telemetry equipment had troubled me that day at Khinganski had turned up safely at Xingkai Hu-Lake Khanka in the early autumn, flown on to another staging area, in Korea's demilitarized zone, and arrived finally, on its winter grounds at Kyushu, in southern Japan. By now, the fierce-eyed bird will have left Kyushu, on its way back north to the Amur Basin, transmitting useful information all the way.

Peter Matthiessen's travels have taken him to remote regions of the world, from the Amazon jungles to the Himalayas. A former commercial fisherman and charter-boat captain, he has always been interested in marine biology and participated in the search for the great white shark that culminated in his book, *Blue Meridian*. He is the author of many fiction and non-fiction works including *At Play in the Fields of the Lord*, *Far Tortuga*, and *The Snow Leopard*.

Invisibility

JON YOUNG

*To gain the ancient knowledge of
the wild, observe the birds.*

A S FOUNDER AND DIRECTOR OF WILDER-
ness Awareness School, it is my job to mentor
trackers and naturalists in not only the modern
language of field ecology and biology, but also the ancient
skills of the scout handed down to me by my two main
teachers. I was lucky to meet and become apprenticed to
tracker, survival expert, and Apache scout-trained teacher,
Tom Brown. He opened my eyes in a new way to the world
of birds.

After nearly a decade as Tom's apprentice in these "lost"
arts, I began instructing at his school and subsequently finished a degree in combined studies of native people and
nature. I then founded the school I now direct. In 1985 I
became an apprentice to a fantastically interesting naturalist, big-game-hunter-turned-photographer and otherwise

wizened elder named Ingwe. His name, which means "the leopard," was first given to him by the Akamba tribesmen, well-known trackers, who mentored him through his childhood and into his adulthood in the wilds of Kenya early this century. Ingwe's own life is a subject of a book called *Ingwe*. Ingwe's influence on the program caused us to reorganize the programs of the school in 1985.

My background in awareness training from Tom and Ingwe helped me to develop a perspective on birds and their relationship to us, The Human Family.

Did you ever wonder why we can co-exist with animals like cougars, bears, and coyotes and yet rarely lay eyes on them? Do bears, cougars, and coyotes know something we don't know? From my experience as a trained tracker, naturalist, and a practitioner of some "older" skills known to the scouts and hunters of the hunter-gatherer societies of the Apache and the Akamba of East Africa, I have learned some important lessons which I can share. You will need to do the work. The combination of your dirt-time, background study, and these perspectives will help you in increasing your success in stealth and invisibility in the forest, while revealing others who are also aware of the "jungle law."

The Akamba, the Apache, and the other native hunters know of a language that I too have learned. I have successfully taught this to many students over the last twelve years. It seems that through working with my two teachers who have much in common, and from studying the native hunter-gatherers around the world, I have distilled down "success" in invisibility into two realms. The first is that there is a language being spoken by many wild creatures, and that there are others who listen attentively to it and use it to their own advantage. The second is that once you know this is going on, *you* can use it to your advantage and in a very real sense, you can become "invisible." There are some definite things we can learn from the cougars, the bears, and the coyotes.

What about the rumored "ancient" bucks with so much wisdom that they choose their own means of death and elude even the most patient and dedicated hunter to their final day? What did the scouts and hunters of the native tribes who lived by hunting and gathering know that could help someone today who would like to get close to one of these elusive animals unseen and unheard? What is the secret to this invisibility? I feel, as do many I work with, that the experienced deer actually learn these same tricks, too. It is as if they gain the knowledge that the cougar possesses.

Among native peoples it is said that the deer can gain "medicine" or knowledge from the cougar's ways. This is a good way to start thinking about the subject. You too can gain "cougar medicine." Knowledge of certain bird behaviors from this perspective is the key to this "medicine."

If you ever watch a wild cat move through its environment you will quickly notice that it moves as if it has honey in its veins. The slow, deliberate, and powerful movements are based on strong muscles, sure-footed accuracy, much practice, and careful planning. Remember this pattern: they move a few steps at a time, they freeze and scan their environment. They look ahead, head held still…They look left, head again held still...They look right...Then up...And often, they look behind them. At this point they move again, ever so slowly and carefully, always staying to the shadows. They always move along the edges, or in the thicket, or under the cover of darkness.

There is very good reason for this stealthy pattern. Use this pattern from now on while going to and from your Secret Spot. This is a way to take this study and bring it to life in rich and powerful ways. The background study of birds and their behavior will only become grounded with your field experience.

Of all the animals in the forest, the big cats are most like us in their dominant sense patterns. They use their eyes to the greatest effect, their ears less so, and their nose even less. This is a lot like our own pattern. Yet we as humans often mimic more the movement of the dog family. We move quickly and continuously, often looking at the ground, as if we could "smell" its many hidden secrets.

Many of you have already broken this pattern in your own movement, especially when in the forest, but we can always strive to be better "cats." For if you think about it, there are young, inexperienced cats, and there are older, wiser and more experienced cats who might just as well be spirits for they go for many years completely unseen by human eyes. We only know of their existence when they leave tracks in the snow, or when a pack of hounds manages to get one into the open to give us a fleeting glance.

Why should we bother learning from these cats? What does this have to do with invisibility? For one thing, cats are the masters and for another, they know the secret to the "alarm system" of the forest. They know you are coming, long before you get there. So does the bear, the coyote, and the wise, old buck. There are certain birds, especially those of the thicket, who watch our approach and signal our arrival with their body language, flight patterns, and mostly, their voices.

When we move like cats, we see these birds before we alarm them. That is if we stand still longer that they do. Once the bird sees you are not "pushing" its way, but pausing, the bird will go back to its business. Only then should you proceed. *But*, you must go around the bird, or it will "complain" as it is "moved off." In time you will learn from these birds how much space they need and how you need to "honor" them so as not to upset them. For once they announce your arrival, there is no turning back. The coyote has already lifted her head, and the deer has paused in his feeding. The cougar has climbed to a point of advantage to see far. The bear is statue-still and testing the breeze for more information. It is too late.

For now, learn from the cougar, the bear, and the coyote. Stop and listen to birds. Stop and watch for them. See what they tell you. Here is a little native lore, "Never disturb a singing bird, for it is performing its Thanksgiving Song." I will take it one step further: learn to honor any bird that you see. Observe what it is doing, and avoid disturbing its routine if at all possible. That is the lesson from the cougar and the deer. This perspective will bring real power to your studies.

Jon Young, inspired by his childhood mentoring with tracker and author Tom Brown Jr., has pioneered blending natives' mentoring techniques from around the world with the tools of modern field ecology. Under Jon's guidance, the Wilderness Awareness School, originally founded as a high school nature club, has grown to reach students around the world with its programs that help people reconnect with their native environments. For more information, visit their Web site at http://www.natureoutlet.com.

With No Direction Home

JON CARROLL

The wonder of bird migration clarifies the nature of "home."

I LOVE THE THINGS THAT SCIENCE DOES NOT know. Science knows so much that I do not know—to put it another way: There is so much real knowledge out there that is inaccessible to me, even though it is real knowledge about the world in which I too live—that when science and I are together baffled by a natural phenomenon, my heart soars.

Science does not know how birds migrate. There have been theories, of course. The angle of the sun. The prevailing wind currents. The stars. The fluctuations in the magnetic field surrounding the earth.

Somehow, it was believed, a bird senses one or more of these constants in the terrestrial environment, and it uses these constants to find its way back to the very same tiny island in the middle of the South Atlantic where it first broke shell three years before.

Then scientists did experiments. Some of these experiments involved doing things to birds that were perhaps not nice, but that's all behind us now. Anyway, every explanation was eliminated.

Angle of sun: Birds were required to migrate only at night, still came home. Fixed stars: Birds were required to migrate only by day, still came home. And so on—I'm not sure how all the experiments were designed, but in the end actual professional scientists pronounced themselves baffled.

So then a fellow in Britain decided to change the rules. He performed an experiment that did nothing to change the world's net supply of bewilderment but did increase the wonder quotient quite a bit.

He moved the home.

He had some homing pigeons. He raised them in a coop that was in fact a trailer hooked up to a small truck. At first, he let them go and they did their thing and circled back and came home.

Then, one day, as soon as he released the pigeons, he got in the truck and moved the home. Off it went down the byways of Britain; off it went into a another county entirely. Same home, same little perches and whatnot, but a different location on the planet.

The pigeons found it. How did the pigeons find it? See above. No one knows how migration works; all they know now is that it is not based on specific geography as we understand it. It is based on the idea of "home," which is more powerful than the idea of "place."

Of course, birds have very tiny brains and have no idea

that "home" is an idea. They just get tired of flying and think, "You know, some nice seed would go down fine just about now," and then they head off to the seed location. If the seed location has moved, their tiny brains are not puzzled.

They know that home is not necessarily a single point on the planet. Home is where the heart is, where the food is; home is the wide place in the road where the perch is.

Home is where you go when you go home.

This happens to a lot of us, does it not? They keep moving home on us. We think we know where it is, and then the people who made it home move, or die, or go crazy, or they stay sane and alive and stable but they don't want us anymore.

And we have to know where home is anyway. That is our challenge. We have to understand that it is not one specific spot on the globe. Science has now taught us that we are none of us homeless. That is the important thing to remember. We are merely temporarily confused about the location of home because they have moved the damn thing again.

But we know. Not by the stars or the sun or the fluctuations in the magnetic field, but by something else—we know. And as long as we know there is something to know, there is hope. Every journey has a goal, and every goal is real.

This despite massive confusion. This despite odd British people who have loaded our perches onto lorries and driven them to lay-bys, as the English say. We have to know only that we know, and all the rest is flying. It's a proven fact.

Jon Carroll writes a daily column for the *San Francisco Chronicle*.

Epiphany

LEONARD NATHAN

*Is birding just another form of hunting,
or something deeper?*

EPIPHANY—I WANT IT TO MEAN SIMPLY A rare and free showing forth of vital presence. But it's an ancient term and won't be easily stripped of its religious associations; the presence, by its sudden intensity, will seem not inappropriate. Birds seem radically different from other creatures.

Donald Culross Peattie tells why:

Man feels himself an infinity above those creatures who stand, zoölogically, only one step below him, but every human looks up to the birds. They seem to us like emissaries of another world which exists about us and above us, but into which, earth-bound, we cannot penetrate. It is not the strength of the lion that we give to angels, but wings....

A male hooded warbler was reported seen in the park seven minutes from my house. I am out there in six, but a half dozen others have arrived ahead of me. It's 9:30, a cool, clear spring morning. First-rate for seeing birds. We take the trail where the warbler was last spotted. Up the hill and into the oak woods, then down and into pines, then willows. There the trail ends. No bird. The others decide to take the same trail back; I go solo down the parallel lower trail. They say they'll shout if they see the warbler. Ten minutes later I hear shouting. Could it be? It could be. But I'm halfway down now, and it would take me some minutes to run back and up the other trail. And suppose it was someone else, shouting for something other than birds? I go on, come out at the end and meet them, who of course, have seen the bird. They go, and I stay to wander the trails till noon, then give up and go home.

Next morning I am out again but earlier, take the upper trail and find nothing. Do I hear a fragment of song? Perhaps from the lower trail. I studied pictures of the bird last night. A little beauty—black hood, bright yellow face and undersides, lovely and complex song.

I don't hesitate—down the lower trail. I take no more than fifteen steps, look up and see it perched a little above eye level in a willow to the left of the trail and not more than ten feet ahead. It begins to sing, and I would like to sing with it, but instead address it with terms of endearment and do a restrained two-step shuffle. There it is, *Wilsonia citrina*—is it really lemon colored? I see it and see it. There is a wonderful convergence here—of its freedom and my purpose. This is epiphany or nothing is. I am a happy—no, an ecstatic—man. Even when it flies. As it now does and with my best wishes.

When I tell Lewis all this, he shrugs: "You know, you may merely have experienced the hunter's joy at capturing and subduing his prey—not quite epiphany, I believe."

"But I'm *not* a hunter. I wasn't trying to capture or subdue." My voice rises in denial. "All I wanted was to see as wholly as I could."

"Perhaps it only seems that way because civilization has domesticated hunting to the point that the desire to capture and subdue is disguised as passive observation. What you do is so refined that the old passion for the blood hunt has been attenuated into gazing through several layers of lens." Lewis thrusts his pipe into the air. I'm about to get a lecture.

"Lewis…," I say.

"No. No. Listen, you ought to know your origins. The tradition of your genteel pastime goes back to the eighteenth century—the great age of the amateur—when leisured members of the educated middle class began collecting bird lore. Partly as a contribution to scientific knowledge but mostly for the fun of it—a hobby, I'm afraid. And behind this hobby lay an older tradition that lives on into our century: birding—collecting birds, dead or alive, for food, for plumage, for pets, for study."

"That's precisely why I resist the term 'birding,'" I say.

"Well, you can resist all you want but you're going to lose on that one. Bird-watching these days sounds a little quaint, a silly old-fashioned pastime of English eccentrics. And besides, the word 'birding' has some zip to it, some active purpose. When I think of bird-watching, I see comfortable elders lollygagging over a little wildflower just off the trail, or stooping to pick up an odd seashell."

"But birding," I say, "according to Peterson anyway, tends to be associated with list making, with identification."

"Well, yes, the old hunting impulse at work there—the list is a substitute for the kill."

"I don't think, in any case, that birding as you define it has much to do with what I'm talking about. Just the opposite. It reduces the real presence of a bird to a name and number."

"If you exclude birders from your religion," here Lewis points his pipestem at me, like a gun barrel, "you'll have to exclude along with them lots of others: for instance, people who just want to get away from it all, and who find birds nice enough but no reason to change their church affiliation. And those to whom interest in birds is just a part of an interest in all nature. All these you're going to deny the privilege of your epiphany? That leaves the poets and like-minded sensitive souls. A rather exclusive club, I'd say!"

Here a silence ensues. I believe Lewis is wrong but have no good answer to his question and now he asks another one, "By the by, how do you *tell* when you've had one of these epiphanies?"...

Lewis is on a field trip. I write him a note: "(1) Epiphany can happen to anyone capable of receiving. (2) You *know* you have an epiphany when you experience the shock of recognition. I hope this answers your question."

Lewis replies in his tiny, beautifully clear hand: "Shock of recognition?"

And I back: "'Shock of recognition,' borrowed by Edmund Wilson from Herman Melville. Wilson meant meeting of a good writer with bad one. Melville meant meeting a genius with genius (Melville meets Hawthorne?). I mean the electric experience when epiphany occurs, when hope or surprise meets intense presence. Why are watchers reluctant to lower their binoculars? To make sure of the identity of the bird, yes, but also from a strong desire to prolong so special a seeing, not the consummation of the hunt, but the experience of knowledge. The meaning and mystery of otherness."

Lewis's prodding reply after: "Knowledge?"

My answer: "Shock because we live insulated by habit, convention, ideas—all devices by which we shelter ourselves from dangerously direct contact with actuality. Direct contact is what shocks us. But we dearly need such shocks to keep ourselves engaged in our real circumstances, which, if full of peril, are also full of life-giving wonder and beauty. How's that?"

From Lewis: "Mmmmm. Rather mystical, don't you think?"

Me again, out of pique:

"There is throughout nature something mocking, something that leads us on and on, but arrives nowhere, keeps no faith with us. All promise outruns the performance. We live in a system of approximations. Every end is prospective of some other end, which is also temporary; a round and final success

nowhere. We are encamped in nature, not domesticated...Our music, our poetry, our language itself
are not satisfactions, but suggestions."

I mean to shake him up a little with this specimen from
Emerson, but manage also to do the same to myself. But I
think Ralph Waldo is more on my side than on Lewis's. And
I'm glad to have him there.

Leonard Nathan is the author of nine books of poetry, one of which was
nominated for the National Book Award. He is a Guggenheim Fellow and
translator, and the author of *Diary of a Left-Handed Birdwatcher*, from which
this story was excerpted.

V

Ascending
Song

Sky Lark

KENN KAUFMAN

And then the song began.

EVEN WITH FOG ON THE WATER I COULD make out islands offshore, evidently the nearest of the San Juans. The character of the islands did not seem to differ from that of the mainland. Shorelines were all black rock, with occasional gravel beaches below, and a solid skyline of evergreen forest above. Gulls of three or four types were flying back and forth, patrolling the shorelines, white wings against the dark trees.

The ferry was a large, multi-tiered craft, with more than enough room for the cars and trucks that were now being maneuvered noisily into lower levels. Up above were observation decks, a passenger lounge, a cafeteria. I bought some coffee and, cradling the hot cup in my hands, walked up on the forward deck to look for birds.

Buffleheads, little black-and-white baby-faced ducks,

were swimming and diving next to the ferry. Numbers of white-winged scoters and surf scoters, dark sea ducks, were floating in the distance. Scanning still farther out, my binoculars picked up two bird silhouettes buzzing over the water on stubby wings: these were certainly alcids of some sort. Rich Stallcup had told me to expect a good variety of alcids on this ride.

At length I heard the muffled roar, felt the sudden vibration underfoot as the ferry's great engines came to life. A few more minutes passed. Then the horizon began to swing slowly around, before the feeling of motion had actually registered; and we were under way.

I was alone on the forward deck. The other passengers were all inside, hidden behind newspapers, looking like morning commuters anywhere. That was their problem; I was excited just to be here. The salty breeze in my face was just cold enough to make me wide awake. I could see a slight swell running in the gray seas, but I could not feel it—all I could feel was the deck throbbing underfoot with the power of the engines. The ferry plowed ahead on a level course, while the engines rolled with a pounding sound, like a train, like a seagoing train....

I stood on the bow with the salt wind in my face, and I thought: How strange that I should be coming here to look for a bird from England.

And then: How strange that I should be arriving by ship to look for a bird that had arrived in North America by ship.

How strange it must have seemed to the sky larks themselves, to be crammed into crates and shipped halfway around the world back in 1903, just because they were unlucky enough to be among the most celebrated songbirds in the world.

How strange it would seem to many of the bird-listers that I should make a major effort to see the sky lark, this alien bird, brought in and released here by humans. No matter that the larks had been surviving on their own here for seventy years now; no matter that their songs were the stuff of poetry and legend—for many birders, nothing could erase the stigma of a nonnative bird, a bird that was "introduced."

I roused myself from these thoughts as the ferry steamed into a natural harbor on the main island, where a town perched on the shore, and maneuvered toward the dock. Back in the interior of the craft there was a stir as people prepared to disembark. Although many passengers were going on across to Victoria, enough were getting off here to create a traffic jam when all those cars came out of the hold; for once I was lucky to be on foot. I walked down the ramp, onto the main street of Friday Harbor.

Now to go find the sky larks. The spot was the "American Camp," whatever that was, at the south end of the island. Shouldering my pack, I was out of town and into the country within minutes.

It was now midmorning. The gray sky overhead was rainwashed and fresh, and a light mist was still falling. The day was warm. It was hard to remember just how far north this place was: to reach this latitude on the Atlantic Coast, one would have to travel to Newfoundland, where the land would still be locked in hard winter. But the Pacific Northwest benefits from warm ocean currents, which keep the climate moderate all year. Rather like the situation in the British Isles. London lies even farther north than the San Juan Islands, but enjoys relatively mild winters, thanks to the moderating influence of the Gulf Stream current.

The road I walked on San Juan Island was partly paved, partly gravel, totally deserted, running through rural country. The landscape was a study in soft tawny yellows and browns, dark greens in the woodlots, occasional views of the steely sea, all the colors muted today under the gray sky.

Somehow it all reminded me of scenes from the writings of British naturalists.

I might have imagined whatever resemblance I pleased, since I had never been to England. But I had read so much about that country. So many of the great naturalists, ornithologists, and nature writers were from the British Isles. It seemed odd that they could love nature so much in a land that was so thoroughly tamed...but then, perhaps that explained it. Their land was civilized. They had no wilderness—no Grand Canyon, no rattlesnakes, no Mount McKinley, no mountain lions, no badlands. No wonder they could afford to think generously of their countryside. They had room, and reason, to appreciate those small elements of nature that would be overlooked entirely in the rip-roaring American frame of reference.

Haunting the library as a kid, reading poetry books when I was not reading bird books, I had been astonished at how often birds were mentioned in British poetry. Songsters like nightingales and sky larks appeared in literally dozens of works, going back beyond Shakespeare, back beyond

Chaucer. Entire poems dedicated to such birds were written by Tennyson, Wordsworth, Shelley, Keats, and many lesser-known poets. I had run across half a dozen British poems just about sky larks; Thomas Hardy had even written a poem about Shelley's poem about the sky lark. The love of birds and of the English language were intermingled in British literary history.

Somehow we Americans had failed to import this English love of birds along with the language, except in a diluted form. But we had imported a few of the English birds themselves—along with birds from practically everywhere else....

I had wandered down the road to the edge of the tall grass, before I realized it. This was the place: somewhere in these fields, the sky larks lurked. Walking out across the fields might have been the fast way to flush them, but I was reluctant to cause such disturbance to a colony that was evidently small and vulnerable. So I put down my backpack and stood at the edge of the taller grass, and watched.

And I waited.

There was nothing there: only the dark earth and tawny grass, damp from late-winter rains, lying silent, awaiting spring. Beyond these fields the ocean grumbled ceaselessly. Away to the south I could see no further land—only gray waters stretching away to blend into gray mist and sky.

Spring had not yet begun here, I told myself; perhaps by the calendar, but not in reality. Spring might arrive here even tomorrow, but not on a day like this. Men might walk the empty fields on such a day, eagles might fly out to sea and not return, but the bird of the poets would not sing from the dark and wintry sky. Not today, I said.

...and then the song began.

It grew out of wave-noise and wind-sound, beginning in low trilled notes, soft but clear, one following rapidly on another. The sound arose from the fields somewhere between me and the shoreline, and it was at once so natural and so alien to the scene that it seemed to be a song without a singer. These first notes were identical in pitch, they did not ascend or descend the scale, but the source of the voice seemed to be rising; too late it occurred to me that the bird must be in the air. It was singing as it flew straight upward. Then the invisible singer seemed to reach a stationary peak in the sky, and the song burst into a cascade of clear notes. The sound grew louder and then softened again, broke into loud warbling passages and then receded through quiet chirring trills; and the song went on and on, without pause, from somewhere up above.

With a start, I realized that I was standing open-mouthed and staring at nothing. I began to look for the singer — wanting reassurance that it was a bird, not imagination or the spirits of the island. My eyes strained against the emptiness of the clouds.

There! So high above the earth that it was almost beyond vision, the sky lark hovered on the wind. Binoculars resolved this speck into the silhouette of a bird, suspended in the sky, its wings barely quivering to hold it aloft. It seemed incredible that any bird should have the strength to fly at the same time that it delivered this song: this amazing torrent of song, which came down so clearly and so continuously. On and on went the song. Finally the bird closed its wings further and began a series of steep glides toward the ground.

The song ceased abruptly.

I stood stunned, waiting for the performance to be repeated. And, in a few minutes, it was. Again the lark rose into the sky to deliver his flight-song, and again I stood listening, unbelieving. The beauty of the song went beyond any details of musical formula: it was the spirit that was so moving. The bird sang from a stage of immense proportions, sang as the soloist before the orchestral growling of the surf. I imagined a title: "Concerto for Sky Lark and Pacific Ocean." The sky lark was the speck of life, the hope of spring, in a gray wilderness.

More, I wanted to hear more. For a couple of hours I wandered the edges of the fields, seeing and hearing other sky larks. A few times, singers coming down from the sky landed near me, and I was able to study them at close range. Visually they were designed for camouflage: streaky and brown. Gaudy hues would have been wasted, since the colors would not be visible from the ground when the bird performed his sky dance.

All the sky larks I found were along less that half a mile of the road. All were between the roadway and the beach. They appeared to occupy an area of a few hundred acres at best. What a small foothold it seemed, and what a vulnerable position; the whole population could be wiped out by one winter storm.

Even the Victoria sky larks were far from their native land. Their ancestors had been trapped out of the pastures of England and crated halfway around the world, to the shadow of Alaska. And the birds that had founded the San Juan Island group must have been lost themselves, storm-driven perhaps, from the population at Victoria. *This is really the lost colony*, I said to myself. *It's alone in the wilderness, an outpost cut off from the fatherland for eternity.*

Once more I walked down to the edge of the tall grass, to the border of the larks' world, and stood looking upward. A single sky lark was up there now, towering on quivered wings, high above the earth. The song that came rippling and running and trilling down spoke defiance to raging seas and rockbound coasts, to the wintry cast of the sky, to the spirits of this northwestern island. It seemed then that even the elements must acknowledge this singer for the eloquence of his futile challenge. At length another sky lark came up to the west, and another off to the east; the voices rang down the sky, on and on, as if the song would go on forever.

Kenn Kaufman also contributed "Close to the End" in Part Three. This story was excerpted from his book *Kingbird Highway: The Story of a Natural Obsession That Got a Little Out of Hand.*

Recommended Reading

Abram, David. *The Spell of the Sensuous: Perception and Language in a More-Than-Human World*. New York: Pantheon, 1996.

Ackerman, Diane. *The Rarest of the Rare: Vanishing Animals, Timeless Worlds*. New York: Random House, 1995.

Attenborough, David. *Life of Birds*. Princeton: Princeton University Press, 1998.

Bird, David M., Ph.D. *The Bird Almanac: The Ultimate Guide to Essential Facts of the World's Birds*. Buffalo, NY: Firefly Books, 1999.

Bodsworth, Fred. *Last of the Curlews*. Washington, D.C.: Counterpoint, 1995.

Dunne, Pete. *Small-Headed Flycatcher: Seen Yesterday, He Didn't Leave His Name, And Other Stories*. Austin: University of Texas Press, 1998.

Dunne, Pete. *Tales of a Low-Rent Birder*. Austin: University of Texas Press, 1986.

Erdrich, Louise. *The Blue Jay's Dance: A Birth Year*. New York: HarperPerennial, 1996.

Heinrich, Bernd. *One Man's Owl*. Princeton, NJ: Princeton University Press, 1993.

Hogan, Linda, Deena Metzger, and Brenda Peterson (eds). *Intimate Nature: The Bond Between Women and Animals*. New York: Fawcette Columbine, 1998.

Kaufman, Kenn. *Kingbird Highway: The Story of a Natural Obsession That Got a Little Out of Hand.* New York: Houghton Mifflin, 1997.

Kilgo, James. *Deep Enough for Ivorybills.* Chapel Hill, NC: Algonquin of Chapel Hill, 1988.

Morton, H. V. *In Search of South Africa.* New York: Dodd Mead & Co., 1948.

Nathan, Leonard. *Diary of a Left-Handed Birdwatcher.* Saint Paul, Minn.: Graywolf Press, 1996.

Naveen, Ron. *Waiting to Fly: My Escapades with the Penguins of Antarctica.* New York: William Morrow & Co., 1999.

Olson, Sigurd F. *Listening Point.* New York: Alfred A. Knopf, 1958.

Page, Jake. *Songs to Birds.* Boston: David R. Godine Publishers, 1993.

Walker, Alice. *Living By the Word: Selected Writings 1973-1987.* Orlando: Harcourt Brace Jovanovich, 1988.

Weidensaul, Scott. *Living on the Wind: Across the Hemisphere with Migratory Birds.* New York: North Point Press, 1999.

Williams, Terry Tempest. *Refuge: An Unnatural History of Family and Place.* New York: Vintage, 1992.

Winn, Marie. *Red-Tails in Love: A Wildlife Drama in Central Park.* New York: Pantheon Books, 1998.

Index

Acknowledgements

Completing a book is never an easy task, but this one has been more pleasure than pain because of several people, foremost of whom is coeditor Amy Greimann Carlson, whose hard work and clear vision were instrumental in bringing this book home to roost. Special thanks for your wise touch and for being such a pleasure to work with, as always.

Many thanks also to my co-workers at Travelers' Tales, especially James, Wenda, Sean, and Tim O'Reilly, Lisa Bach, Susan Brady, Deborah Greco, Raj Khadka, Jennifer Leo, Natanya Pearlman, and Tara Weaver. Thanks also to Diana Howard for contributing her considerable design talents, Patty Holden for her enduring patience and unerring eye, and Randy Johnson for bringing the cover illustrations to vibrant life.

Special thanks to the late Sister Clara Louise of St. Peter's School in Richfield, Minnesota, who through her love for my brother Gene and her passionate interest in birds helped us both get out into the wilds in ways we might not have otherwise, and to my parents for giving us such free rein at so early an age.

And very special thanks to Paula Mc Cabe and Alanna Habegger Mc Cabe for making every day feel like the first day of spring.

—LARRY HABEGGER

This book has been a joy to compile. I feel blessed to have had the opportunity to read a body of stories so uplifting and inspiring, to surround myself with flight and song. Thank you, James O'Reilly, for once again having the faith in me to fly with this project. I am soaring.

A special thanks to my coeditor, Larry Habegger, for his gentle touch, furrowed brow, lovingly tending to the stories herein. His depth of caring shows in these pages. To the production staff at Travelers' Tales, I say HURRAH to you for all of the hard work you all do to turn these books from idea to reality. It wouldn't be possible without you.

To my parents, Millie and Stan Greimann, who fostered and encouraged my love of the great outdoors and all creatures winged or slithery. Thank you for the opportunity of the woods. To my husband, Reed Carlson, a big hug goes to you for not only "just being there," but also for your insightful critiques and suggestions, even if they were not always taken. To Liz and Rich Caemmerer at the Grunewald Guild, thanks again for granting me the space and time to spread out and weave.

…and last, but not least, I would like to thank God for all of the birds of the air, meadow, and stream. With talon, plumage, beak, and bill, they are a gift to us mortals, gracing us with a presence that soars into a world for which we long.

— AMY GREIMANN CARLSON

Frontispiece from *A Sand County Almanac* by Aldo Leopold. Copyright © 1949, 1966 by Oxford University Press.

"Gift of Seed" by Pete Dunne excerpted from *Small-Headed Flycatcher: Seen Yesterday, He Didn't Leave His Name, And Other Stories* by Pete Dunne. Copyright © 1998 University of Texas Press. Reprinted by permission of the University of Texas Press.

"The Balinese Chicken" by Alice Walker excerpted from *Living By the Word: Selected Writings 1973-1987* by Alice Walker. Copyright © 1988 by Alice Walker. Reprinted by permission of Harcourt Brace & Company and David Higham Associates.

"Wild Owls" by Bernd Heinrich excerpted from *One Man's Owl* by Bernd Heinrich. Copyright © 1993 by Princeton University Press, paperback edition 1993 by Princeton University Press. Reprinted by permission of Princeton University Press.

"The Legend of Jesse Mew" by Pete Dunne excerpted from *Tales of a Low-Rent Birder* by Pete Dunne. Copyright © 1986 by Pete Dunne. Reprinted by permission of the University of Texas Press.

"How the Pimpernel Saved His Pigeons" by Pippa Stuart originally appeared in the May 1, 1996 issue of the *Christian Science Monitor*. Copyright © 1996 by Pippa Stuart. Reprinted by permission of the author.

"Nothing Tastes Like Roadkill" by Robert H. Boyle reprinted courtesy of *Sports Illustrated*, April 7, 1997. Copyright © 1997, Time, Inc. "Nothing Tastes Like Roadkill" by Robert H. Boyle. All rights reserved.

"Close to the End" by Kenn Kaufman excerpted from *Kingbird Highway: The Story of a Natural Obsession That Got a Little Out of Hand* by Kenn Kaufman. Copyright © 1997 by Kenn Kaufman. Reprinted by permission of Houghton Mifflin Company. All rights reserved.

"After the Fires" by Peter Davis published with permission from the author. Copyright © 1999 by Peter Davis.

"The Ramble of Central Park" by Marie Winn excerpted from *Red-Tails in Love: A Wildlife Drama in Central Park* by Marie Winn. Copyright © 1998 by Marie Winn. Reprinted by permission of Pantheon Books, a division of Random House, Inc.

"Actual Field Conditions" by James Kilgo excerpted from *Deep Enough for Ivorybills* by James Kilgo. Copyright © 1988 by James Kilgo. Reprinted by permission of the author.

"The Setting of Wings" by Buddy Levy originally appeared in *Northern Lights* magazine, Missoula, Montana. Copyright © 1996 by Buddy Levy. Reprinted by permission of the author.

"Whimbrels" by Terry Tempest Williams excerpted from *Refuge: An Unnatural History of Family and Place* by Terry Tempest Williams. Copyright © 1991 by Terry Tempest Williams. Reprinted by permission of Vintage Books, a division of Random House, Inc. and Brandt and Brandt Literary Agency.

About the Editors

Larry Habegger, executive editor of Travelers' Tales, has been writing about travel since 1980. He has visited almost fifty countries and five of the six continents, traveling from the frozen arctic to equatorial rain forest, the high Himalayas to the Dead Sea. In the early 1980s he co-authored mystery serials for the *San Francisco Examiner* with James O'Reilly, and in 1985 the two of them began a syndicated newspaper column, "World Travel Watch," which still appears in major newspapers throughout the USA. He was born and raised in Minnesota and lives with his family on Telegraph Hill in San Francisco.

Amy Greimann Carlson inherited a case of wanderlust from her Connecticut family, a malady which has led her to eat *fugu* (blowfish) in Japan, get chased by a Red Guard in Beijing, get kicked out of a casino in Macau, come close to starving in a London garret while writing about William Blake, and generally wander the world with only her backpack for company, staying for a year or two where she found her heart's desire. Currently she has settled down with her husband, Reed, in the mountains of Washington State where she stays busy building a house, teaching poetry, dodging hummingbirds, giving flute lessons, writing, and researching. She is coeditor of *Travelers' Tales Japan*.

TRAVELERS' TALES GUIDES
LOOK FOR THESE TITLES IN THE SERIES

FOOTSTEPS: THE SOUL OF TRAVEL
A NEW IMPRINT FROM TRAVELERS' TALES GUIDES

An imprint of Travelers' Tales Guides, the Footsteps series unveils new works by first-time authors, established writers, and reprints of works whose time has come…again. Each book will fire your imagination, disturb your sleep, and feed your soul.

KITE STRINGS OF THE SOUTHERN CROSS
A Woman's Travel Odyssey
By Laurie Gough
ISBN 1-885211-30-9
400 pages, $24.00, Hardcover

THE SWORD OF HEAVEN
A Five Continent Odyssey to Save the World
By Mikkel Aaland
ISBN 1-885211-44-9
350 pages, $24.00, Hardcover

✑PECIAL INTEREST

THE FEARLESS SHOPPER
How to Get the Best Deals on the Planet
By Kathy Borrus
ISBN 1-885211-39-2, 200 pages, $12.95

Check with your local bookstore for
these titles or visit our web site at
www.travelerstales.com

$\mathscr{S}$PECIAL INTEREST

THE GIFT OF BIRDS:
True Encounters with Avian Spirits
Edited by Larry Habegger & Amy Greimann Carlson
ISBN 1-885211-41-4, 275 pages, $17.95

TESTOSTERONE PLANET:
True Stories from a Man's World
Edited by Sean O'Reilly, Larry Habegger & James O'Reilly
ISBN 1-885211-43-0, 300 pages, $17.95

THE PENNY PINCHER'S PASSPORT TO LUXURY TRAVEL
The Art of Cultivating Preferred Customer Status
By Joel L. Widzer
ISBN 1-885211-31-7, 253 pages, $12.95

DANGER!
Ttue Stories of Trouble and Survival
Edited by James O'Reilly, Larry Habegger & Sean O'Reilly
ISBN 1-885211-32-5, 336 pages, $17.95

FAMILY TRAVEL:
The Farther You Go, the Closer You Get
Edited by Laura Manske
ISBN 1-885211-33-3, 368 pages, $17.95

$\mathscr{S}$PECIAL INTEREST

THE GIFT OF TRAVEL:
The Best of Travelers' Tales
Edited by Larry Habegger, James O'Reilly & Sean O'Reilly
ISBN 1-885211-25-2, 240 pages, $14.95

THERE'S NO TOILET PAPER...ON THE ROAD LESS TRAVELED:
The Best of Travel Humor and Misadventure
Edited by Doug Lansky
ISBN 1-885211-27-9, 207 pages, $12.95

A DOG'S WORLD:
True Stories of Man's Best Friend on the Road
Edited by Christine Hunsicker
ISBN 1-885211-23-6, 257 pages, $12.95

$\mathscr{W}$OMEN'S TRAVEL

A WOMAN'S PASSION FOR TRAVEL
More True Stories from A Woman's World
Edited by Marybeth Bond & Pamela Michael
ISBN 1-885211-36-8, 375 pages, $17.95

SAFETY AND SECURITY FOR WOMEN WHO TRAVEL
By Sheila Swan & Peter Laufer
ISBN 1-885211-29-5, 159 pages, $12.95

$\mathcal{W}$OMEN'S TRAVEL

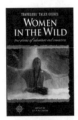

WOMEN IN THE WILD:
True Stories of Adventure and Connection
Edited by Lucy McCauley
ISBN 1-885211-21-X, 307 pages, $17.95

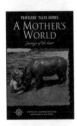

A MOTHER'S WORLD:
Journeys of the Heart
Edited by Marybeth Bond & Pamela Michael
ISBN 1-885211-26-0, 233 pages, $14.95

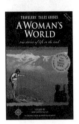

A WOMAN'S WORLD:
True Stories of Life on the Road
Edited by Marybeth Bond
Introduction by Dervla Murphy
ISBN 1-885211-06-6
475 pages, $17.95

**Winner of the Lowell
Thomas Award for Best
Travel Book – Society of
American Travel Writers**

GUTSY WOMEN:
Travel Tips and Wisdom for the Road
By Marybeth Bond
ISBN 1-885211-15-5, 123 pages, $7.95

GUTSY MAMAS:
**Travel Tips and Wisdom for
Mothers on the Road**
By Marybeth Bond
ISBN 1-885211-20-1, 139 pages, $7.95

$\mathscr{B}$ODY & SOUL

THE ADVENTURE OF FOOD:
True Stories of Eating Everything
Edited by Richard Sterling
ISBN 1-885211-37-6, 375 pages, $17.95

---★ ★ ★---
Small Press Book Award Winner and Benjamin Franklin Award Finalist

THE ROAD WITHIN:
True Stories of Transformation and the Soul
Edited by Sean O'Reilly, James O'Reilly & Tim O'Reilly
ISBN 1-885211-19-8, 459 pages, $17.95

LOVE & ROMANCE:
True Stories of Passion on the Road
Edited by Judith Babcock Wylie
ISBN 1-885211-18-X, 319 pages, $17.95

---★ ★ ★---
Silver Medal Winner of the Lowell Thomas Award for Best Travel Book – Society of American Travel Writers

FOOD:
A Taste of the Road
Edited by Richard Sterling
Introduction by Margo True
ISBN 1-885211-09-0
467 pages, $17.95

THE FEARLESS DINER:
Travel Tips and Wisdom for Eating around the World
By Richard Sterling
ISBN 1-885211-22-8, 139 pages, $7.95

COUNTRY GUIDES

AUSTRALIA
True Stories of Life Down Under
Edited by Larry Habegger & Amy Greimann Carlson
ISBN 1-885211-40-6, 375 pages, $17.95

AMERICA
Edited by Fred Setterberg
ISBN 1-885211-28-7, 550 pages, $19.95

JAPAN
Edited by Donald W. George
& Amy Greimann Carlson
ISBN 1-885211-04-X, 437 pages, $17.95

ITALY
Edited by Anne Calcagno
Introduction by Jan Morris
ISBN 1-885211-16-3, 463 pages, $17.95

INDIA
Edited by James O'Reilly & Larry Habegger
ISBN 1-885211-01-5, 538 pages, $17.95

$\mathscr{C}$OUNTRY GUIDES

FRANCE
Edited by James O'Reilly, Larry Habegger
& Sean O'Reilly
ISBN 1-885211-02-3, 517 pages, $17.95

MEXICO
Edited by James O'Reilly & Larry Habegger
ISBN 1-885211-00-7, 463 pages, $17.95

───── ★ ★ ★ ─────

***Winner of the Lowell
Thomas Award for Best
Travel Book–Society of
American Travel Writers***

THAILAND
Edited by James O'Reilly
& Larry Habegger
ISBN 1-885211-05-8
483 pages, $17.95

SPAIN
Edited by Lucy McCauley
ISBN 1-885211-07-4, 495 pages, $17.95

NEPAL
Edited by Rajendra S. Khadka
ISBN 1-885211-14-7, 423 pages, $17.95

COUNTRY GUIDES

BRAZIL
Edited by Annette Haddad & Scott Doggett
Introduction by Alex Shoumatoff
ISBN 1-885211-11-2
452 pages, $17.95

— ★ ★ ★ —
Benjamin Franklin
Award Winner

CITY GUIDES

HONG KONG
Edited by James O'Reilly, Larry Habegger & Sean O'Reilly
ISBN 1-885211-03-1, 439 pages, $17.95

PARIS
Edited by James O'Reilly, Larry Habegger & Sean O'Reilly
ISBN 1-885211-10-4, 417 pages, $17.95

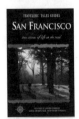

SAN FRANCISCO
Edited by James O'Reilly, Larry Habegger & Sean O'Reilly
ISBN 1-885211-08-2, 491 pages, $17.95

ℛEGIONAL GUIDES

HAWAI'I
True Stories of the Island Spirit
Edited by Rick & Marcie Carroll
ISBN 1-885211-35-X, 416 pages, $17.95

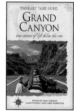

GRAND CANYON
True Stories of Life Below the Rim
Edited by Sean O'Reilly,
James O'Reilly & Larry Habegger
ISBN 1-885211-34-1, 296 pages, $17.95

SUBMIT YOUR OWN TRAVEL TALE

Do you have a tale of your own that you would like to submit to Travelers' Tales? We highly recommend that you first read one or more of our books to get a feel for the kind of story we're looking for. For submission guidelines and a list of titles in the works, send a SASE to:

Travelers' Tales Submission Guidelines
330 Townsend Street, Suite 208, San Francisco, CA 94107

or send email to *guidelines@travelerstales.com*
or visit our Web site at **www.travelerstales.com**

You can send your story to the address above or via email to *submit@travelerstales.com*. On the outside of the envelope, *please indicate what country/topic your story is about*. If your story is selected for one of our titles, we will contact you about rights and payment.

We hope to hear from you. In the meantime, enjoy the stories!